T0215745

Getting Started with the Uno Platform and WinUI 3

Hands-On Building of Cross-Platform Desktop, Mobile, and Web Applications That Can Run Anywhere

Skye Hoefling

Apress®

Getting Started with the Uno Platform and WinUI 3: Hands-On Building of Cross-Platform Desktop, Mobile, and Web Applications That Can Run Anywhere

Skye Hoefling
Rochester, NY, USA

ISBN-13 (pbk): 978-1-4842-8247-2　　　　ISBN-13 (electronic): 978-1-4842-8248-9
https://doi.org/10.1007/978-1-4842-8248-9

Managing Director, Apress Media LLC: Welmoed Spahr
Acquisitions Editor: Joan Murray
Development Editor: Laura Berendson
Coordinating Editor: Jill Balzano

Cover photo by Alice Butenko on Unsplash

Distributed to the book trade worldwide by Springer Science+Business Media LLC, 1 New York Plaza, Suite 4600, New York, NY 10004. Phone 1-800-SPRINGER, fax (201) 348-4505, e-mail orders-ny@springer-sbm. com, or visit www.springeronline.com. Apress Media, LLC is a California LLC and the sole member (owner) is Springer Science + Business Media Finance Inc (SSBM Finance Inc). SSBM Finance Inc is a **Delaware** corporation.

For information on translations, please e-mail booktranslations@springernature.com; for reprint, paperback, or audio rights, please e-mail bookpermissions@springernature.com.

Apress titles may be purchased in bulk for academic, corporate, or promotional use. eBook versions and licenses are also available for most titles. For more information, reference our Print and eBook Bulk Sales web page at http://www.apress.com/bulk-sales.

Any source code or other supplementary material referenced by the author in this book is available to readers on GitHub (https://github.com/Apress). For more detailed information, please visit http://www. apress.com/source-code.

Printed on acid-free paper

*This book is dedicated to my supportive and loving
wife Rebekah and our two wonderful children.
Thank you for supporting me through this journey.*
♥

Table of Contents

About the Author

Skye Hoefling is a lead software engineer and works on cross-platform desktop, mobile, and web apps using Xamarin and .NET technologies. She has been using .NET and Microsoft technologies since 2006 and has a Bachelor of Science from Rochester Institute of Technology in game design and development. Skye has a background in enterprise software, building custom web portals for large corporations as well as small projects used by general consumers. She is an active open source contributor, a Microsoft MVP in Developer Technologies, and a .NET Foundation member. You can find her on Twitter at @SkyeTheDev as well as at her software development blog `https://SkyeThe.Dev` where you will find a wide range of blogs.

About the Technical Reviewer

Nick Randolph currently runs Built to Roam, which focuses on building rich mobile applications. Nick has been identified as a Microsoft MVP in recognition of his work and expertise with the Microsoft application platforms. He is still an active contributor in the device application development space via his blog at `http://nicksnettravels.builttoroam.com`. Nick has been invited to present at a variety of events including TechEd and Ignite Australia & NZ, DDD, NDC, and local user groups. He has also authored multiple books on Visual Studio and Windows development and helped judge multiple world finals for the Imagine Cup. Nick has worked on numerous mobile applications and has helped hundreds of developers build their own mobile applications. He has been involved with applications for well-known brands such as Domain.com.au, ninemsn, AFL, NRL, Qantas, JB Hi-Fi, NAB, Stan, and Boost Juice.

Acknowledgments

This book would not be possible without the various friends and colleagues who have helped me along the way. I would like to acknowledge my wife and partner, Rebekah, who has supported me on this from day one, helping me through many late nights of coding and writing.

A friend and mentor, Mitchel Sellers, extended help before I even started writing the book and guided me through many challenges I faced.

The .NET community volunteered their time to help me complete this book. Nick Randolph, the technical reviewer; Pedro Jesus, the code reviewer; and Christos Matskas, the MSAL code reviewer.

Uno Platform has been so helpful from start to end. Jérôme Laban, the CTO, spent many days chatting with me on GitHub and Discord as I ran into various issues while keeping up with the speed of the technology. Sasha Krsmanovic, the CMO, and Francois Tanguay, the CEO, both helped in early planning and making sure I was able to collaborate with the right people on the internal team.

Thank you to everyone who helped me complete this book.

Introduction

This book is intended for the C# .NET developer who wants to learn how to build cross-platform applications with Uno Platform. Together, we will be going on a journey where we build an application from start to finish that targets Windows, WebAssembly (WASM), Windows Presentation Framework (WPF), GTK (Linux), iOS, Android, and macOS. You do not need any experience in cross-platform or mobile application development. The chapters break everything down, so the only prerequisite needed is to be a C# .NET developer and a fundamental understanding of the language.

The final application is a OneDrive clone that uses Azure AD and the Microsoft Graph. You will be able to translate your authentication and API skills right into an enterprise-grade application. This book builds upon itself chapter over chapter as we implement our OneDrive clone. You will learn concepts such as XAML, Model-View-ViewModel, platform-specific code, Dependency Injection, navigation, and more! The goal of this book is to provide you, the reader, with all the tools to build an Uno Platform application.

CHAPTER 1

Introduction to Uno Platform

There are many options available when building cross-platform applications in the .NET ecosystem, especially when considering the variety of mobile devices and different form factors available today. Some of the popular options are using Uno Platform, .NET MAUI (Multi-platform App UI), Xamarin.Forms, Avalonia UI, and others. This book is all about Uno Platform development, but each framework has advantages and disadvantages over the others.

Uno Platform provides a familiar development experience for Windows developers, especially developers who have used the Universal Windows Platform (UWP) or WinUI. Uno Platform's original vision was to take the UWP (now WinUI) specification and add implementations for the remaining platforms. This has since expanded into UWP and WinUI specifications, but the platform support remains the same.

The major advantage of Uno Platform development is pixel-perfect user interfaces across the various platforms. Where other platforms may strive for a consistent native experience, Uno Platform wants the interface to be as close to identical in the platforms. This opinionated approach makes it an ideal framework when building line-of-business applications such as tools for large enterprises. Uno Platform still uses the native controls unless you are using a specific Skia target such as WPF or GTK.

Note Uno Platform's default look and feel matches the Windows platform, but you can use native styling or one of the style kits provided by Uno Platform, such as Material.

© Skye Hoefling 2022
S. Hoefling, *Getting Started with the Uno Platform and WinUI 3*,
https://doi.org/10.1007/978-1-4842-8248-9_1

Who Is This Book For?All Developers

In this book we will be building an Uno Platform application targeting Windows, WebAssembly (WASM), WPF, GTK (Linux), iOS, Android, and macOS. The only expectation from the reader is that you have a basic understanding of C# and .NET. As we go through each chapter, it will expand on the various topics we are implementing with full code samples.

After reading this book, you should have all the concepts you need to complete your cross-platform project. This book will be a great getting started guide for new developers as well as a good reference guide for developers who have been building apps for many years. There are concepts you only do once on a project and you need a refresher on for your next project.

Our goal is to build an Uno Platform application regardless of your background. It is not required to have experience with Xamarin.Forms, .NET MAUI, WPF, UWP, or other technologies.

.NET MAUI and Xamarin.Forms Developers

If you are a .NET MAUI or Xamarin.Forms developer, some of the concepts will appear familiar. I would encourage you to follow along as there are often subtle differences that you should be aware of. The XAML specification is not standardized across the various frameworks in the ecosystem. The fundamentals of XAML are the same, but since Uno Platform uses the UWP and WinUI specifications, many of the objects will have different names as well as different techniques.

As a .NET MAUI or Xamarin.Forms developer, you will have experience with the application development model of Uno Platform where you will be using a combination of XAML and C# technologies. Model-View-ViewModel design is a best practice in both, and the skills transfer over to Uno Platform quite well. Outside of the views, your view models have the same problems and similar solutions.

Universal Windows Platform (UWP) and WinUI Developers

UWP and WinUI developers will feel right at home using Uno Platform as the original vision of Uno Platform was to implement the UWP specification for the various platforms. Many of the concepts in this book will be reviewed for UWP or WinUI developers, and you may find this book useful as a reference. This will be especially true when you are trying to accomplish Uno Platform–specific techniques.

When using Uno Platform in the non-Windows platforms, you are still using the `Windows.*` or `Microsoft.*` namespaces and APIs. On those platforms the core code has native implementations to perform the requested task. This gives the Windows developers a great starting point as they do not need to learn any new APIs.

Even though Uno Platform provides a great shared API for all the platforms, you will still need to write native code from time to time. A Windows developer will need to familiarize themselves with the native targets when they have a task that is not supported.

Windows Presentation Framework (WPF) Developers

Windows Presentation Framework (WPF) came before UWP, and there are many similarities in the specification as well as differences and lessons learned when Microsoft set out to create UWP. WPF developers will have a good starting point with the user interface layer as there are similarities in controls used between WPF and UWP. The APIs for performing operations other than the user interface will be mostly new.

Developers with experience with WPF will have a similar learning curve as Xamarin. Forms and .NET MAUI developers. The skills you have learned using XAML, data binding, and more are directly applicable in Uno Platform. You will need to familiarize yourself with native APIs and WinUI.

.NET and C# Developers

Do not worry if you are a .NET developer with no user interface experience. This book will be covering new concepts. Each chapter will include detailed code snippets to help you along the way.

Upon completing this book, you will have the skills to build applications with Uno Platform. Uno Platform is built on top of .NET technologies, which you are already familiar with. While many concepts will be new, the libraries and programming skills you have today are still relevant.

What Is Uno Platform

Uno Platform is a WinUI bridge that allows developers to use the WinUI specification to compile applications for various platforms such as iOS, Android, WebAssembly (WASM), macOS, Linux, and more. Conceptually it is like Xamarin.Forms or .NET MAUI but is a different implementation that takes different architectural design choices.

Pixel Perfect

Mobile development is difficult, and there are so many options available that can be overwhelming for developers. Do you pick a technology that provides native controls, or do you use something that uses rendered controls? The end users of your application typically only care if they can complete their task and not what toolkit and frameworks were used to compile it. In modern mobile development, it is common to have a similar look and feel across the different platforms. The user should feel at home and familiar with your app as they use it on different devices. If a user has been using your application on Android and then they open the web version, it should be using the same icons, themes, and overall look and feel.

Uno Platform provides pixel-perfect development across their platforms, which means you will write your application once and it will look the same across the platforms. The user interface toolkit comes styled across the different platforms to match Fluent Design from Microsoft. If this doesn't work for your application, you can style them to match your branding strategy or even use the platform native styles. Uno Platform gives you complete control on how your application looks.

Architecture

Uno Platform creates a WinUI bridge to the other platforms it supports. This means you can write WinUI code and compile it for the various platforms. The platform uses various techniques to support the different platforms such as Xamarin Native, WebAssembly, and SkiaSharp depending on the target. See the Uno Platform architecture diagram in Figure 1-1.

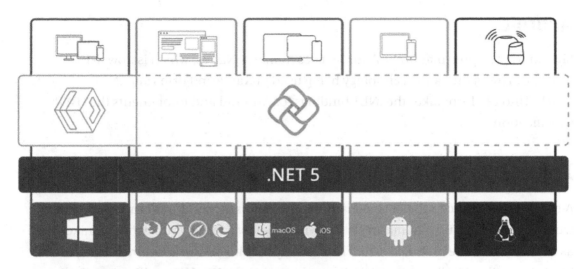

Figure 1-1. *Uno Platform architecture diagram*

Windows

Since Uno Platform is a reimplementation of the WinUI specification, there is nothing special in the Windows target. It does come preconfigured to use WinUI and Project Reunion, so your environment is ready to go with the latest technology.

WebAssembly

The web implementation for Uno Platform uses WebAssembly (WASM), which takes each WinUI control and builds its implementation that is sent to the DOM. There is no need to write any JavaScript as the code is compiled as native WASM that the browser can understand.

If you want to write an application for WASM that depends on JavaScript, there are interoperability features built into the platform so it will work together.

macOS and iOS

Xamarin Native, which is now .NET iOS and .NET macOS, is used to support iOS and macOS. This is the same technology that Xamarin.Forms and .NET MAUI use to support the Apple platforms. Uno Platform doesn't specifically use Xamarin.Forms or .NET MAUI, but it uses the same underlying technology to create the native controls.

Android

Similar to the Apple platforms, Android uses Xamarin Native, which is now .NET Android. This is the same technology being used in Xamarin.Forms and .NET MAUI. Uno Platform takes the .NET bindings for Android and implements the UWP specification.

Xamarin Is Not Xamarin.Forms

A common misconception of Uno Platform is that it uses Xamarin.Forms, which is not true. Uno Platform uses Xamarin Native, which is now a target framework moniker such as net6.0-ios or net6.0-android. The best way to think of Uno Platform is a separate implementation similar to Xamarin.Forms but using the WinUI specification. Both technologies rely on the same underlying technology.

Uno Platform has built custom renderers for Xamarin.Forms, which allows existing Xamarin.Forms applications to be compiled under Uno Platform.

Conclusion

This chapter is a general overview of cross-platform application development. We set expectations for developers of varying backgrounds as we build a full Uno Platform application throughout this book. In the next chapter, we will be getting started with our Uno Platform project so we can start developing.

CHAPTER 2

New Project

In this book we are going to build a cross-platform app that uses Uno Platform and WinUI 3 as the application framework. Then we will leverage public APIs from OneDrive and the Microsoft Graph. You will learn the basics of user interface development, application architecture, and accessing native APIs as we build our app, at least initially, offline first.

This chapter is going to help us get started by creating our brand-new Uno Platform and WinUI 3 project. We will cover how to get your development environment set up and ready to build your application on the various target platforms of Uno Platform.

To begin you should be ready to install Visual Studio and all the necessary tools to create a new project in Uno Platform. This will be a complete guide on setting up your development environment and getting the Uno Platform template to compile and run applications that target Windows, WebAssembly (WASM), WPF, Linux (GTK), Android, iOS, and macOS.

Visual Studio

When using Uno Platform, I recommend using the latest version of Visual Studio for Uno Platform development. If you want to target iOS, you can use a connected macOS or remotely connected macOS or directly use Visual Studio for Mac on the macOS machine. In the connected scenario, there is an iOS Simulator viewer built into Visual Studio. If you want to target macOS, your only option is to run it from macOS hardware. There is no connected approach or viewer like there is with iOS. We will be using Visual Studio for this book with a remotely connected macOS machine. When we need to run macOS builds, we will be using Visual Studio for Mac directly on macOS hardware.

Most of the screenshots you will see throughout this book will be using Visual Studio on Windows unless needed for iOS or macOS actions.

© Skye Hoefling 2022
S. Hoefling, *Getting Started with the Uno Platform and WinUI 3*,
https://doi.org/10.1007/978-1-4842-8248-9_2

> **Note**   You are not limited to just Visual Studio for building Uno Platform projects. You can use Visual Studio for Mac, Visual Studio Code, JetBrains Rider, and others. Some of these tools provide installers to ensure you have the necessary dependencies installed, but there is an easier way.

Requirements

Uno Platform development depends on several different Visual Studio workloads to be preinstalled:

- Universal Windows Platform development

- Mobile development with .NET

- ASP.NET and web development

It is best to install the correct workloads using the latest version of the Visual Studio installer. If Visual Studio is already installed, you can modify your installation and make your selections via the Visual Studio installer.

The Universal Windows Platform development workload, selected via the Visual Studio installer, is required for the core UWP components and Windows target. See Figure 2-1 for the workload screenshot.

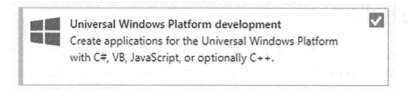

Figure 2-1. *Visual Studio component: Universal Windows Platform*

Mobile development with .NET is required for iOS, macOS, and Android development. If you plan to develop an app for Apple hardware, you will need a macOS machine. See Figure 2-2 for the workload screenshot.

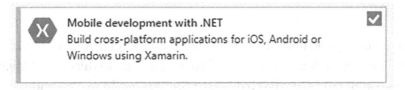

Figure 2-2. *Visual Studio component: Mobile development with .NET*

ASP.NET and web development is required for the WebAssembly (WASM) target. See Figure 2-3 for the workload screenshot.

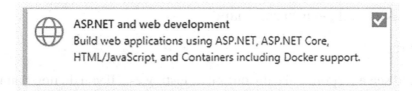

Figure 2-3. *Visual Studio component: ASP.NET and web development*

Project Templates

To start building Uno Platform projects, you will need to download the Visual Studio extension, which includes the project templates. The extension is needed if you plan to create your projects through the Visual Studio new project wizard:

```
https://marketplace.visualstudio.com/items?itemName=nventivecorp.uno-
platform-addin
```

Uno Check

The Visual Studio installer does not always install all the tools you need, such as the latest mobile Software Development Kits (SDKs). To properly develop cross-platform applications, you will need SDKs for Android, Windows, GTK, WASM, and any platform you plan to compile. This is where Uno Check is so useful as it goes through all your installed components and ensures everything is installed so you can start your Uno Platform development.

Uno Check is a dotnet command-line interface (CLI) that will download and install items upon your approval. Let's see how it works.

Requirements

You will need to ensure you have the latest version of dotnet installed. We are going to be using .NET 6. If you don't have it installed, you can go to the official Microsoft Downloads page at https://dotnet.microsoft.com/download. You will want to download .NET 6 or newer for your operating system. If you are using Visual Studio 2022, it should already be preinstalled on your machine.

To test that .NET is installed correctly, you can run the command from Listing 2-1 in your CLI of choice.

Listing 2-1. .NET CLI get info command

```
dotnet --info
```

You should see a response like the output in Listing 2-2. If you do not, that means .NET is not installed correctly or not added to your path. Go back and double-check that it is installed correctly.

Listing 2-2. .NET CLI response

```
.NET SDK (reflecting any global.json):
 Version:   6.0.100
 Commit:    9e8b04bbff

Runtime Environment:
 OS Name:     Windows
 OS Version:  10.0.19043
 OS Platform: Windows
 RID:         win10-x64
 Base Path:   C:\Program Files\dotnet\sdk\6.0.100\

Host (useful for support):
  Version: 6.0.0
  Commit:  4822e3c3aa

.NET SDKs installed:
  5.0.301 [C:\Program Files\dotnet\sdk]
  6.0.100 [C:\Program Files\dotnet\sdk]

.NET runtimes installed:
```

```
Microsoft.WindowsDesktop.App 5.0.7 [C:\Program Files\dotnet\shared\
Microsoft.WindowsDesktop.App]
Microsoft.WindowsDesktop.App 6.0.0 [C:\Program Files\dotnet\shared\
Microsoft.WindowsDesktop.App]
```

```
To install additional .NET runtimes or SDKs:
```

```
  https://aka.ms/dotnet-download
```

Once .NET is installed correctly, you can move on to the next step. Uno Check is a dotnet CLI tool, and it is required to run.

Installing Uno Check

To install Uno Check, open up your CLI of choice and run the dotnet command seen in Listing 2-3.

Listing 2-3. .NET CLI install tool for Uno.Check.

```
dotnet tool install -global Uno.Check
```

This command will install Uno Check as a global tool that can be invoked using the command uno-check.

Run Uno Check

Now that Uno Check is installed, you can run the CLI utility, and it will check everything for you and request permission to install missing items. See example output in Listing 2-4.

Listing 2-4. Uno Check response output

uno-check

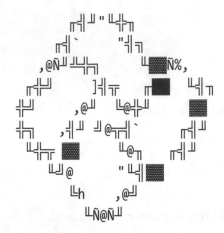

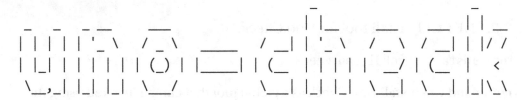

☼ Uno Platform Check v1.1.0.0 ☼

This tool will check your Uno Platform development environment.
If problems are detected, it will offer the option to try and fix them for
you, or suggest a way to fix them yourself.

» Synchronizing configuration... ok
» Scheduling appointments... ok

A new window will display that shows the output from Uno Check as it looks for
SDKs and runtimes required for Uno Platform development. As it goes through and
validates everything on your development machine, it will request permission to fix
missing dependencies.

Once you give it permission, it will install the missing dependency and perform the
check again. If that is successful, it will let you know, and you can start development.

Other IDEs

Uno Platform is designed to help you build cross-platform applications; you will need to use other tools besides Visual Studio as it is only supported on Windows. There are a variety of choices such as Visual Studio for Mac, Visual Studio Code, JetBrains Rider, and others. Throughout this book we will be focusing on Visual Studio for Windows and switch to Visual Studio for Mac when needed for iOS and macOS development.

UWP vs. WinUI

Uno Platform allows you to create a project using UWP or WinUI, which gives you the latest features from the Windows App SDK. WinUI is an evolution of UWP that is not coupled to the Windows operating system. Many of the familiar controls from UWP have been ported over to WinUI. A common problem with UWP development is to get the latest features you need for your customers to be on a certain build of Windows. WinUI resolves that problem by not making anything dependent on the OS.

If you are migrating an existing UWP application to Uno Platform, you may want to use the Uno Platform UWP projects. This will reduce your time than porting everything over to WinUI. If you are working on a brand-new project, it is best to start with WinUI.

Create a New Project

The best way to create an Uno Platform project is to use the official dotnet CLI template. You can still use the Visual Studio templates and the wizard experience. To get started open your favorite CLI and enter the command seen in Listing 2-5.

Listing 2-5. Download Uno Platform .NET CLI templates

```
dotnet new -i Uno.ProjectTemplates.Dotnet
```

This will download and install all the Uno Platform .NET CLI templates for creating new projects, libraries, and more. You can verify that it installed them correctly by listing out all project templates tagged with the keyword "Uno Platform". Use the command seen in Listing 2-6 to verify. To see a complete list of all the available .NET Templates see Table 2-1.

Listing 2-6. .NET CLI list of "Uno Platform" templates

```
dotnet new -l --tag "Uno Platform"
```

Table 2-1. *A Listing of Available Uno Platform .NET Templates*

Template Name	Short Name
Cross-Platform App (Prism)	unoapp-prism
Cross-Platform Library	unolib
Cross-Platform UI Tests	unoapp-uitest
Cross-Runtime Library	unolib-crossruntime
Multi-Platform App	unoapp
Multi-Platform App (net6)	unoapp-net6
Multi-Platform App (WinUI)	unoapp-winui
Multi-Platform App net6 (WinUI)	unoapp-winui-net6
Uno Platform WebAssembly Head	wasmxfhead

After verifying that the templates are installed, we can start the process of creating our project. Create a new directory called "UnoDrive" where all our code will live for this project and then run the new template command as seen in Listing 2-7.

Listing 2-7. Create a new Uno Platform app using the dotnet template

```
C:\> mkdir UnoDrive
C:\> cd UnoDrive
C:\UnoDrive> dotnet new unoapp-winui-net6
```

These commands will create your new .NET 6 WinUI 3 Uno Platform application. We can go and open the solution file with Visual Studio to start exploring what has been created for us. See Figure 2-4 for a view of the Visual Studio Solution Explorer of the new project.

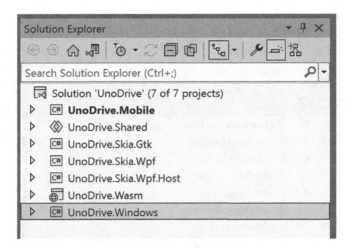

Figure 2-4. *Visual Studio Solution Explorer after creating the Uno app*

The Solution Explorer contains all the various target platform heads and shared code. I find it easier to organize your projects into two groups, platform heads and shared code. The first thing to do is to create a solution folder called "Platforms" and move all the project heads into that folder:

- UnoDrive.Mobile

- UnoDrive.Skia.Gtk

- UnoDrive.Skia.Wpf

- UnoDrive.Skia.Wpf.Host

- UnoDrive.Wasm

- UnoDrive.Windows

Once you have everything moved into your new solution folder, your Solution Explorer should look like the screenshot in Figure 2-5.

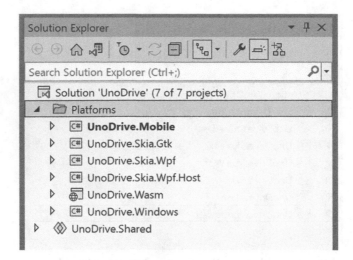

Figure 2-5. *Visual Studio Solution Explorer with the new Platforms solution folder*

In Uno Platform your shared code should be included in your shared project. A shared project varies from a standard .NET project as it doesn't compile on its own. To compile a shared project, you must reference it from another .NET project or in our case a target platform head. This allows us to write all our code for the various projects in the one shared project. At compile time the code will be treated as part of the .NET project that is compiling and not another dependency.

If you choose, you can convert your shared project to a .NET standard project or even a multi-targeting project. It is recommended to use multi-targeting techniques as it will be easier to manage your various platform-specific code. In a multi-targeting project, you will have one .csproj file that represents all the platforms that project can target. On the other hand, the shared project will just use pre-processor directives for platform-specific code. You can learn more about multi-targeted class libraries and projects at the Uno Platform docs. See the following link:

- `https://platform.uno/docs/articles/cross-targeted-libraries.html`

Our examples in this book will follow the recommendation from Uno Platform, which is to use shared projects.

Why Shared Projects?

One of the major benefits of using a shared project is there is no need to manage additional dependencies as the code is treated as part of the target platform that is currently being compiled. This means that any dependency, pre-processor directive, or other items that may exist in one project and not the other can seamlessly be used in the shared project.

In the Uno Platform ecosystem, it is recommended to use the WinUI dependencies for the Windows project and then the Uno Platform forks if they exist for the various target platforms. Typically the package naming convention adds the prefix `Uno.*`, which means you will have different dependencies for the Windows project vs. other target platforms. If you were to try using a `netstandard2.0` project or even a multi-targeting project, you would need to manage the dependency tree for each target platform. By using a shared project, this maintenance problem goes away completely, as dependencies for each platform are added to the appropriate target platform head project.

As you work on your cross-platform app, you will need to access native APIs for the various platforms that are not implemented in Uno Platform or don't have a good mapping to the WinUI API specification. In this case you will be using a pre-processor directive or another means of getting the code to compile for that specific platform. By using the shared project, you will have access to all the pre-processor directives from each target platform head project as the code will be compiled just as if it was included in that project.

Since a shared project is referenced directly by the project head, there is no additional assembly to build. This means your final binary size is smaller and you get better performance in Visual Studio. If you choose to build a multi-targeted project, you will be fighting the tooling as each platform will need to compile when you build inside of Visual Studio.

These are some of the reasons why it is recommended to use a shared project. If a shared project isn't going to work for you, I strongly recommend looking at a multi-targeting project as you will be able to manage dependencies for each platform.

Shared Code: UnoDrive.Shared

Exploring our codebase, the UnoDrive.Shared shared project is where most of your coding will be happening. If you expand the project out, it looks very similar to a Windows project as Uno Platform is a reimplementation of the UWP specification. See screenshot in Figure 2-6.

Right now, there isn't much to look at, but we have our basic building blocks:

- Assets folder

- Strings folder

- App.xaml

- MainPage.xaml

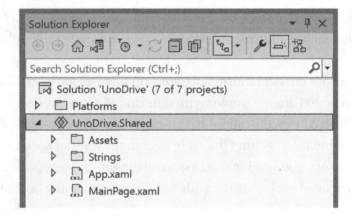

Figure 2-6. *Visual Studio Solution Explorer – shared project*

The App.xaml is your entry point to the Uno Platform application, and the template generated some Uno Platform–specific code that you may not have seen in traditional Windows development. I would not worry too much about changing them; it configures logging for some of the platforms so you can see messages in the console.

The MainPage.xaml is your main page of the application. Currently it is a simple Hello World that displays a message in a window. We will start editing this in the next chapter.

Windows Target: UnoDrive.Windows

The Windows target project is called `UnoDrive.Windows`. This code uses the Microsoft implementation Windows App SDK and WinUI 3 API. There aren't any changes here when using Uno Platform. See screenshot of Visual Studio Solution Explorer in Figure 2-7.

Figure 2-7. *Visual Studio Solution Explorer – Windows project*

In the non-Windows platforms, there is a little bit of code that uses the platform's specific way of creating a page. That code then invokes the Uno Platform entry point. In the Windows target, none of this is needed, and it can reference the shared project.

Launching the Windows project requires you to set the configuration correctly:

- *Configuration*: Debug

- *Platform*: x86, x64, or arm64

  - It will not work with any CPU.

Once you have successfully built and launched the Windows project, you should see the Uno Platform Hello World page, see screenshot in of application running in Figure 2-8.

Figure 2-8. *Windows application – Hello World*

WebAssembly: UnoDrive.Wasm

WebAssembly, otherwise known as the WASM target, is found in the UnoDrive.Wasm project. This project is an ASP.NET Core project. If you are familiar with how those projects look, things will be very familiar to you. See screenshot of Visual Studio Solution Explorer in Figure 2-9.

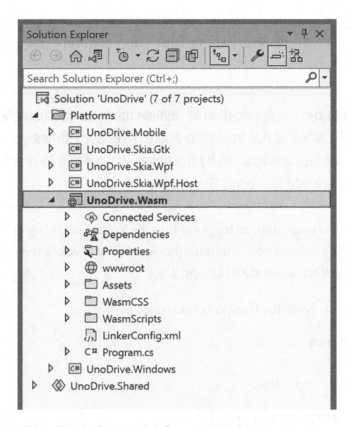

Figure 2-9. *Visual Studio Solution Explorer – WASM project*

The WASM project is broken into several folders:

- *wwwroot*: Anything public such as other HTML files you want served with the web application

- Assets

- WasmCSS

- WasmScripts

After the folders you will have two important files, the LinkerConfig.xml and the Program.cs.

A compilation linker is a tool that removes unused APIs to reduce the size of the final binary. This is a technique that is very useful in building mobile apps when you want to ensure your final binary is small to ship to the app store. This same concept applies to WASM projects as the end user is using a web browser to download your binaries. The smaller they are, the faster the page will load.

As you include more and more dependencies to your Uno Platform project, you will need to edit the `LinkerConfig.xml` to ensure important APIs aren't removed at compile time.

Tip   It is useful to run the application in release mode as you complete features to validate that the linker is not being too aggressive. Sometimes you need to manually edit what files are ignored by the linker. We put this to practice in Chapter 13 when we add Microsoft Graph APIs.

The `Program.cs` is your main entry point into the WASM target upon starting the application. This file contains your main method and then invokes the `App.xaml.cs` from your shared project, see code in Listing 2-8.

Listing 2-8. Startup code for the WebAssembly project

```
public class Program
{
    private static App _app;

    static int Main(string[] args)
    {
        Windows.UI.Xaml.Application.Start(_ =>
            _app = new App());

        return 0;
    }
}
```

Compiling the WASM target can be a little slow on the first compile. Once build binaries and generated source code are cached, the build goes much faster. To start the WASM target, you will select the following configuration:

- *Configuration*: Debug

- *Platform*: Any CPU

Once you have selected the configuration and platform, you can run the WASM target. After it has successfully compiled and launched, you should have a web browser open with a similar page that says "Hello, world!". See screenshot of WASM application running in Figure 2-10.

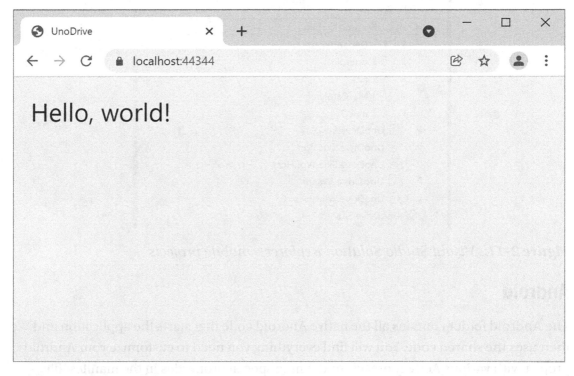

Figure 2-10. WASM application – Hello World

Mobile Targets

To compile and run any of the mobile targets, you will use `UnoDrive.Mobile`. The mobile targets include Android, iOS, macOS, and MacCatalyst, which are using a .NET 6 multi-targeted project. .NET MAUI (Multi-platform App UI) uses this same technique, and Uno Platform leverages the new features in the tooling. To start any of the mobile projects, use a .NET multi-targeted project file named `UnoDrive.Mobile`.

The single .NET project for mobile targets allows us to contain Android, iOS, MacCatalyst, and macOS in one project. See screenshot of Visual Studio Solution Explorer in Figure 2-11.

Figure 2-11. *Visual Studio Solution Explorer – mobile projects*

Android

The Android folder contains all the native Android code that starts the application and then uses the shared code. You will find everything you need to customize your Android project with various Activity objects or defining special properties in the manifest file.

Expanding the Android folder, we can explore the various items that are configured for our Uno Platform application by default. See screenshot of Visual Studio Solution Explorer in Figure 2-12.

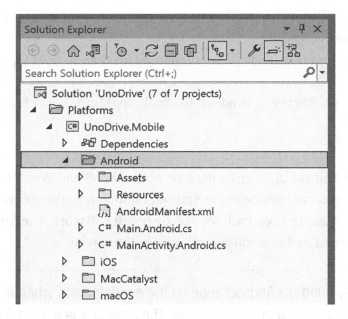

Figure 2-12. *Visual Studio Solution Explorer – Android project*

The Android project has the following items:

- *Assets*: Used for Android-specific assets

- *Resources*: Used for Android-specific resources

- Main.cs

- MainActivity.cs

In the Android ecosystem, every page is an Activity. Uno Platform uses the
MainActivity to render the application. As pages change in the app, it will update this
Activity, and there is no need to launch other activities.

As you work on your Uno Platform application, you will need to come back to the
Android target to configure permissions and adjust Android-specific configurations.
Most of the code required to start up your application exists in the Uno Platform parent
class, which makes our MainActivity very small, see code in Listing 2-9.

Listing 2-9. Startup code for the Android project

```
[Activity(
        MainLauncher = true,
```

```
        ConfigurationChanges = global::Uno.UI.ActivityHelper.
        AllConfigChanges,
        WindowSoftInputMode = SoftInput.AdjustPan | SoftInput.StateHidden
    )]
public class MainActivity : Windows.UI.Xaml.ApplicationActivity
{
}
```

Debugging an Android app can be done on both macOS and Windows hardware using a physical connected device or the Android Emulator. Nothing compares to testing your app on real hardware as you will see exactly how it will work. The Android Emulator is a great development tool as it will get you most of the way there.

Note   I typically build my Android apps on the emulator and when it is time to release do my final testing on a real device. The emulator is a good tool, but always validate on real hardware.

We are going to use the Android Emulator in this book. The Android target requires the Android Emulator to be running. If you have not configured your Android Emulator, you can quickly do this through Visual Studio. Open the Android Device Manager as seen in Figure 2-13 by going to Tools ➤ Android ➤ Android Device Manager.

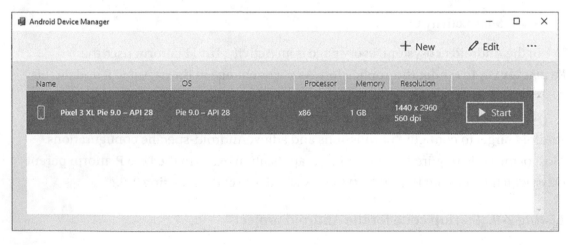

Figure 2-13. *Android Device Manager*

Once you have the Android Device Manager opened, you can see all your emulators and create a new one. If you have not created one yet, go ahead and create one. We already have an emulator created, so we are going to launch it.

Note   Typically, you do not need to manually start the emulator; it should start automatically when selected at project startup.

With your emulator started, go ahead and start the Android project. Since the mobile project can target multiple platforms, you will need to select Android. Next to the green debug button, which may read Simulator or UnoDrive.Shared, click the down arrow. This opens the menu to select the various emulators and simulators. Open "Android Emulators" and select the emulator you are currently running. See Figure 2-14 for a screenshot of the menu selecting the Android Emulator.

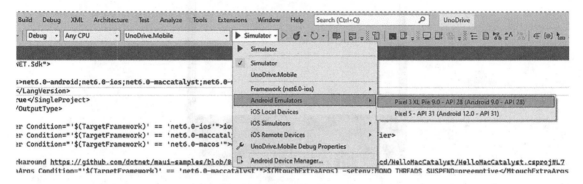

Figure 2-14. *Visual Studio debug menu selecting an Android Emulator for UnoDrive.Mobile*

Select the following configuration:

- *Configuration*: Debug

- *Platform*: Any CPU

- *Emulator*: Pixel 3 XL Pie 9.0 (this will vary depending on emulator name)

After your Android target compiles and launches into the emulator, you should see our "Hello, world!" application.

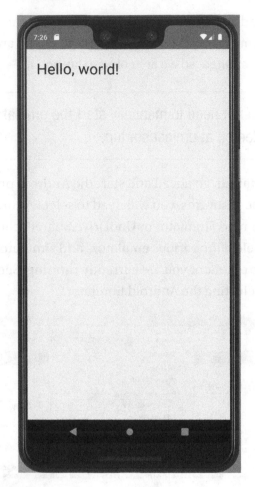

Figure 2-15. *Android application – Hello World*

iOS

The iOS folder contains the iOS-specific code, and it uses .NET for iOS, which gives us native iOS bindings to compile the project. In this project you will be configuring any iOS-specific settings such as permissions.

Expanding the iOS folder will show you all the existing files for your native iOS application.

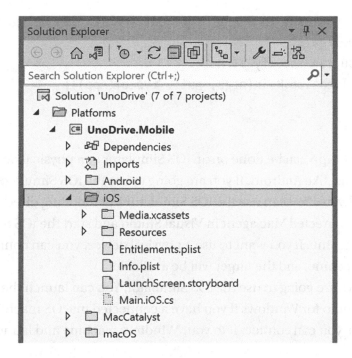

Figure 2-16. *Visual Studio Solution Explorer – iOS project*

The main items in the iOS project are

- *Media.xcassets*: Asset catalogs

- Resources

- Entitlements.plist

- Info.plist

- Main.cs

The startup code for iOS apps is simple and just invokes our main App.xaml.cs from the shared code, see code in listing 2-10.

Listing 2-10. Startup code for the iOS project

```
Public class Application
{
    // This is the main entry point of the application.
    Static void Main(string[] args)
    {
```

```
        // if you want to use a different Application Delegate class from
        "AppDelegate"
        // you can specify it here.
        UIApplication.Main(args, null, typeof(App));
    }
}
```

Building an iOS app can be done on an iOS Simulator or a physical device connected to your machine just like Android. If you are going to use the iOS Simulator, you must have macOS hardware. You can use the iOS Simulator by compiling directly from macOS, or you can use a connected Mac agent in Visual Studio and start the iOS Simulator from your Windows machine. If you want to use a physical device, you can connect it directly to your macOS machine, and the target will be available.

In this book we are going to use the iOS Simulator. You can launch the iOS app right through Visual Studio for Windows if you have a connected macOS machine. If you have a physical iPhone, you can connect it to your Windows machine and launch it that way as well.

- *Configuration*: Debug.

- *Platform*: iPhoneSimulator or iPhone.

- *Target*: Select from your list of targets.

Figure 2-17. *iOS application – Hello World*

To distribute iOS apps, you will need macOS hardware, and there is no substitute for this. You can compile the binaries on Windows, but the final deployment to an iOS Simulator or physical device must be done from a macOS machine. Once you have the hardware, you can either use Visual Studio for Windows or Visual Studio for Mac. It is recommended to do as much work as possible through Visual Studio for Windows as the development experience is the best there.

The latest Uno Platform project templates will include a special macOS slnf file, which is a solution filter that tells Visual Studio and MSBuild which projects to load. This file is safe to open in Visual Studio for Mac. If it doesn't exist, you can manually unload or create your own slnf file.

If you are not using the slnf (solution filter), it is best to unload all projects except UnoDrive.Mobile. This means you should unload the following projects:

- UnoDriveSkia.Wpf
- UnoDrive.Skia.Wpf.Host
- UnoDrive.Windows

macOS

The macOS folder uses an almost identical SDK as iOS. This project contains the desktop-specific project settings for macOS applications. You will be modifying settings in this project to control platform-specific settings such as permissions.

Since macOS uses an almost identical SDK to iOS, the project structure is very similar. See screenshot of Visual Studio Solution Explorer in Figure 2-18.

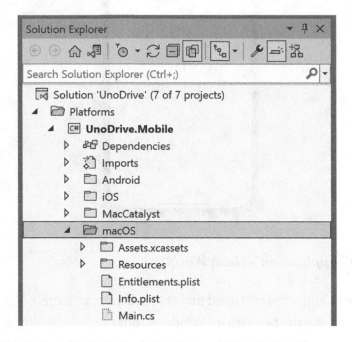

Figure 2-18. *Visual Studio Solution Explorer – macOS Project*

- Asset catalog

- Resources

- Entitlements.plist

- Info.plist

- Main.cs

The startup code is very simple and just instantiates the shared code `App.xaml.cs`, see code in Listing 2-11.

Listing 2-11. Startup code for the macOS project

```
static class MainClass
{
    static void Main(string[] args)
    {
        NSApplication.Init();
        NSApplication.SharedApplication.Delegate = new App();
        NSApplication.Main(args);
    }
}
```

Launching the macOS target is currently only supported in Visual Studio for Mac as there is no remote simulator like iOS. On your Mac device, select the following build settings:

- *Configuration*: Debug

- *Platform*: iPhoneSimulator

- *Target*: My Mac

You can see a screenshot of how to configure Visual Studio for Mac in Figure 2-19.

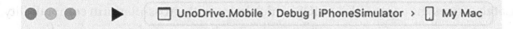

Figure 2-19. *Visual Studio for Mac configuration – select to run on "My Mac"*

Once you select iPhoneSimulator for your platform, you will see My Mac appear as a launch target. Now you should be able to launch the app and see your native macOS application. See Figure 2-20 for a screenshot of the macOS application running.

If you run into build issues on Visual Studio for Mac, try unloading projects you are not using.

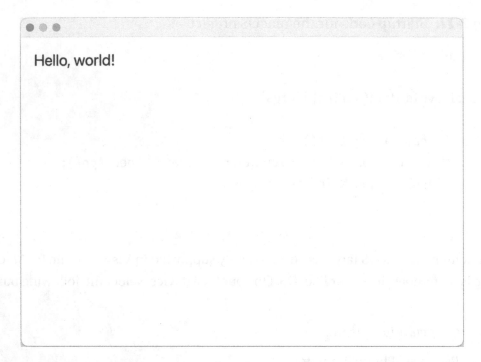

Figure 2-20. *macOS application – Hello World*

MacCatalyst

MacCatalyst uses the same UIKit as iOS, which helps with cross-platform compatibility in the Apple ecosystem. Since Uno Platform is already cross-platform, you can just as easily use macOS or MacCatalyst. The advantage of using MacCatalyst is fewer problems since iOS and MacCatalyst use the same UIKit. If you choose macOS, it uses AppKit, which will be like supporting an entirely different platform.

The MacCatalyst folder contains all the native code specific to your MacCatalyst application. MacCatalyst allows you to use Apple's UIKit for desktop applications instead of AppKit. There are not many changes from your Uno Platform code since our code sharing strategy is part of the platform. The value proposition of MacCatalyst is more code reusability between iOS and Mac desktop apps as they are using the same UI library.

For the purpose of this book, we are going to focus on macOS. We will leave MacCatalyst in the code samples as a point of reference.

WPF Target: UnoDrive.Skia.Wpf

SkiaSharp is a 2D graphics library used throughout the .NET ecosystem, which is a .NET wrapper around the Google 2D graphics library Skia. Some platforms such as WPF use SkiaSharp to create a rendered user interface instead of mapping Uno Platform controls to their native controls.

The WPF target uses SkiaSharp to render the user interface, which is different from some of the other platforms. Instead of native controls, your project will use a drawn user interface that uses the Skia 2D graphics engine to render the controls. This is a popular technique used in tools such as Google's cross-platform toolkit Flutter and a future direction for React Native. If you want to learn more about Skia or SkiaSharp, follow these links:

- `https://github.com/mono/SkiaSharp`

- `https://skia.org/`

The WPF target is broken into two projects, which are the main project of `UnoDrive.Wpf` and the host project of `UnoDrive.Wpf.Host`. To run the WPF project, you will select the host project as your target platform. If you need to make any changes to the WPF project such as adding a new dependency, it will happen in the WPF main project. If you need to add specific startup code or similar, you will edit it in the WPF host project. They are separated out as the WPF main project is a netstandard project and the host project is a .NET Core 3.1 project. As the .NET ecosystem marches toward one .NET with .NET 6 and newer, this may change.

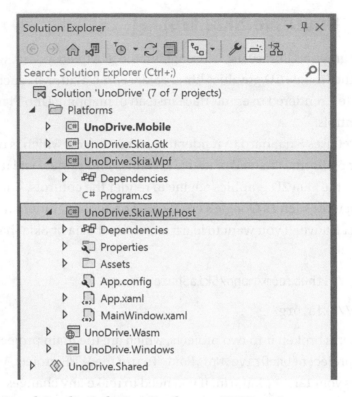

Figure 2-21. *Visual Studio Solution Explorer – WPF projects*

In the host project, you will find your WPF startup code that looks like Windows startup code. The WPF project requires startup code that instantiates the Uno Platform app and loads the shared code. Even though WPF code is similar to WinUI and UWP, the namespaces and controls are not identical, so it needs to start the Uno Platform app just like other targets, see startup code in Listing 2-12.

- App.Xaml

- MainWindow.xaml

Note   Just like in the Windows project, the ***App.xaml*** is our main entry point into the WPF application, and ***MainWindow.xaml*** is where our page is rendered. In this project if you open the ***MainPage.xaml.cs***, you will see the startup code that invokes the shared project to launch the app.

Listing 2-12. Startup code for the WPF project

```
/// <summary>
/// Interaction logic for MainWindow.xaml
/// </summary>
public partial class MainWindow : Window
{
    public MainWindow()
    {
        InitializeComponent();

        root.Content = new global::Uno.UI.Skia.Platform.WpfHost(
            Dispatcher, () => new UnoDrive.App());
    }
}
```

To properly launch the WPF host project, you will need to select the following configuration settings:

- *Configuration*: Debug

- *Platform*: Any CPU

Ensure you select the host project `UnoDrive.WPF.Host`.

Figure 2-22. *WPF application – Hello World*

GTK Target: UnoDrive.Skia.Gtk

The GTK target project contains the GTK that will allow you to run the project on Linux operating systems. Just like the WPF project, the GTK project uses SkiaSharp, and it is a drawn user interface instead of native controls.

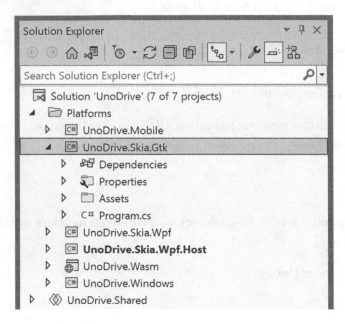

Figure 2-23. *Visual Studio Solution Explorer – GTK project*

The GTK project contains the following items:

- Assets

- Program.cs

The entry point to the GTK application registers an exception listener so the application can exit safely. Then it starts our application using the same shared code, see code in Listing 2-13.

Listing 2-13. Startup code for the GTK project

```
class Program
{
    static void Main(string[] args)
    {
        ExceptionManager.UnhandledException +=
```

```
        delegate (UnhandledExceptionArgs expArgs)
    {
        Console.WriteLine(
            "GLIB UNHANDLED EXCEPTION" +
            expArgs.ExceptionObject.ToString());
        expArgs.ExitApplication = true;
    };

    var host = new GtkHost(() => new App(), args);

    host.Run();
    }
}
```

Before we can get started with the GTK project, we will need to install additional requirements. While GTK is supported on Windows and macOS, we are going to focus on Linux as we have other target projects for those platforms.

As we are doing the majority of our development from a Windows machine, we are going to leverage Windows Subsystem for Linux 2 (WSL2) to run our Linux code. As WSL continues to evolve, there may be a better solution out of the box, but right now we can use an X11 Server for Windows. In the Linux ecosystem, an X11 Server is your GUI server, which is needed to render any graphical user interface.

This is not an easy plug-and-play environment as there are a lot of moving parts. We will be configuring WSL2 to run an X11 GUI that will connect to our Xserver, which will be hosted on our Windows host machine. This means when we debug our applications, it will almost feel like a remote desktop into the Linux environment.

We need to install the following components:

- WSL2 running Ubuntu 18.04 or later

- *Visual Studio feature*: .NET debugging with WSL2

- *vcXsrv*: X11 Server for Windows

- GTK3 runtime on Windows and Linux

You can get this working with WSL1, but the setup will be different as the networking has changed between WSL1 and WSL2.

Install WSL2

To get started you will need to install WSL2 if you have not done so already. You can follow the official documentation from Microsoft to install WSL2: `https://docs.microsoft.com/en-us/windows/wsl/install`. Once you have that completed, you can come back here for the rest of the guide. The installation will automatically install WSL2 and the Ubuntu distribution. See command in Listing 2-14 to check WSL status.

Listing 2-14. Check WSL status

```
wsl --status
```

Visual Studio: .NET Debugging on WSL2

If you are using Visual Studio 16.8 or earlier, you will need to download the preview extension as it was released into Visual Studio in 16.10. In cross-platform development, it is always recommended to use the latest and greatest version of Visual Studio as the technology changes at a very rapid pace.

1. Close any open instances of Visual Studio.

2. Open the Visual Studio installer.

3. Select your installation. You want to enable WSL debugging and select the "Modify" button.

4. Select the "Individual Components" tab.

5. Ensure the ".NET Debugging with WSL" checkbox is checked and select the "Modify" button.

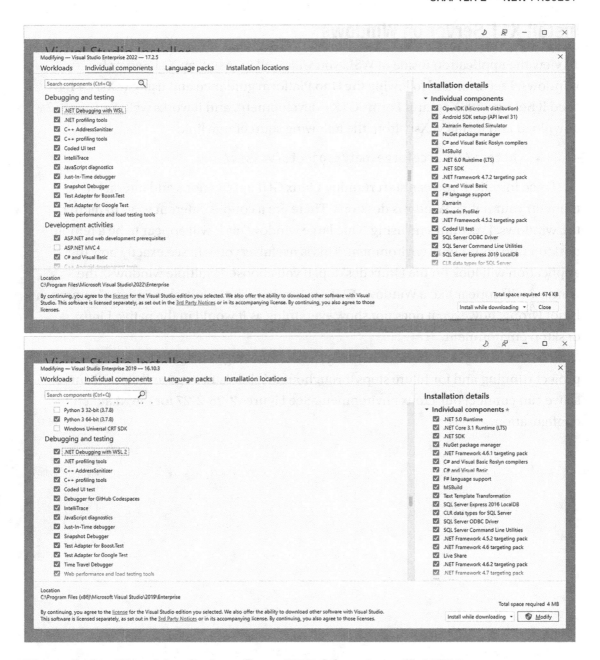

Figure 2-24. *Visual Studio Installer – .NET debugging with WSL2*

Install X11 Server on Windows

To view the application inside of WSL, you will need to install an X11 Server for Windows. I recommend following the Uno Platform guidance and using vcXsrv. I have used it before with Xamarin.Forms GTK+ development, and it works well. You can download and install vcXsrv from the following sourceforge link:

- `https://sourceforge.net/projects/vcxsrv/`

Once installed, you can start running Linux GUI applications and interact with them on your native Windows desktops. There are a couple different ways to render the windows. I recommend using "One large window" as it will appear to be a remote desktop into your Linux environment. This is useful as you will see exactly how the application will look on the Linux desktop. If you choose "Multiple windows," the window will appear like a Windows GUI application. The "Multiple windows" approach is not wrong; however, it does not show everything as it would in the native Linux desktop environment.

The choice is yours, but we are going to use "One large window" for getting the project running and for future steps throughout this book. Let's go and start XLaunch so we can connect our Linux environment. See Figures 2-25-2-27 for the XLaunch configuration.

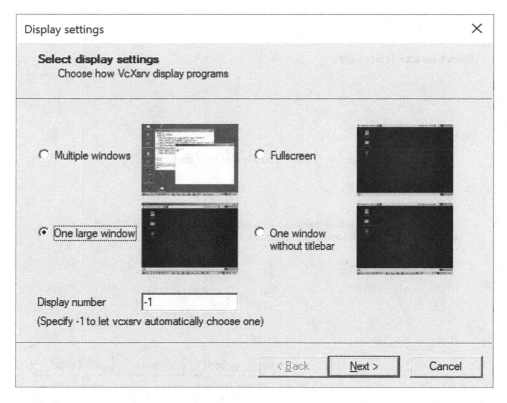

Figure 2-25. *XLaunch display settings*

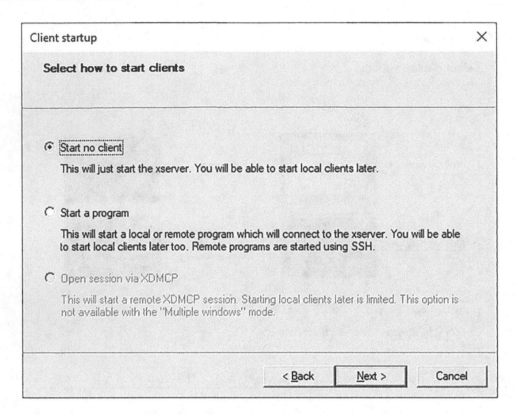

Figure 2-26. *XLaunch client startup*

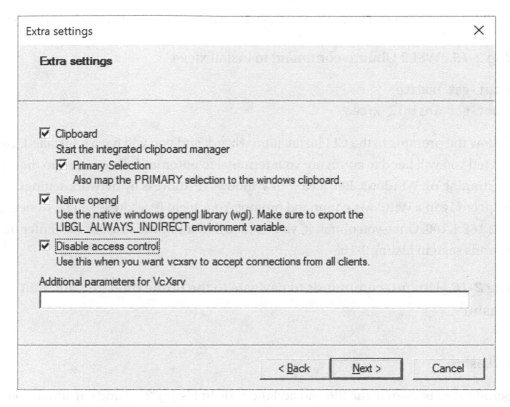

Figure 2-27. *XLaunch extra settings*

In Figure 2-27 we select "Disable access control," which is okay to do on a protected network. It allows any X11 Server to connect to your XLaunch viewer that has access to your machine. In our case it is safe to do this, but if you are using a public network, you may want to configure more of the security settings on XLaunch.

After following the startup wizard, your X11 Server will be running, and you can see it in your Windows System Tray. If you open the XLaunch application, you will see a black screen. This is perfectly normal as we haven't connected our WSL2 to the running X11 Server. Once we start it in Linux, we will have a full desktop environment to interact with.

Install X11 on WSL2

We are going to use xfce4, which is a lightweight desktop environment that works with WSL2. It technically falls outside official support for WSL2 as their goal is to focus on command-line tools in Linux. This is a known and documented working solution in the WSL2 community, so it is safe for us to use.

Open your WSL2 terminal and enter the commands in Listing 2-15 to install xfce4.

Listing 2-15. WSL2 Ubuntu command to install xfce4

```
sudo apt-get update
sudo apt-get install xfce4
```

Follow the prompts in the CLI installation wizard, and you will have it installed. Once completed you will need to configure your terminal to automatically connect to the X11 Server running on Windows. Retrieve your Windows IP address by network settings or enter ipconfig in a Windows command prompt. Your local IP address will be something like 192.168.1.100. Once you obtain it, you need to add it to your .bashrc file. Enter the commands seen in Listing 2-16.

Listing 2-16. Ubuntu commands to navigate to the home directory and edit the .bashrc

```
cd ~/
nano .bashrc
```

Scroll to the bottom of the file and add the code in Listing 2-17 and substitute your IP address.

Listing 2-17. Code to export your current IP address for XLaunch

```
export DISPLAY=192.168.1.100:0.0
```

Now close your WSL2 terminal and reopen it. We can start our desktop environment and connect it to our X11 Server on Windows. To start xfce4 run the command seen in Listing 2-18.

Listing 2-18. Ubuntu command to start xfce4, which will connect to XLaunch

```
startxfce4
```

Open XLaunch to view your running Linux desktop environment. If everything worked, you will see the xfce4 desktop environment instead of the black screen as seen in Figure 2-28.

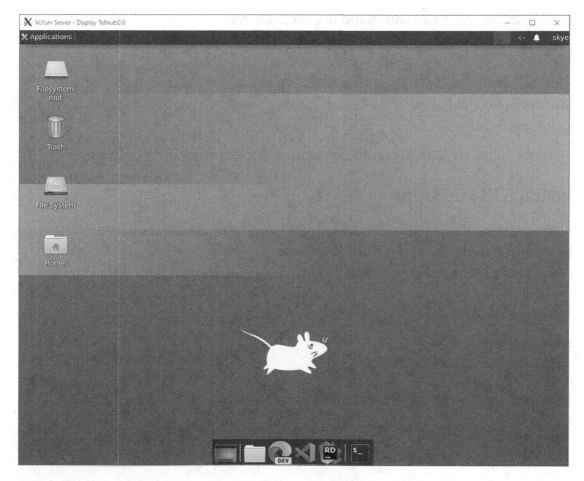

Figure 2-28. *xfce4 desktop running on WSL2 and XLaunch*

Install .NET 6

Using the Ubuntu package manager, we can easily install .NET 6. Enter the command seen in Listing 2-19 into your Linux terminal and follow the prompts.

Listing 2-19. Ubuntu apt-get to install .NET 6.0 SDK

```
sudo apt get install dotnet-sdk-6.0
```

If it installed correctly, you can check by running the command in Listing 2-20.

Listing 2-20.   .NET CLI command to check the info

```
dotnet -info
```

If you are having issues installing .NET 6, you can always refer to the official Microsoft documentation. You will want to follow the links to your distribution and the specific version:

- https://docs.microsoft.com/en-us/dotnet/core/install/linux

Install GTK3 on Linux

Again, using the Ubuntu package manager, we can easily install the necessary dependencies into our Linux environment on WSL2. What version of Ubuntu you have will dictate what commands you enter. See Listing 2-21 for Ubuntu 20.04 and Listing 2-22 for Ubuntu 18.04.

Listing 2-21.   Install GTK3 on Ubuntu 20.04

```
sudo apt-get update
sudo apt-get install libkit-3-dev
```

Listing 2-22.   Install GTK3 on Ubuntu 18.04

```
sudo apt-get update
sudo apt-get install gtk3+3.0
```

Once your installation has finished successfully, we can move on and get ready for debugging our application.

Install GTK3 Runtime on Windows (Optional)

This step is optional, but it is useful to be able to debug the application in a Windows and Linux environment as GTK3 is a cross-platform GUI library. Installing the GTK3 runtime on Windows is as easy as running the installer. You can grab the latest runtime installer from GitHub:

- https://github.com/tschoonj/GTK-for-Windows-Runtime-
  Environment-Installer/releases

Run the installer, and you should be able to run and debug the UnoDrive.Skia.Gtk on the local Windows machine.

Configure Default WSL2

Before we can debug our application, we need to make sure that our default Linux environment is the correct one. If you are only running one Linux environment on WSL2 or WSL1, then you can skip this section. If you are running multiple, you will need to check and set the correct one as the default.

Using the Windows command prompt or PowerShell running on the Windows host machine, run the command seen in Listing 2-23 and see Listing 2-24 for the output. This will tell us what Linux environments are installed.

Listing 2-23. WSL command to list installed versions of Linux

```
wslconfig /l
```

Listing 2-24. Command output from Listing 2-23 – Windows Subsystem for Linux distributions

```
Ubuntu (Default)

Ubuntu-20.04
```

I am using Ubuntu 20.04, so I need to update my default WSL instance using the command in Listing 2-25.

Listing 2-25. WSL command to switch to "Ubuntu-20.04"

```
wslconfig /s "Ubuntu-20.04"
```

Now everything is ready for us to debug our GTK application.

Debug UnoDrive.Skia.Gtk

Our Linux environment is ready, and we can debug the application. In Visual Studio select UnoDrive.Skia.Gtk as your startup project. Then pick WSL next to the green debug arrow.

Note   If you already have GTK installed on your Windows machine, you can debug by selecting UnoDrive.Skia.Gtk. Our goal with GTK is to showcase Linux support. In this book we will be using WSL2 for GTK.

You should now have a new `launchSettings.json` file located under Properties for this target platform. Update your WSL2 launch settings environment variables to look like this. You will need to swap out the IP address for your local IP on the Windows machine:

```
"environmentVariables": {
    "DISPLAY": "192.168.1.192:0.0"
}
```

Now everything is configured, and we can launch our application. Compile and debug it in WSL2. Once it successfully launches, you should see it in the XLaunch window that we started earlier with the application running. See Figure 2-29 for a screenshot of the GTK application running.

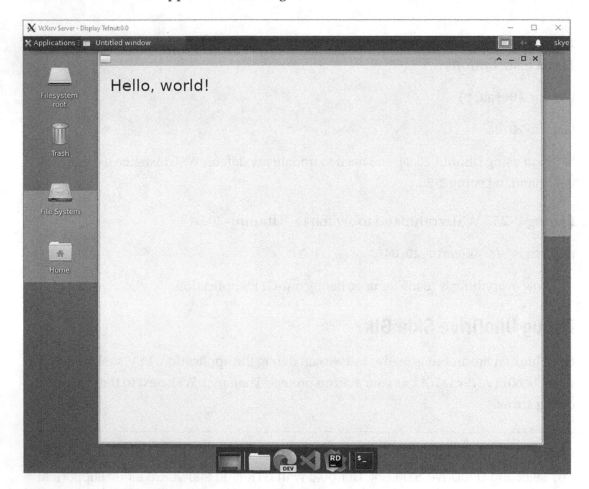

Figure 2-29. *GTK application (Linux) – Hello World*

Conclusion

At this point you should now have your development environment completely set up for each target platform that Uno Platform supports and have your project configured. It is important to be able to run the Hello World application for each target as this is our test to make sure we can develop in those platforms.

In the next chapter, we are going to begin our journey as we start to write Uno Platform code for our new application. If you had any trouble creating the template, you can download all the code in this chapter from GitHub: `https://github.com/SkyeHoefling/UnoDrive/tree/main/Chapter%202`.

CHAPTER 3

Your First Page

In the previous chapter, we learned about setting up our Uno Platform development environment, and we created our new UnoDrive application using the .NET 6 and WinUI 3 project templates. In this chapter we are going to build the very first page of our application that the user will see, which is the login screen.

Moving forward we will be using the code from each chapter. If you get stuck along the way, you can always download the code samples to have a clean start at each chapter. The completed code for Chapter 2 is the starting point for Chapter 3. This can be used as we progress through the book. The recommendation for developing with Uno Platform is to build your application using the Windows target first, which gives you the best developer experience. Some features in your app will require you to focus on a non-Windows target first such as building a mobile-only app or accessing native APIs that are not available in a Windows target.

When building the main user interface and business logic, follow the recommendation and start in the Windows target. Once things appear to be working, go and work in the other platforms.

The Login Page

Before we begin adding any code, we need to define our specification of what we want to accomplish in our login page. In this chapter the goal is to just focus on the basic user interface. We will work on business logic and platform-specific styles in chapters that follow.

Our login page should have the following components:

- Welcome message
- Login button

© Skye Hoefling 2022
S. Hoefling, *Getting Started with the Uno Platform and WinUI 3*,
https://doi.org/10.1007/978-1-4842-8248-9_3

The Uno Platform template creates a MainPage.xaml, but our main page is a login page, so we are going to rename this page to LoginPage.xaml, which is a more descriptive name. A typical page consists of two files: the markup known as the XAML file and the code behind, which is typically a C# code file. When you start changing the name of a page, you will need to update the names of the MainPage.xaml and MainPage.xaml.cs. You will also need to update the class names in both files, which gives us four items to change.

Note   You can create user interface pages entirely in code using C# if you do not want to use XAML. The most used technique is XAML with a code behind.

Let's start by updating the file names first. You see the changes in Figure 3-1, which shows a screenshot of the Visual Studio Solution Explorer.

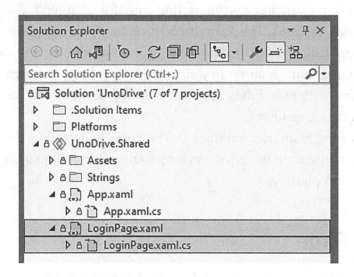

Figure 3-1. *Visual Studio Solution Explorer – LoginPage*

Now that the files have been renamed to LoginPage.xaml and LoginPage.xaml.cs, we need to update the class declaration to match. In both the XAML and the code behind, update the name to be LoginPage.

In the top section of the XAML, you need to update the x:Class attribute as seen in Listing 3-1.

Listing 3-1. Class declaration name in LoginPage.xaml

```
x:Class="UnoDrive.LoginPage"
```

The final XAML code should look like the snippet in Listing 3-2.

Listing 3-2. LoginPage.xaml

```
<Page
  x:Class="UnoDrive.LoginPage"  xmlns="http://schemas.microsoft.com/
  winfx/2006/xaml/presentation"
  xmlns:x="http://schemas.microsoft.com/winfx/2006/xaml"
  xmlns:local="using:UnoDrive"
  xmlns:d="http://schemas.microsoft.com/expression/blend/2008"

  mc:Ignorable="d">

  <Grid
    Background="{ThemeResource ApplicationPageBackgroundThemeBrush}">
    <TextBlock
      Text="Hello, world!"
      Margin="20"
      FontSize="30" />
  </Grid>
</Page>
```

In the code behind, you will update the class declaration and the constructor to be LoginPage. Your new code can be seen in Listing 3-3.

Listing 3-3. LoginPage code behind

```
Namespace UnoDrive
{
    public sealed partial class LoginPage : Page
    {
        public LoginPage()
        {
```

```
        this.InitializeComponent();
    }
  }
}
```

Changing the page name from MainPage to LoginPage requires us to make additional changes to the startup of the application. The App.xaml.cs is the class that contains the main application. It is the class that will launch the LoginPage by creating a Frame and navigating to the page. The App.xaml.cs has a lot of code in it, and it can be overwhelming at first. We can just focus on the small code change we need to make to start the application using the LoginPage.

In the App.xaml.cs go to the method OnLaunched and scroll down until you find the navigation code that launches the MainPage. You can search for the code snippet in Listing 3-4.

Listing 3-4. App.xaml.cs original Navigate command for MainPage

```
rootFrame.Navigate(typeof(MainPage), args.Arguments);
```

Update this code block to use LoginPage, which looks like the code snippet in Listing 3-5.

Listing 3-5. App.xaml.cs Navigate command updated to use LoginPage

```
rootFrame.Navigate(typeof(LoginPage), args.Arguments);
```

Now everything is all set. You should be able to compile the application and run it using x86, x64, or arm64 with the Windows target. You should still see the "Hello, world!" message that we saw in the last chapter as we haven't changed any of the XAML user interface code.

Adding Controls

The default template starts us out with a Grid control as the main control with a TextBlock on the inside of it that reads "Hello, world!" A Grid control is a container control that renders other controls in it. Other common containers are StackPanel, ListView, and GridView. The Grid control is a powerful control that allows us to define a custom grid on the screen to place other user interface items on the screen. This grid can have any number of columns and rows with varying widths and heights. It is a little bit too powerful for what we want to display on our first login page.

A StackPanel is a simple container that renders controls in either a vertical or horizontal stack. It is recommended to use a StackPanel first before using a Grid as it can keep your visual tree smaller and easier for the native platforms to handle.

First, start off by changing our Grid control to a StackPanel that renders our controls in a vertical stack. This is the default setting for a StackPanel, so there is no need to add any custom attributes to the markup. See the code snippet of an empty StackPanel declaration in Listing 3-6.

Listing 3-6. Empty StackPanel declaration in XAML

```
<StackPanel>
</StackPanel>
```

Once we have our StackPanel in place, you can update the contents to contain two TextBlock controls to display messages above our login button. They should display the following messages:

- Welcome to UnoDrive
- Uno Platform ♥ OneDrive = UnoDrive

See updated StackPanel with TextBlock controls in Listing 3-7.

Listing 3-7. StackPanel that contains two TextBlock controls

```
<StackPanel>
  <TextBlock Text="Welcome to UnoDrive " />
  <TextBlock Text="Uno Platform ♥ OneDrive = UnoDrive " />
</StackPanel>
```

The application should compile and run. We haven't added any special styling, but let's give it a try and see how it looks. It is a good idea when building user interfaces to test often and leverage hot reload. This keeps your inner development loop as fast as possible.

Hot reload is a feature built into Visual Studio and other editing tools that allows you to edit your user interface and see the results without recompiling the application. Be wary that your app state may get lost if you are working on a complicated page. Most of the time you can just save your changes in the XAML file and see the changes instantly. See the screenshot of the Windows app in Figure 3-2.

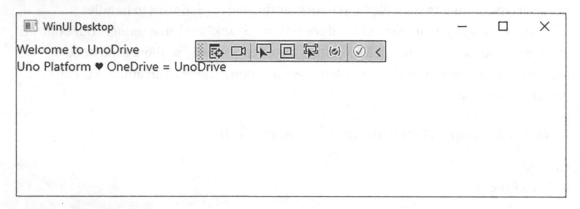

Figure 3-2. *Windows desktop app with basic title and header messages*

The messages we have added to the screen need some styling; otherwise, they will be drawn at the top left of the screen with the standard styles. To update the size, you will use the FontSize attribute. See updated TextBlock controls with styling in Listing 3-8.

Listing 3-8. Adds FontSize to the TextBlock controls

```
<TextBlock
    Text="Welcome to UnoDrive!"
    FontSize="40" />
<TextBlock
    Text="Uno Platform ♥ OneDrive = UnoDrive"
    Fontsize="24"/>
```

Now when we run our application, the messages will be bigger. On a login page, typically all the content is centered. It makes sense for us to create a page-wide style, which will center all the controls. You can create page- or control-wide styles using a ResourceDictionary. Let's start by defining an empty one just above our StackPanel. See Listing 3-9 for code snippet.

Listing 3-9. Empty ResourceDictionary for adding styles

```
<Page.Resources>
  <ResourceDictionary>
  </ResourceDictionary>
</Page.Resources>
```

This is a basic introduction to styles, and we will cover them in more depth in Chapter 4.

The ResourceDictionary contains all the styles and applies them to each control being specified by that dictionary. We can define our styles using the Style object, which specifies the exact TargetType. Nested inside of the Style object are Setter elements that define the properties you want to set in the style. The following code creates a style that defines HorizontalTextAlignment and HorizontalAlignment, which will be applied to all TextBlock controls on this page. See the style code snippet in Listing 3-10.

Listing 3-10. Style targeting TextBlock that centers text and aligns horizontally

```
<Style TargetType="TextBlock">
    <Setter Property="HorizontalTextAlignment" Value="Center" />
    <Setter Property="HorizontalAlignment" Value="Center" />
</Style>
```

Once the style is added, if we run our application, all the messages we added will be centered. See the screenshot of the Windows app with styled content in Figure 3-3.

Figure 3-3. *Windows desktop app with larger text that is horizontally centered*

Our controls are looking much better, as we have the first message that acts as our header and the second message that acts as a subheader. Let's add some more centering and update the StackPanel to position the controls vertically centered. See the updated StackPanel code snippet in Listing 3-11 and a screenshot of the Windows application in Figure 3-4.

Listing 3-11. StackPanel with VerticalAlignment set to Center

```
<StackPanel VerticalAlignment="Center">
```

Figure 3-4. *Windows desktop app with vertically centered text*

Perfect! Now our header messages are centered on the screen vertically and horizontally. It is clear to the user that this is your landing page and, in our case, a welcome and login page.

The next steps are going to be adding the login button, which will perform authentication with Microsoft Identity. Once authenticated we will be able to communicate with the Microsoft Graph API to retrieve our OneDrive data. Right now, we are just focused on the user interface, and we will write the authentication later in future chapters.

After `<TextBlock>` controls we will add a standard `<Button>` with a content of "Login to UnoDrive". See the code snippet in Listing 3-12.

Listing 3-12. Button control

```
<Button Content="Login to UnoDrive" />
```

Now that you have added the button, we need to add some styling to it so it looks just right on the page. Set the `FontSize` to 40, Padding to "40, 10", and `HorizontalAlignment` to `Center`. See the updated `Button` control in Listing 3-13.

Listing 3-13. Button control with updated styles

```
<Button
  Content="Login to UnoDrive"
  Background="LightGray"
  FontSize="40"
  Padding="40, 10"
  HorizontalAlignment="Center" />
```

Padding and Margin properties are used throughout controls, and it is useful to understand how they work. These properties use a Thickness to define the amount of space. Like other user interface toolchains, it uses four variables: left, top, right, and bottom. When you want to set all four variables to the same value, you can just add one number. See the code snippet in Listing 3-14.

Listing 3-14. Padding with one value

```
Padding="40"
```

In our preceding case, we wanted to set the left and right padding to 40 and the top and bottom padding to 10. If we were to write this as a formula, it would look like {left-right}, [top-bottom}. See the code snippet in Listing 3-15.

Listing 3-15. Padding with two values

```
Padding="40, 10"
```

Finally, if we want to set each variable in the Thickness, we can use all four. It will go clockwise around the screen starting with left: {left}, {top}, {right}, {bottom}. See the code snippet in Listing 3-16.

Listing 3-16. Padding with four values

```
Padding="30, 40, 25, 10"
```

Once you have added the button, you can run the application, and you should see the new login button. See the screenshot of the Windows app in Figure 3-5.

Figure 3-5. *Windows desktop app with the login button*

Customize Layout and Controls

We have added some of the basic controls to build our new landing and welcome page, and it has all the components. Let's start adding some more complex styling techniques to get our page to look just right. We are going to use a combination of the Grid control and the StackPanel control to complete this page. Earlier, we mentioned that the Grid control is very powerful for customizing our layout. Let's convert our StackPanel to a Grid and learn how it works.

Start by updating the StackPanel container to be a Grid. In this section we will define two rows, one row for the headers and another for the button. When defining a grid's row or column, you have several options. See Table 3-1.

Table 3-1. *Grid Row or Column Definition Types and Example Values*

Definition Type	Description	Example
Numeric size	The value gets converted into screen dimension and sets it to use exactly that amount of space. This option does not use pixels but a calculated dimension of space for the width and height.	100
Auto	Sets the row or column definition to take up space that is exactly the size of your control.	Auto
Wildcard or asterisk	Sets the row or column definition to use a percentage of screen space. For example, if you have two row definitions both set to a Height= "*", this means each row will take up 50% of the vertical screen space. You can apply numbers to the asterisk, which gives you various percentages. If we take the same example and change the first row to Height="2*", this will then have the first row take up twice as much space as the second.	* or 2*

These concepts can be used together to make a truly customized display. For now, we are going to keep it simple and create two rows with the wildcard. This will create two rows that take up 50% of the Grid screen space. See the code snippet in Listing 3-17.

Listing 3-17. Grid RowDefinitions using the wildcard asterisk technique

```
<Grid.RowDefinitions>
  <RowDefinition Height="*" />
  <RowDefinition Height="*" />
</Grid.RowDefinitions>
```

Once you have defined your rows, you can define what controls are applied to a row or column using the syntax Grid.Row="0 " or Grid.Column="0 ". This can be applied to any item in the Grid. Before we start defining controls for a row, we need to add two StackPanel controls. The first one will wrap the headers, and the second one will wrap the Button.

In the first StackPanel, add Grid.Row="0 ", and in the second StackPanel, add Grid.Row="1 ". See the updated code in Listing 3-18.

Listing 3-18. Updated StackPanels to use Grid.Row

```
<StackPanel Grid.Row="0">
  <TextBlock
    Text="Welcome to UnoDrive!"
    FontSize="40" />
  <TextBlock
    Text="Uno Platform ♥ OneDrive = UnoDrive"
    Fontsize="24"/>
</StackPanel>
<StackPanel Grid.Row="1">
  <Button
    Content="Login to UnoDrive"
    FontSize="40"
    Padding="40, 10"
    HorizontalAlignment="Center" />
</StackPanel>
```

We want the second StackPanel to be centered on the screen vertically. The preceding code will only center work in the bottom half of the screen. To solve this, we can set the row to the first one and define a RowSpan. This tells the user interface that it should take up more than one row. See the code snippet in Listing 3-19.

Listing 3-19. Updated StackPanel to use Grid.RowSpan

```
<StackPanel Grid.Row="0 " Grid.RowSpan="2 ">
```

Now let's add our VerticalAlignment and HorizontalAlignment, update the parent Grid to center the controls horizontally, and update both StackPanel controls to center controls vertically. See our current working code in Listing 3-20.

Listing 3-20. Current working code for LoginPage.xaml

```
"""""<Grid HorizontalAlignment="Center">
  <Grid.RowDefinitions>
    <RowDefinition Height="*" />
    <RowDefinition Height="*" />
  </Grid.RowDefinitions>
```

```
<StackPanel Grid.Row="0" VerticalAlignment="Center">
  <TextBlock
    Text="Welcome to UnoDrive!"
    FontSize="40" />
  <TextBlock
    Text="Uno Platform ♥ OneDrive = UnoDrive"
    FontSize="24"/>
</StackPanel>
<StackPanel
  Grid.Row="0"
  Grid.RowSpan="2"
  VerticalAlignment="Center">
  <Button
    Content="Login to UnoDrive"
    Background="LightGray"
    FontSize="40"
    Padding="40, 10"
    HorizontalAlignment="Center" />
</StackPanel>
</Grid>
```

If you go ahead and launch the application, you will see the new styles have been applied, and your application should look like the screenshot in Figure 3-6.

Figure 3-6. *Windows desktop app using Grid layout*

Earlier in this chapter, we talked about page-wide styles. We have a few items we can put in the page-wide style to help simplify our XAML code. In the `ResourceDictionary` at the top of the page, add a style for the `Grid` and the `StackPanel`. For each of them, you will add the `HorizontalAlignment` and the `VerticalAlignment`, respectively. See the style code snippet in Listing 3-21.

Listing 3-21. Grid and StackPanel styles

```
<Style TargetType="Grid">
  <Setter Property="HorizontalAlignment" Value="Center" />
</Style>

<Style TargetType="StackPanel">
  <Setter Property="VerticalAlignment" Value="Center" />
</Style>
```

Now that we have defined styles for these controls, we can remove the explicit attributes for all `Grid` and `StackPanel` controls on this page. See our final code for this page in Listing 3-22.

Listing 3-22. Final code for LoginPage.xaml

```xml
<Page
  x:Class="UnoDrive.LoginPage"
  xmlns="http://schemas.microsoft.com/winfx/2006/xaml/presentation"
  xmlns:x="http://schemas.microsoft.com/winfx/2006/xaml"
  xmlns:local="using:UnoDrive"
  xmlns:d="http://schemas.microsoft.com/expression/blend/2008"

  mc:Ignorable="d">

  <Page.Resources>
    <ResourceDictionary>
      <Style TargetType="TextBlock">
        <Setter
          Property="HorizontalTextAlignment"
          Value="Center" />
        <Setter
          Property="HorizontalAlignment"
          Value="Center" />
      </Style>

      <Style TargetType="Grid">
        <Setter
          Property="HorizontalAlignment"
          Value="Center" />
      </Style>

      <Style TargetType="StackPanel">
        <Setter
          Property="VerticalAlignment"
          Value="Center" />
      </Style>
    </ResourceDictionary>
  </Page.Resources>

  <Grid>
    <Grid.RowDefinitions>
```

```
        <RowDefinition Height="*" />
        <RowDefinition Height="*" />
      </Grid.RowDefinitions>
      <StackPanel Grid.Row="0">
        <TextBlock
          Text="Welcome to UnoDrive!"
          FontSize="40" />
        <TextBlock
          Text="Uno Platform ♥ OneDrive = UnoDrive"
          FontSize="24" />
      </StackPanel>
      <StackPanel Grid.Row="0" Grid.RowSpan="2">
        <Button
          Content="Login to UnoDrive"
          Background="LightGray"
          FontSize="40"
          Padding="40, 10"
          HorizontalAlignment="Center"/>
      </StackPanel>
    </Grid>
</Page>
```

Test Cross-Platform

Now that the application is working how we want on the Windows project, it is time to validate everything is working across the various platforms we want to support. In Visual Studio select each target platform and run the application to ensure things are working correctly. In this chapter we are using basic controls, so there isn't anything special we need to do for each platform.

It is a very good practice and is the recommendation of Uno Platform to test each target platform as you implement a feature. It becomes increasingly difficult to build the entire Windows application and add support for the various platforms afterward. See screenshots of the running apps in Figure 3-7 for WASM, Figure 3-8 for Android, Figure 3-9 for iOS, Figure 3-10 for macOS, Figure 3-11 for Linux, and Figure 3-12 for WPF.

WebAssembly

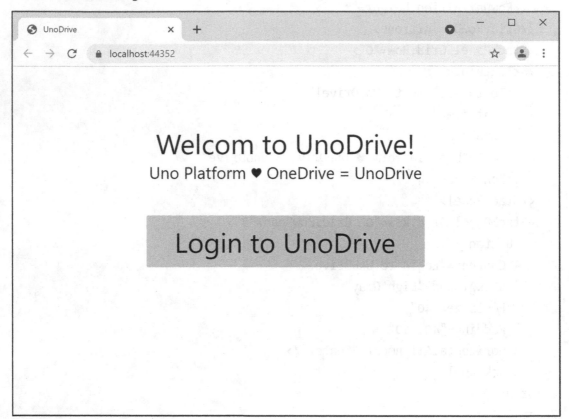

Figure 3-7. *WebAssembly application*

Android

Figure 3-8. *Android application*

iOS

Figure 3-9. *iOS application*

macOS

Figure 3-10. *macOS application*

Linux

Figure 3-11. *Linux application*

WPF

Figure 3-12. *WPF application*

Conclusion

In this chapter we learned how to create a cross-platform page in Uno Platform using some of the basic containers and controls. Our focus was just on the look and feel of our application as we did not need to write any platform-specific styles or code.

In the next chapter, we are going to expand on some of these concepts. If you have trouble with any of the code, you can download the completed sample code for Chapter 3 from here: https://github.com/SkyeHoefling/UnoDrive/tree/main/ Chapter%203.

CHAPTER 4

Application Styles

In the previous chapter, we built our first page, which is the login page. As we learned our way around the WinUI 3 tools, we added several styles that we are using in multiple controls. It is important to set a standard in your application from the beginning of how you want styles to be configured. If this is not done early on, it will be difficult to go back and do it afterward. In this chapter we will go over different techniques for implementing application-wide reusable styles and how to best manage them depending on the size of your application.

Style Implementations

Styles help simplify your user interface customization, so your XAML code isn't repeating itself in every file. For example, if you have a blue button, instead of setting the color of every button, you can use a style. An added benefit of reusable styles is when you need to change the color of the button, all the buttons in the app are updated at once.

A style object is defined in a special XAML object called a `ResourceDictionary,` which can be used in various objects throughout your application. A `ResourceDictionary` is a special dictionary that is attached to a page, a control, and the global application and contains `Style` and `DataTemplate` objects. These objects are then implicitly or explicitly controls where the `ResourceDictionary` is defined. In this section we are going to go through several examples of a `ResourceDictionary`.

Using our example of a blue button, our style will set the `Background`. When we implement the `Style,` if we do not give it a unique identifier using `x:Key`, it is considered an implicit `Style,` which means it is automatically applied to all controls that are using that `ResourceDictionary`. See the code snippet in Listing 4-1.

© Skye Hoefling 2022
S. Hoefling, *Getting Started with the Uno Platform and WinUI 3*,
https://doi.org/10.1007/978-1-4842-8248-9_4

Listing 4-1. Button style setting Background to Blue

```
<ResourceDictionary>
  <Style TargetType="Button">
    <Setter Property="Background" Value="Blue" />
  </Style>
</ResourceDictionary>
```

When creating a style, the element requires a `TargetType`. This defines what type of control the `Style` will be applied to. In the preceding example, we created a style that will be used in `Button` controls, so our `TargetType` is `Button`.

There are three different scopes when adding styles:

- Control styles

- Page styles

- Application styles

In addition to the three scopes, there is also the concept of a named style, which can be used in any of the scopes: control, page, and application. This technique uses a unique identifier by `x:Key` on the `Style` object. To use this, the control will need to explicitly reference this style.

Control Styles

A control style is applied to all controls contained within another control. In other words, typically a container such as a `StackPanel` or `Grid` will have multiple controls to render its layout. In this example, the `StackPanel` or `Grid` can have its `ResourceDictionary` that will be applied to only its controls. If you are working with multiple container controls, you can specify a custom `ResourceDictionary` for each. This provides great flexibility when adding common controls on a page where the styles need to be slightly different between the containers.

In the code snippet in Listing 4-2, we have two `StackPanel` controls that set the `Foreground` color of TextBlocks depending on which container they are in.

Listing 4-2. Control style example using a StackPanel

```
<StackPanel>
  <StackPanel>
    <StackPanel.Resources>
      <ResourceDictionary>
        <Style TargetType="TextBlock">
          <Setter Property="Foreground" Value="Blue" />
        </Style>
      </ResourceDictionary>
    </StackPanel.Resources>
    <TextBlock Text="Hello - this text is blue" />
  </StackPanel>

  <StackPanel>
    <StackPanel.Resources>
      <ResourceDictionary>
        <Style TargetType="TextBlock">
          <Setter Property="Foreground" Value="Red" />
        </Style>
      </ResourceDictionary>
    </StackPanel.Resources>
    <TextBlock Text="Hello - this text is red" />
  </StackPanel.
</StackPanel>
```

Control styles are a useful technique but add a lot of verbosity and noise to your code.

Note   Control styles are very useful but are not used that much because of verbosity. They are best used when you need to override the default style and your container contains many controls of that type. Consider you have a `StackPanel` with one hundred controls of the same type. In that case you may want to use a control style.

Page Styles

The next level up from control styles are page styles, which are applied to the entire page. These styles are useful when you have settings specific to the entire page. If you want all the buttons on your page to have a specific color, font size, etc., you can set it in the page style and not have to manually set it at the control.

See Listing 4-3 where we will set the background color of all buttons to orange.

Listing 4-3. Page style example setting the background of all buttons to orange

```
<Page>
  <Page.Resources>
    <ResourceDictionary>
      <Style TargetType="Button">
        <Setter Property="Background" Value="Orange" />
      </Style>
    </ResourceDictionary>
  </Page.Resources>

  <StackPanel>
    <Button Content="Hello Button 1" />
    <Button Content="Hello Button 2" />
  </StackPanel>
</Page>
```

Page styles are most useful when you want to style items just for a specific page. When you know the control or layout rules on the page won't be used on other pages, it is best to use the page style technique.

Application Styles

Application styles are the next level up after page styles and are the most general type of style you can create. A style defined as an application style is used on any page or any control in your application.

To define your application styles, you will add a `ResourceDictionary` in your `App. xaml` file, and you can start adding all the styles there.

See the code snippet in Listing 4-4 that sets all Button controls to have an orange background and all TextBlock controls to have a blue foreground. These styles are applied to all controls in the entire application.

Listing 4-4. Application style example that sets all Button and TextBlock colors

```
<Application>
  <Application.Resources>
    <ResourceDictionary>
      <Style TargetType="Button">
        <Setter Property="Background" Value="Orange" />
      </Style>

      <Style TargetType="TextBlock">
        <Setter Property="Foreground" Value="Blue" />
      </Style>
    </ResourceDictionary>
  </Application.Resources>
</Application>
```

Once you have defined your application-wide styles, you can add controls, and these styles will automatically be applied.

Named Styles

A separate technique in XAML styling is using named styles, which are independent of the previous scopes and can be used in all of them. When you name a style, you aren't explicitly setting all controls to use that style but allowing a control to use that style if it is required. You can do this by setting the Style property on any control.

When applying a named style, you use the StaticResource markup extension, which understands how to find the correct item in the ResourceDictionary:

```
Style="{StaticResource MyStyle}"
```

The preceding code tells the styling engine to find the Style with the key of "MyStyle".

Consider the page style technique from earlier. If we want to set button 1 to use the default style and button 2 to use our named style, our new XAML will look like the code in Listing 4-5.

Listing 4-5. Page style example using a named style and default style

```
<Page>
  <Page.Resources>
    <ResourceDictionary>
      <Style x:Key="MyStyle" TargetType="Button">
        <Setter Property="Background" Value="Orange" />
      </Style>
    </ResourceDictionary>
  </Page.Resources>

  <StackPanel>
    <Button Content="Hello Button 1" />
    <Button
      Style="{StaticResource MyStyle}"
      Content="Hello Button 2" />
  </StackPanel>
</Page>
```

This technique can be used in any `ResourceDictionary`, but it is commonly used in application or page styles to denote different styles for the same control.

Style Inheritance

The three different style scopes can be used together in an inheritance tree when you have general styles that you want to override or overwrite the closer you get to the control. When you add an implicit style in the application scope, it is applied to all controls of that type. If you decide to create that same implicit style in the page or control scope, those changes will be overriden.

Consider you have a `Button` control whose `Background` you want to set to blue throughout your application. Then on a particular page, you want that `Background` to be green. See Listing 4-6 for the application style and Listing 4-7 for the page style.

Listing 4-6. Application style example setting Background to Blue

```
<Application>
  <Application.Resources>
    <ResourceDictionary>
      <Style TargetType="Button">
        <Setter Property="Background" Value="Orange" />
      </Style>
    </ResourceDictionary>
  </Application.Resources>
</Application>
```

Listing 4-7. Page style example that overwrites the application style setting Background to Green

```
<Page>
  <Page.Resources>
    <ResourceDictionary>
      <Style TargetType="Button">
        <Setter Property="Background" Value="Green" />
      </Style>
    </ResourceDictionary>
  </Page.Resources>

  <StackPanel>
    <Button Content="Hello Button 1" />
  </StackPanel>
</Page>
```

Note   When using the overriding technique demonstrated in Listings 4-6 and 4-7, the original style is replaced, and any of the properties will not be retained.

When working with Style inheritance and you need to add minor changes to an existing Style, you can override the behavior instead of overwriting as demonstrated in Listings 4-6 and 4-7. When overriding a Style, you will use the keyword BasedOn that references the existing style.

To demonstrate Style overriding, start with an explicit Style in the application scope that has a unique identifier using the x:Key notation. We will use the same example from Listings 4-6 and 4-7 where we change the Background. Then in the page scope, you will update the Style object to use the BasedOn keyword referencing the original Style by its unique identifier. See example code in Listings 4-8 and 4-9.

Listing 4-8. Application style example – explicit style

```
<Application>
  <Application.Resources>
    <ResourceDictionary>
      <Style x:Key="ButtonStyle" TargetType="Button">
        <Setter Property="Background" Value="Orange" />
      </Style>
    </ResourceDictionary>
  </Application.Resources>
</Application>
```

Listing 4-9. Page style example that overrides the application style by using BasedOn

```
<Page>
  <Page.Resources>
    <ResourceDictionary>
      <Style
        x:Key="CustomButtonStyle"
        TargetType="Button"
        BasedOn="{StaticResource ButtonStyle}">
        <Setter Property="Background" Value="Green" />
      </Style>
    </ResourceDictionary>
  </Page.Resources>
```

```
<StackPanel>
  <Button
    Content="Hello Button 1"
    Style="{StaticResource CustomButtonStyle}" />
</StackPanel>
</Page>
```

Organizing Styles

XAML can be very verbose, and creating styles regardless of technique can become messy quickly. It is a good idea to set your standard for organizing your styles as early in the project as possible. It is not easy to go back afterward and create custom styles for the application. This is because controls vary slightly from page to page, making it difficult to create a one-size-fits-all style. If you implement a good convention at the beginning, it is easier to override the styles downstream in your page or control scope.

We are going to cover two popular techniques for organizing styles and explain the benefits and disadvantages of each:

- App.xaml styles
- Grouped styles

App.xaml Styles

The App.xaml styles are no different from the application-wide styles we covered earlier. The ResourceDictionary in the App.xaml will contain all the styles for your application. As your application grows, this file will grow, and it can be cumbersome to manage. If you have over a thousand unique styles, you may be looking at 10,000 or even 100,000 lines of XAML code in your App.xaml. However, this technique provides a nice and simple location where all the application-wide styles can be stored.

A good rule to follow is if you are building a small app, you can use App.xaml-based styles. If you are building a large app with hundreds of pages, it is going to be best to use another technique as this technique does not scale very well.

Benefits

- Simple and easy to find all styles

- Useful on smaller projects

Disadvantages

- Difficult to maintain on large applications

- No structure on where styles are located

- Lends itself to using lots of XML comments to solve the structure problem

Real-World Experience

If you are building a smaller app, this technique is a great solution.

I have seen this technique used on many large applications for WPF, UWP, Xamarin. Forms, and other XAML-based toolchains. All of these have fallen into the same trap where one file for all the styles does not scale. The App.xaml file has grown to thousands upon thousands of lines of XAML code with no way to identify where styles exist. Even adding comments that explain the sections becomes difficult and unmaintainable. If you think you will be adding lots of styles, read on to the next section.

Grouped Styles

Another technique for organizing styles is creating grouped styles, which breaks your styles down to simple XAML files that cover one part of your application. You may have various Button styles for all the different Button controls throughout your application. You can put all of these styles in a Button.xaml file, and now you have one simple place to edit them.

Grouped styles are not set up for you out of the box and will require a little bit of configuration and understanding additional controls such as the ResourceDictionary. MergedDictionaries. A benefit of this technique is you can choose how simple or complicated you want your groupings to be.

Benefits

- Clearly separates concerns between styles
- Scales for large applications that require many custom styles
- Easy to find a specific style

Disadvantages

- Adds extra complexity to your style management
- Requires a merged `ResourceDictionary`
- Convention driven
- Preview windows not working as well

Real-World Experience

Using grouped styles provides a powerful way to manage all of your styles. After stumbling through many projects that only had styles in `App.xaml`, I always try and use this technique. The setup time is often offset by the ease of use and maintenance cost.

Implement Grouped Styles

In our application we are going to use grouped styling as the convention lends itself nicely to separation of concerns and scales nicely for large applications. Let's look at how we can break up our application styles. In our application we are building, we need to add styles for controls and application-wide items such as converters. This breaks our grouped convention down into two categories:

- Control styles
- Application styles

The plan will be to create a simple XAML file for each grouped item of styles. In the previous chapter we built a simple login screen that has `TextBlock` and `Button` controls. We will be adding the styles to these controls in our new grouped style. Before we can do that, we need to understand our structure and what we want to accomplish.

In a grouped style convention, you will create an entry point style XAML page, which then orchestrates your application- and control-specific styles. Each of these will then add additional styles based on the complexities of your application. To start we are going to add two style pages for controls. Our resulting file and folder structure will look like Figure 4-1.

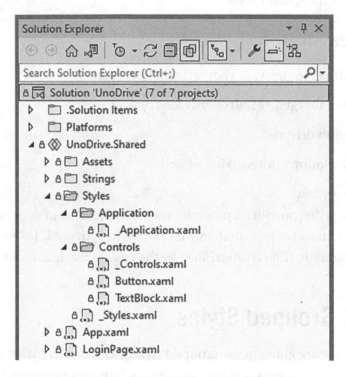

Figure 4-1. *Visual Studio Solution Explorer – grouped styles*

Create Entry Point

Let's start by creating our top-level XAML files, _Styles.xaml, _Controls.xaml, and _Application.xaml. All these files are prefixed with an underscore to prevent a naming conflict with the folder name. Go ahead and create the necessary files as a simple XML file. See code in Listing 4-10.

Listing 4-10. Styles directory structure and files

```
Styles/_Styles.xaml
Styles/Application/_Application.xaml
Styles/Controls/_Controls.xaml
```

The _Styles.xaml file will be your entry point into your grouped style files and will need to reference both _Application.xaml and _Controls.xaml. Update the entry point style file to use the XAML code as seen in Listing 4-11.

Listing 4-11. Application style that uses a merged dictionary to put application and control styles in separate areas

```
<ResourceDictionary>

  <ResourceDictionary.MergedDictionaries>
    <ResourceDictionary Source="Application/_Application.xaml" />
    <ResourceDictionary Source="Controls/_Controls.xaml" />
  </ResourceDictionary.MergedDictionaries>

</ResourceDictionary>
```

This code tells the system to use the resource dictionaries from both _Application.xaml and _Controls.xaml. At this point we are still orchestrating what ResourceDictionary objects are loaded into the application. Earlier we mentioned that grouped styles rely on the ResourceDictionary.MergedDictionaries, which is an object that allows us to append multiple dictionaries. This allows us to reference the multiple files, which are ResourceDictionary objects.

Go and update your _Controls.xaml and _Application.xaml to contain an empty ResourceDictionary. We will be coming back to them in just bit. See the code snippet in Listing 4-12.

Listing 4-12. _Controls.xaml – ResourceDictionary with an empty MergedDictionary.

```
<ResourceDictionary>

  <ResourceDictionary.MergedDictionaries>
  </ResourceDictionary.MergedDictionaries>

</ResourceDictionary>
```

Now that we have the scaffolding in place, we can update the App.xaml to use our new grouped styles. Since we are using the Uno Platform template for .NET 6 and WinUI 3, we need to ensure the WinUI controls are still loaded. See the code snippet in Listing 4-13.

Listing 4-13. XAML statement to load WinUI controls

```
<XamlControlsResources xmlns="using:Microsoft.UI.Xaml.Controls" />
```

If you navigate to the definition of the preceding code, you will notice that XamlControlsResources inherits from ResourceDictionary. This means we can add it to our ResourceDictionary.MergedDictionaries just like we plan to do with our other dictionaries. Go ahead and add it to the merged dictionary in the _Application.xaml. See code in Listing 4-14.

Listing 4-14. Adds WinUI statement to _Application.xaml

```
<ResourceDictionary>

  <ResourceDictionary.MergedDictionaries>
    <XamlControlsResources xmlns="using:Microsoft.UI.Xaml.Controls" />
  </ResourceDictionary.MergedDictionaries>

</ResourceDictionary>
```

Now that we have moved the WinUI ResourceDictionary, we should not have anything else left over in the App.xaml file. Let's update the ResourceDictionary in this file to point to our _Styles.xaml file, which will complete the configuration of the grouped styles. See code in Listing 4-15.

Listing 4-15. App.xaml final XAML call to our Styles directory

```
<Application.Resources>
  <ResourceDictionary>
    <ResourceDictionary.MergedDictionaries>
      <ResourceDictionary Source="Styles/_Styles.xaml" />
    </ResourceDictionary.MergedDictionaries>
  </ResourceDictionary>
</Application.Resources>
```

At this point you should have the following XAML flow: App.xaml ➤ _Styles.xaml ➤ _Controls.xaml and _Application.xaml. Everything should compile and run as we haven't changed anything; we just organized our styles differently. We even made sure to include the WinUI resources. In the next few sections, we will be adding control-specific styles so we can remove them from the LoginPage.xaml.

Add TextBlock Styles

Now that we have the basic building blocks for our grouped styles implemented, we can start adding TextBlock styles for the login page. We have two separate types of TextBlock controls that need to be styled: a standard header and subheader. Both controls need to be centered horizontally, but they differ in their FontSize. Extracting the properties out from our LoginPage.xaml, we can create the style.

Let's create a named style for both concepts, denoting one as Header and the other as Subheader. We will use the named style technique that we learned earlier.

Add the following code to your TextBlock.xaml file. See Listings 4-16 and 4-17.

Listing 4-16. TextBlock.xaml header style

```
<Style x:Key="Header" TargetType="TextBlock">
  <Setter Property="FontSize" Value="40" />
  <Setter Property="HorizontalTextAlignment" Value="Center" />
  <Setter Property="HorizontalAlignment" Value="Center" />
</Style>
```

Listing 4-17. TextBlock.xaml subheader style

```
<Style x:Key="Subheader" TargetType="TextBlock">
  <Setter Property="FontSize" Value="24" />
  <Setter Property="HorizontalTextAlignment" Value="Center" />
  <Setter Property="HorizontalAlignment" Value="Center" />
</Style>
```

Your completed TextBlock.xaml file should look like the code in Listing 4-18.

Listing 4-18. TextBlock.xaml completed style

```
<ResourceDictionary>

  <Style x:Key="Header" TargetType-"TextBlock">
    <Setter Property="FontSize" Value="40" />
    <Setter Property="HorizontalTextAlignment" Value="Center" />
    <Setter Property="HorizontalAlignment" Value="Center" />
  </Style>
```

```
<Style x:Key="SubHeader" TargetType="TextBlock">
  <Setter Property="FontSize" Value="24" />
  <Setter Property="HorizontalTextAlignment" Value="Center" />
  <Setter Property="HorizontalAlignment" Value="Center" />
</Style>
```

```
</ResourceDictionary>
```

Now that we have added our style successfully, it needs to be applied to the
LoginPage.xaml. Update each TextBlock control, by removing all the custom attributes
and then explicitly setting the style by using the StaticResource markup extension. Be
sure to leave the Text attribute, as that should be defined here and not in the style. See
code in Listing 4-19.

Listing 4-19. Explicit style statement to use the TextBlock style Header

```
Style="{StaticResource Header}"
```

Update your TextBlock controls to match the code in Listing 4-20.

Listing 4-20. Update TextBlock controls in LoginPage.xaml to use explicit styles

```
<TextBlock
    Text="Welcome to UnoDrive!"
    Style="{StaticResource Header}" />
<TextBlock
    Text="Uno Platform ♥ OneDrive = UnoDrive"
    Style="{StaticResource SubHeader}" />
```

Note   Many developers in the Uno Platform ecosystem prefer to place the Style
property as the first one before any other properties. This is purely coding style and
doesn't change how the properties are loaded.

Add Button Styles

Now it is time to add styles for the `Button` control and update it in the `LoginPage.xaml`. Let's start by referencing the attributes we want to set as default styles: `FontSize`, `Padding`, and `HorizontalAlignment`. Open the `Button.xaml` file and add the following custom named style. See the code snippet in Listing 4-21.

Listing 4-21. LoginButton style

```
<Style x:Key="LoginButton" TargetType="Button">
  <Setter Property="Background" Value="LightGray" />
  <Setter Property="FontSize" Value="40" />
  <Setter Property="Padding" Value="40, 10" />
  <Setter Property="HorizontalAlignment" Value="Center" />
</Style>
```

Now that the style is defined, we can update the code in the `LoginPage.xaml` for the `Button` control to reference the style. While we do this, we can remove all the specific attribute declarations as they are present in the style. Be sure to leave the `Content` attribute as this is specific to the control and not part of the style. See updated code in Listing 4-22.

Listing 4-22. LoginPage.xaml Button control using the new explicit style

```
<Button
  Content="Login to UnoDrive"
  Style="{StaticResource LoginButton}" />
```

Update LoginPage.xaml

All the custom styles have been migrated from the `LoginPage.xaml` to their respective control style files for `TextBlock` and `Button` styles. While we have updated the `LoginPage.xaml` to use the explicitly named styles, we have some stale code that needs to be removed.

In the `ResourceDictionary` at the top of the page, remove the `TextBlock` style declaration as there are no other `TextBlock` controls on this page. All the `TextBlock` controls are using explicit styles on this page. See complete `LoginPage.xaml` code in Listing 4-23.

Listing 4-23. LoginPage.xaml completed code

```xaml
<Page x:Class="UnoDrive.LoginPage">

  <Page.Resources>
    <ResourceDictionary>
      <Style TargetType="Grid">
        <Setter Property="HorizontalAlignment" Value="Center" />
      </Style>

      <Style TargetType="StackPanel">
        <Setter Property="VerticalAlignment" Value="Center" />
      </Style>
    </ResourceDictionary>
  </Page.Resources>

  <Grid>
    <Grid.RowDefinitions>
      <RowDefinition Height="*" />
      <RowDefinition Height="*" />
    </Grid.RowDefinitions>
    <StackPanel Grid.Row="0">
      <TextBlock
        Text="Welcome to UnoDrive!"
        Style="{StaticResource Header}" />
      <TextBlock
        Text="Uno Platform ♥ OneDrive = UnoDrive"
        Style="{StaticResource SubHeader}" />
    </StackPanel>
    <StackPanel Grid.Row="0" Grid.RowSpan="2">
    <Button
      Content="Login to UnoDrive"
      Style="{StaticResource LoginButton}" />
    </StackPanel>
  </Grid>

</Page>
```

Now you can go and run your application, and everything should look the same across all the platforms. We haven't changed any functionality or how the user interface looks. We have just moved our styles from the one page to our new grouped style implementations.

Note   After making changes like this, it is always a good idea to make sure things still work correctly.

Conclusion

Styling in Uno Platform is very useful for creating a standard look and feel for your application. In this chapter we covered the basic technique of placing your styles in the `App.xaml` vs. a grouped style technique and creating a system of reusable styles. Both techniques are correct, and there is no wrong way to build your application. Pick the solution that is going to work best for you and your team.

Uno Platform provides prebuilt themes that implement Material, Cupertino, and Fluent. These themes provide a great starting point to make your application look great. We are not including Uno.Themes in this book; you can learn more at the official documentation: `https://platform.uno/docs/articles/external/uno.themes/doc/themes-overview.html`.

As we continue to build out our UnoDrive application, we will be using the grouped style technique that we implemented in this chapter. It is easier to set the building blocks up at the beginning of the project than trying to retrofit it at the end.

If you got lost along the way, be sure to check out the completed code sample on GitHub: `https://github.com/SkyeHoefling/UnoDrive/tree/main/Chapter%204`.

CHAPTER 5

Platform-Specific Code and XAML

Even with all the abstractions in Uno Platform, you will still need to write platform-specific code or XAML. When interacting with native APIs, you will always need to write code for those APIs. In the user interface, there may be spacing issues on controls not lining up just right, and you'll need to add platform-specific XAML. In this chapter we are going to cover the various techniques of adding platform-specific code and XAML for Uno Platform.

In this chapter we will learn how to add platform-specific code in C# and XAML. We will be using the existing code that we have written up to now, but the completed code in this chapter will not be used in subsequent chapters. Our goal is to learn the concepts and apply them as we need them.

Note The code contained in this chapter is example code only and will not be used in any other chapter of this book.

In Uno Platform you can write platform-specific code or XAML using several techniques:

- *Pre-processor directives*: #if
- *XAML*: xmlns
- Multi-targeting project

© Skye Hoefling 2022
S. Hoefling, *Getting Started with the Uno Platform and WinUI 3*,
https://doi.org/10.1007/978-1-4842-8248-9_5

Pre-processor Directives

A pre-processor directive is a compile-time symbol that will tell the compiler what code to omit or include in compiling that platform. The most common pre-processor directive is #if DEBUG, which only runs code if the binary has been compiled in debug mode.

Note   The DEBUG pre-processor directive is typically set in the debug configuration. In most if not all projects, it will always work. If the DEBUG constant is not set, the #if DEBUG will not work.

Uno Platform has multiple pre-processor directives that are included in the templates. There are symbols for each platform, so it easy enough to add it to your code, and it will only run on that platform.

XAML: XML Namespaces

XML namespaces or xmlns are defined in your XAML typically at the root node, which is typically your <Page> declaration. You are already using xmlns for loading different control libraries or even the default libraries that come with Uno Platform and WinUI 3.

Uno Platform allows you to define several namespaces that will only compile or load the XAML for a specific platform or set of platforms. This acts just like a pre-processor directive that we just learned about as we only have xmlns in XAML and in C# we have pre-processor directives.

Multi-targeting Project

Uno Platform development is best done using shared projects, but sometimes a multi-targeted project is going to work best for you. This could be an upstream library that you want to work with Uno Platform, or you want to use it for your shared code.

The advantage in multi-targeted projects is you will not need to use pre-processor directives or use them as much. You will create special C# code files that only compile for specific platforms. This can then leverage newer language features such as partial methods and have those methods implemented in the correct platform C# code files.

This is a very advanced technique and comes with a new set of risks. It should only be used if you are prepared to handle additional problems that may come up. It is a very powerful technique and is becoming more commonplace in the multi-platform .NET community.

The project template we are using is leveraging a multi-targeted project for the .NET MAUI target heads: Android, iOS, and macOS. Notice it is one project file but it allows you to compile under the various targets.

Pre-processor Directives

The pre-processor directive approach makes adding platform-specific C# code an easy process. The overview section explains the basic concepts of pre-processor directives, which you have probably seen as a #if DEBUG statement that only compiles the code if the binary is built in debug mode. A pre-processor directive is used at compile time and tells the compiler what code to omit or include depending on the values of the directive.

Uno Platform includes all the platform-specific pre-processor directives for you out of the box. Since it is recommended to use a shared project, you can simply just add them into any code file that you want to.

If you are using a multi-targeted project as opposed to a shared project, you will need to ensure the pre-processor directives are defined.

You can find all the documentation for platform-specific C# code at the Uno Platform official documentation page. It is a good idea to reference this for changes as Uno Platform continues to evolve:

- https://platform.uno/docs/articles/platform-specific-csharp.html

Table 5-1. *Pre-processor Directives for Platform-Specific Code*

Platform	Symbol
Windows	NET6_0_OR_GREATER && WINDOWS
Android	__ANDROID__
iOS	__IOS__
macOS	__MACOS__
WebAssembly (WASM)	__WASM__
Skia	HAS_UNO_SKIA
WPF	HAS_UNO_SKIA_WPF

Note The Windows platform needs to use NET6_0_OR_GREATER && WINDOWS as the WINDOWS constant is used for both UWP and WinUI.

Tip It may be easier to manage to create a special constant in the Windows project head so you do not need to include verbose constants when you want to run Windows-specific C#.

Using Table 5-1 we can add a pre-processor directive to any C# file in the shared project, and it will only run on the corresponding platform. Let's look at some code!

In our app, we have created a login page, which has a code behind file named LoginPage.xaml.cs. Let's add a pre-processor directive to only run code on the Windows platform. See the code snippet in Listing 5-1.

Listing 5-1. Add the Windows pre-processor directive to Console.WriteLine

```
public partial class LoginPage
{
  public LoginPage()
  {
    InitializeComponents();
```

```
#if NET6_0_OR_GREATER && WINDOWS
    Console.WriteLine("Login Page created for Windows");
#endif
  }
}
```

The code in Listing 5-1 adds a statement to the console only for Windows as we are using the NET6_0_OR_GREATER && WINDOWS pre-processor directive. This is a good sample to get the basics, but let's add some code to the XAML page so we can have more direct interaction with the platform-specific code.

Update the header TextBlock to have the attribute x:Name="header". This will allow us to access the object in the code behind and update the text. See code in Listing 5-2.

Listing 5-2. Update the TextBlock control in LoginPage.xaml to use x:Name

```
<TextBlock
  x:Name="header"
  Text="Welcome to UnoDrive"
  Style="{StaticResource Header}" />
```

Before we see the header property in the code behind, you must compile the application. This is because code generators need to run, which create the private variable. In the code behind, we can remove the Console.WriteLine() statement and update the text of our header TextBlock. Let's update the header to say "Hello from Windows".

Add the code snippet in Listing 5-3 into the pre-processor directive.

Listing 5-3. Code snippet to update the header TextBlock text for a Windows-specific message

```
header.Text = "Hello from Windows";
```

See complete code in Listing 5-4.

Listing 5-4. LoginPage.xaml.cs complete code with a Windows-specific message

```
public partial class LoginPage
{
  public LoginPage()
  {
    InitializeComponents();
```

```
#if net6_0_OR_GREATER && WINDOWS
    header.Text = "Hello from Windows";
#endif
  }
}
```

If you go and run the Windows application, you should see the header text updated, and if you run the other platforms, it is still the original value. See the screenshot in Figure 5-1.

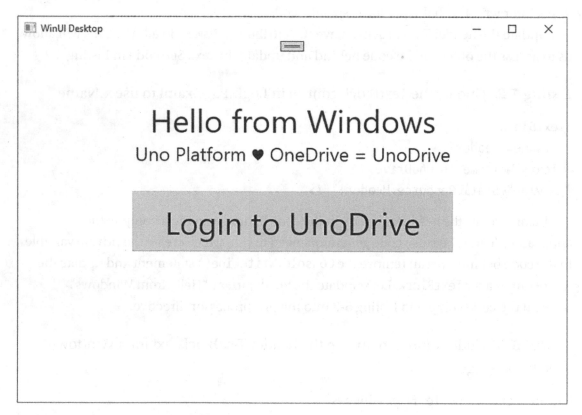

Figure 5-1. *Windows desktop application showing a Windows-only message*

Now that we have the standard Windows pre-processor directive working, let's add the remaining platforms in with similar messaging. See code in Listing 5-5.

Listing 5-5. LoginPage.xaml.cs with platform-specific code for all the platforms

```
public partial class LoginPage
{
  public LoginPage()
  {
    InitializeComponents();

#if NET6_0_OR_GREATER && WINDOWS
    header.Text = "Hello from Windows";
#elif __ANDROID__
    header.Text = "Hello from Android";
#elif __IOS__
    header.Text = "Hello from iOS";
#elif __MACOS__
    header.Text = "Hello from macOS";
#elif HAS_UNO_WASM
    header.Text = "Hello from WASM";
#elif HAS_UNO_SKIA
    header.Text = "Hello from Skia";
#endif
  }
}
```

Now you can go ahead and run the app for each platform and see the different Hello World messages. See Android and iOS screenshots in Figure 5-2. See the macOS screenshot in Figure 5-3. See the WASM screenshot in Figure 5-4. See the WPF screenshot in Figure 5-5. See the Linux screenshot in Figure 5-6.

Figure 5-2. *Android and iOS platform-specific header messages*

Figure 5-3. *macOS application showing a macOS-only header message*

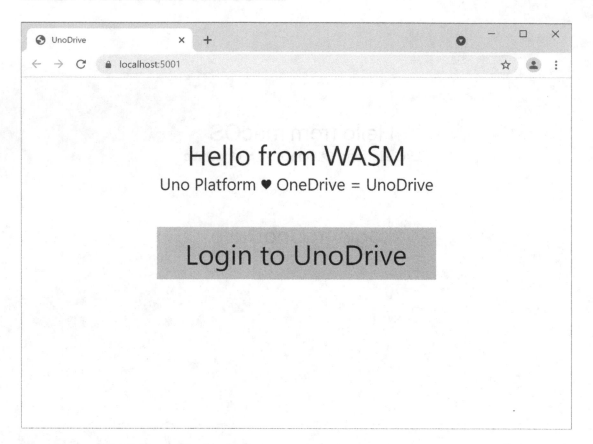

Figure 5-4. *WebAssembly displaying a web-only message*

Figure 5-5. *WPF application showing the Skia-only message*

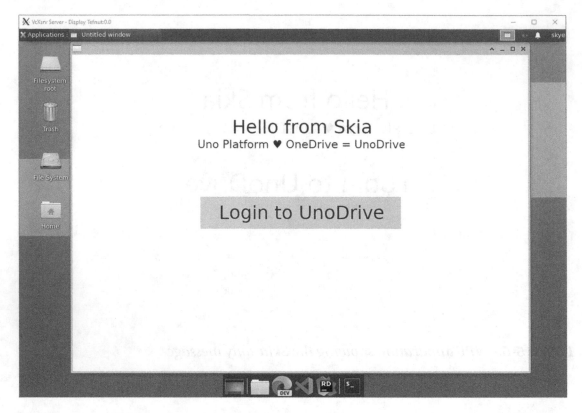

Figure 5-6. *Linux application showing the Skia message*

Code Organization

Adding many pre-processor directives like this can become messy quickly. It is best used for ad hoc platform-specific code. If you find yourself writing large chunks of code for each platform, you may want to create C# code files for that platform entirely.

When building cross-platform applications, you can use a partial method, which is a special C# language feature that allows you to define a method in a partial class and implement it in another file for that same partial class.

Update the code from earlier by removing all of the pre-processor directives and adding a partial method called SetHeaderText(). See the code snippet in Listing 5-6.

Listing 5-6. Adds partial method declaration

```
partial void SetHeaderText();
```

When defining a partial method, it has no implementation; it will be implemented in another file for the partial class. See completed LoginPage.xaml.cs code in Listing 5-7.

Listing 5-7. LoginPage.xaml.cs completed code with partial method declaration

```
public partial class LoginPage
{
  public LoginPage()
  {
    InitializeComponents();
    SetHeaderText();
  }

  partial void SetHeaderText();
}
```

Now you can create multiple files for the platform-specific implementations of this partial method:

- LoginPage.android.cs

- LoginPage.ios.cs

- LoginPage.macos.cs

- LoginPage.skia.cs

- LoginPage.windows.cs

- LoginPage.wasm.cs

In each file you will wrap the entire code in a pre-processor directive for that platform. For example, prior to implementation, our Android code will look like the snippet in Listing 5-8.

Listing 5-8. Android – LoginPage.xaml.cs empty partial class

```
#if __ANDROID__
namespace UnoDrive
{
  public partial class LoginPage
  {
```

```
    }
  }
#endif
```

Since we have defined the partial method in our `LoginPage.xaml.cs` code behind file, we can now create the implementation of that method in each platform. Remember, if you try and compile the application and the partial method is not implemented, the build will fail. Update the partial classes as seen in Listing 5-9 for Android, Listing 5-10 for iOS, Listing 5-11 for macOS, Listing 5-12 for Skia, Listing 5-13 for Windows, and Listing 5-14 for WASM.

Listing 5-9. Android – LoginPage.xaml.cs partial class with partial method implementation

```
#if __ANDROID__
namespace UnoDrive
{
  public partial class LoginPage
  {
    partial void SetHeaderText()
    {
      header.Text = "Hello from Android";
    }
  }
}
#endif
```

Listing 5-10. iOS – LoginPage.xaml.cs partial class with partial method implementation

```
#if __IOS__
namespace UnoDrive
{
  public partial class LoginPage
  {
    partial void SetHeaderText()
    {
```

```
      header.Text = "Hello from iOS";
    }
  }
}
#endif
```

Listing 5-11. macOS – LoginPage.xaml.cs partial class with partial method implementation

```
#if __MACOS__
namespace UnoDrive
{
  public partial class LoginPage
  {
    partial void SetHeaderText()
    {
      header.Text = "Hello from macOS";
    }
  }
}
#endif
```

Listing 5-12. Skia – LoginPage.xaml.cs partial class with partial method implementation

```
#if HAS_UNO_SKIA
namespace UnoDrive
{
  public partial class LoginPage
  {
    partial void SetHeaderText()
    {
      header.Text = "Hello from Skia";
    }
  }
}
#endif
```

Listing 5-13. Windows – LoginPage.xaml.cs partial class with partial method implementation

```
#if NET6_0_OR_GREATER && WINDOWS
namespace UnoDrive
{
  public partial class LoginPage
  {
    partial void SetHeaderText()
    {
      header.Text = "Hello from Windows";
    }
  }
}
#endif
```

Listing 5-14. WASM – LoginPage.xaml.cs partial class with partial method implementation

```
#if HAS_UNO_WASM
namespace UnoDrive
{
  public partial class LoginPage
  {
    partial void SetHeaderText()
    {
      header.Text = "Hello from WASM";
    }
  }
}
#endif
```

This technique is a nice way to blend a multi-targeted csproj while still using the shared project. It is a convention-based technique, and there is nothing specific being done with file extensions at the compiler level. If you use the __ANDROID__ directive in a file that ends with .ios.cs, it will still run the code on Android and not iOS.

You and your team will need to ensure you follow good convention best practices when adding new code files.

Special Cases with Skia

When building your application for a Skia target, you need to ensure that you know your target audience and are careful with your code. The Skia target is used in both the GTK project, which can be run on Linux, macOS, and Windows, and the WPF project, which can only be run on Windows. This means the pre-processor directive of HAS_UNO_SKIA could be used on Linux, macOS, or Windows. If you need to access native Windows APIs using Skia, you will need to add the specific WPF directive HAS_UNO_SKIA_WPF.

XAML: XML Namespaces

Uno Platform allows you to write platform-specific XAML that makes it very easy to add controls or user interface changes for a specific platform. When you define any XAML class such as a page or control, you can add multiple XML namespaces or xmlns definitions. These definitions can be used throughout your XAML code file.

If you aren't familiar with xmlns but have been working with XAML, you are probably using it and not even realizing it. Take the code snippet in Listing 5-15.

Listing 5-15. LoginPage.xaml with standard xmlns definitions

```
<Page
  x:Class="UnoDrive.LoginPage"
  xmlns="http://schemas.microsoft.com/winfx/2006/xaml/presentation"
  xmlns:x="http://schemas.microsoft.com/winfx/2006/xaml"
  xmlns:local="using:UnoDrive"
  xmlns:d="http://schemas.microsoft.com/expression/blend/2008"

  mc:Ignorable="d">

  <!-- Omitted markup -->

</Page>
```

In this code snippet, we are using four different xmlns definitions: x, local, d, and mc. You are probably most familiar using the x namespace as it is used to add keys, names, and other items throughout your page.

In Uno Platform you can add xmlns definitions at the top of your page. When used, the XAML engine will include or omit the code depending on the platform. The Uno Platform official documentation provides details on what can be used:

- https://platform.uno/docs/articles/platform-specific-xaml.html

Table 5-2 documents different namespaces you can include on your page to run platform-specific XAML. Many of the namespaces require to be placed in the mc:Ignorable attribute; otherwise, you will get tooling errors with Visual Studio.

Table 5-2. xmlns Definitions for Platform-Specific XAML

Prefix	Platforms	Excluded Platforms	Namespace
win	Windows	Android, iOS, WASM, macOS, Skia	http://schemas.microsoft.com/winfx/2006/xaml/presentation
xamarin	Android, iOS, WASM, macOS, Skia	Windows	http://uno.ui/xamarin
not_win	Android, iOS, WASM, macOS, Skia	Windows	http://uno.ui/not_win
android	Android	Windows, iOS, WASM, macOS, Skia	http://uno.ui/android
ios	iOS	Windows, Android, Web, macOS, Skia	http://uno.ui/ios
wasm	WASM	Windows, Android, iOS, macOS, Skia	http://uno.ui/wasm
macos	macOS	Windows, Android, iOS, Web, Skia	http://uno.ui/macos
skia	Skia	Windows, Android, iOS, Web, macOS	http://uno.ui/skia
not_android	Windows, iOS, Web, macOS, Skia	Android	http://schemas.microsoft.com/winfx/2006/xaml/presentation
not_ios	Windows, Android, Web, macOS, Skia	iOS	http://schemas.microsoft.com/winfx/2006/xaml/presentation
not_wasm	Windows, Android, iOS, macOS, Skia	WASM	http://schemas.microsoft.com/winfx/2006/xaml/presentation
not_macos	Windows, Android, iOS, Web, Skia	macOS	http://schemas.microsoft.com/winfx/2006/xaml/presentation
not_skia	Windcws, Android, iOS, Web, macOS	Skia	http://schemas.microsoft.com/winfx/2006/xaml/presentation

This table can be very confusing and difficult to understand when to use the various namespaces. Let's break it down to the simple cases first.

If I want to create a page and display a special message only on Android and no other platforms, I will add the xmlns for Android, which is `http://uno.ui/android`. With that added, I can now append any control on the page with that namespace, and it will only be visible on Android. Add the Android-specific xmlns as seen in Listing 5-16.

Listing 5-16. Android-specific xmlns definition

```
xmlns:android="http://uno.ui/android
```

Add `TextBlock` to only render on Android as seen in Listing 5-17.

Listing 5-17. Only render TextBlock when using the Android platform via xmlns

```
<android:TextBlock Text="Hello on Android" />
```

See complete LoginPage.xaml code in Listing 5-18.

Listing 5-18. LoginPage.xaml completed code with Android-specific xmlns

```
<Page
  x:Class="UnoDrive.LoginPage"
  xmlns="http://schemas.microsoft.com/winfx/2006/xaml/presentation"
  xmlns:x="http://schemas.microsoft.com/winfx/2006/xaml"
  xmlns:local="using:UnoDrive"
  xmlns:d="http://schemas.microsoft.com/expression/blend/2008"

  xmlns:android="http://uno.ui/android"
  mc:Ignorable="d android">

  <!-- Omitted markup -->

  <android:TextBlock Text="Hello on Android" />
</Page>
```

If you go and run this code, it will only display the message on Android and none of the other platforms.

This can make your XAML very verbose. If you need to change just one or two properties on a control, the same style syntax can be applied. However, instead of appending the namespace to the control, you can append it to the attribute. Given the preceding example, we can adjust the TextBlock to display different messages to different platforms.

Update the xmlns definitions to include the major platforms as seen in Listing 5-19.

Listing 5-19. LoginPage.xaml – add platform-specific xmlns definitions for Android, iOS, macOS, Skia, and WASM

```
xmlns:android="http://uno.ui/android"
xmlns:ios="http://uno.ui/ios"
xmlns:macos="http://uno.ui/macos"
xmlns:skia="http://uno.ui/skia"
xmlns:wasm="http://uno.ui/wasm"
```

Now update the TextBlock so it renders on all platforms and update the Text property to change depending on the platform. See code in Listing 5-20.

Listing 5-20. LoginPage.xaml – TextBlock control using xmlns to change the Text property

```
<TextBlock
  Text="Hello from Windows"
  android:Text="Hello from Android"
  ios:Text="Hello from iOS"
  macos:Text="Hello from macOS"
  skia:Text="Hello from Skia"
  wasm:Text="Hello from WASM" />
```

If you go and run the code, you will see a custom message displaying on the screen for each platform.

Native Controls

Adding controls or updating properties using the namespace definitions is a powerful technique to get your application looking just right. Uno Platform allows you to use this technique and add native platform code via XAML. Yes, if you are on Android and you want to add a native `TextView` or `TextEdit`, just add it to the XAML for your namespace:

```
<android:TextView
  Text="Hello native Android Control"
  TextSize="22 />
```

The `TextView` control is a native Android control that is part of the Android implementation for Uno Platform's `TextBlock`. In practice it is best to use the Uno Platform control, but this demonstrates complex capabilities for using native controls. If you go and run the code, it will display a new native `TextView` control that is using the default styles for Android instead of the custom styles we implemented for this page.

There is no need for building any custom abstractions around the native controls. You can simply place them in your XAML as you would any other control. When Uno Platform creates the view, it will add the native one in the correct place.

Note   Native controls are most useful when there is a very specific native control you want to use. We used `TextView` as a concrete example to see it in action.

Multi-targeted Projects

The Uno Platform templates use a shared project as the recommended approach for building your application. If you want to create a multi-targeted project, you may run into problems that a shared project does not run into. There are still many benefits of using a multi-targeted project. We will not be using one in our application, but let's go over some of the concepts for getting this to work and why you may want to use one.

Using a multi-targeted project will not solve all platform-specific problems, but it will certainly solve your C#-related ones.

Benefits

- Removes pre-processor directives

- Separates platform-specific code from shared code

Disadvantages

- Complicated to configure

- Difficult to maintain packages

- Difficult to distinguish between WASM and WPF since they both use the .NET 6.0 target framework moniker

A multi-targeted project is a concept supported by csproj and modern .NET tooling. The idea is you add multiple `<TargetFrameworks>` for all the platforms you want to support. In Uno Platform you will still need to maintain all the project heads, and your shared code will just be a compiled binary instead of being included in the project head. This means you will effectively be creating two binaries, one with your shared code and the other with executable or application code. The shared project approach includes all code in the root executable or application code.

To isolate your platform-specific code, you will need to implement special `<ItemGroup>` definitions in your csproj file. These will tell the compiler what to compile for which platform:

1. Add `<TargetFrameworks>` you need to support.

2. Set default compilation to false `<EnableDefaultCompilationItems>`.

3. Add target framework–specific `<ItemGroup>` to define compilation strategy. For example, Android should compile all files that end in `android.cs`.

The goal of this section isn't to fully document multi-targeting but to give you enough to understand how it works.

Conclusion

In this chapter we learned how to add platform-specific code in both C# and XAML, which allows us to ensure the application we are building looks just right between the various platforms. The code in this chapter will not directly be used in the following chapters but creates a foundation for the techniques we will be using later in the book.

If you had trouble with this chapter, you can view all the code on GitHub: `https://github.com/SkyeHoefling/UnoDrive/tree/main/Chapter%205`.

CHAPTER 6

Master-Detail Menu and Dashboard

Our application is going to have a main dashboard where all the operations of the authenticated user occur. You may also refer to this type of page as the main page or an application shell. In our application we will call it the dashboard, which is going to be our first deep dive into layout and menus. In Uno Platform you have several different ways to build your view stack and menus. In this chapter we are going to highlight some of the standard techniques and then build a flyout menu–style dashboard.

Navigation Types

When building any application, you need to decide what type of navigation you want to implement. There are several options to choose from, and each of them has its own advantages:

- Frame-based navigation (view stack)

- Tabbed menu

- Master-detail menu

These standard techniques are not mutually exclusive and can be combined to create the right user experience.

Frame-Based Navigation (View Stack)

Frame-based navigation, also known as view stack navigation, is when you display a new page on top of an existing page. Consider your page hierarchy as a stack data structure that is First-In-Last-Out, which means the newest item is the first to be

© Skye Hoefling 2022
S. Hoefling, *Getting Started with the Uno Platform and WinUI 3*,
https://doi.org/10.1007/978-1-4842-8248-9_6

removed. When we use the term *view stack*, nothing changes, and the data structure works just as defined. This means as you push new pages onto your view stack, you go back to the previous page by popping the most recent page off the stack. See diagram of View Stack in Figure 6-1.

Figure 6-1. *View stack diagram from Microsoft Docs(https://docs.microsoft. com/en-us/windows/apps/design/basics/navigation-basics)*

View stack navigation is typically used with other navigation techniques. Consider you are building a shopping app and a user selects an item they want to purchase and see more details of. You could use a view stack and push a new page onto the screen that displays all the details. When they click the back button, the page is popped off the view stack, and they are back to the list of items.

Tabbed Menu

A tabbed menu is when you have several menu options always available as quick icons in a tab bar. When the user selects the tab, the main display area updates to the new page. By design all major pages are one tap away for the user, which makes it very easy to navigate to the various pages in your application.

You are not limited to where you display the tabs. You can place your tabbed menu horizontally on the top or bottom of the page. You can also place your tabbed menu vertically on the left or right of the page.

A challenge with tabbed menus is you can only display so many tabs on the screen at once. In smaller devices such as the typical Android or iOS phone, you can only have four or five menu options.

Master-Detail Menu

A master-detail menu is popular on small form factor devices such as mobile phones where there is an icon with three horizontal lines commonly called the "hamburger" icon, which opens the menu. This menu can open from the left or the right portion of the screen depending on application design. The master-detail menu is popular because it is an easy way to store several options that can't be displayed in a tabbed menu or another navigation structure.

The master-detail menu is not just for small form factor devices but is very useful on tablets as well as desktop or laptop computers. In the larger form factors, the menu is typically always opened with the content area in the middle of the application. The menu can then be made responsive for the desktop or laptop scenario. As the screen size shrinks, it will fall back to a traditional flyout menu that is activated by the "hamburger" icon.

Combination

When building your application, you are not limited to just one navigation structure. It is common to mix and match these techniques where it makes the most sense. You may end up using all these techniques or even some that aren't listed.

A common pairing is tabbed menus and flyout menus, where the popular options are listed in the tabbed menu. Then there is a "More" or "Settings" icon that opens a master-detail menu, which has the less common options.

Create a Dashboard Layout

The first thing we need to do is build our dashboard core layout. Once we have this built, we can start adding menu options and event handlers to properly implement the master-detail design pattern.

In Uno Platform there are many ways to implement your master-detail menu:

- Master-detail control

- NavigationView

- Visual state manager

We are going to use the NavigationView as it provides everything we need to create a simple master-detail menu and it allows us to customize the menu completely. The NavigationView control is a powerful control that provides a master-detail implementation that we can customize. On larger displays we can have a left pane or top pane that is always visible. On smaller displays we can have it collapsed or hidden and only display it when we want to perform an operation in the pane menu. You can learn more about the NavigationView from the official WinUI documentation:

- https://docs.microsoft.com/en-us/windows/apps/design/
  controls/navigationview

To get started we need to create a new Views folder in the shared project. This folder will contain all of our user interface pages, as well as any helper class to support those pages.

Note   The typical convention in XAML-based applications is to have a Views folder or a Pages folder. It stores the various pages and sometimes more. This is entirely convention based and is up to you and your team. We are going to use a Views folder for this book.

We are going to be creating some new views in this chapter. Once you have the new folder created, move the existing LoginPage into this folder and then add four new blank Uno Platform pages called Dashboard, MyFilesPage, RecentFilesPage, and SharedFilesPage. See Figure 6-2 for a screenshot of the Visual Studio Solution Explorer.

Note   It is best to create your XAML files using the Visual Studio extension, which will generate the XAML file and code behind correctly. If you have trouble, the complete code snippets included with this chapter will help you out.

Figure 6-2. *Visual Studio Solution Explorer – Views folder*

In the Dashboard.xaml update your XAML to have the basic structure for the NavigationView. Inside the control add the following elements: PaneCustomContent, MenuItems, Header, and a standard Frame. See code snippet in Listing 6-1.

Listing 6-1. Dashboard.xaml – basic layout with NavigationView. The xmlns have been omitted

```
<Page>

  <!-- root container for the dashboard -->
  <NavigationView x:Name="menu">

    <!-- flyout menu header content -->
```

```
    <NavigationView.PaneCustomContent>
    </NavigationView.PaneCustomContent>

    <!-- flyout menu items -->
    <NavigationView.MenuItems>
    </NavigationView.MenuItems>

    <!-- main content area header -->
    <NavigationView.Header>
    </NavigationView.Header>

    <!-- main content area -->
    <Frame x:Name="contentFrame" />

  </NavigationView>

</Page>
```

PaneCustomContent

This allows you to place any content that will render above the menu items in the flyout menu. This will be used to display information about the user such as name and their profile photo.

MenuItems

This defines all the menu options that the user can navigate to from the flyout menu. In this container you will specify a list of NavigationViewItems, and each one will define an icon and text to keep a consistent menu experience.

Header

This specifies a standard content object where you can control what your page header looks like. The page header is the content that is rendered just above the main content area to the right of the flyout menu.

Frame

The content frame is where the current page or main content is rendered.

Now that we have the basic structure, we can start implementing various pieces to the dashboard page. Let's start by overriding some of the default values and configuring the platform targets.

Next, start adding properties to the `NavigationView` element. Update the control to match the code snippet in Listing 6-2.

Listing 6-2. Dashboard.xaml – NavigationView properties

```
<NavigationView x:Name="menu"
  IsBackButtonVisible="Collapsed"
  IsPaneOpen="False"
  IsSettingsVisible="False"
  ItemInvoked="MenuItemSelected">

  <!-- omitted code -->

</NavigationView>
```

These controls will configure the look and feel of the `NavigationView` to best match a standard flyout menu for the Windows target. The last property `ItemInvoked` configures an event listener that we will be using later. You will need to go into the code behind and create a method stub; otherwise, your application won't compile. See the method stub for the code behind in Listing 6-3.

Listing 6-3. Dashboard.xaml.cs – MenuItemSelected method stub for the event in NavigationView

```
Void MenuItemSelected(
  NavigationView sender,
  NavigationViewItemInvokedEventArgs args)
{
  // todo - add implementation
}
```

In the `<Page>` declaration at the top of the XAML file, add the following xmlns definitions to allow us to add specific rules for the various target platforms. See xmlns definitions in Listing 6-4.

Listing 6-4. Dashboard.xaml – XAML xmlns definitions

```
xmlns:win="http://schemas.microsoft.com/winfx/2006/xaml/presentation"
xmlns:android="http://uno.ui/android"
xmlns:ios="http://uno.ui/ios"
xmlns:macos="http://uno.ui/macos"
xmlns:wasm="http://uno.ui/wasm"
xmlns:skia="http://uno.ui/skia"
```

When adding platform-specific xmlns to the root element, you need to make sure they are added to the Ignorable attribute; otherwise, you will get compilation errors. See ignorables in Listing 6-5.

Listing 6-5. Dashboard.xaml – XAML xmlns ignorables

```
mc:Ignorable="d android ios macos wasm skia"
```

Let's add special configuration rules in for those so we can have the `NavigationView` render correctly across the platforms. Update your `NavigationView` to match the code snippet in Listing 6-6.

Listing 6-6. Dashboard.xaml – NavigationView updated pane display rules for the various target platforms

```
<NavigationView
  x:Name="menu"
  IsBackButtonVisible="Collapsed"
  IsPaneOpen="False"
  win:PaneDisplayMode="Left"
  wasm:PaneDisplayMode="Left"
  skia:PaneDisplayMode="Left"
  android:PaneDisplayMode="LeftMinimal"
  ios:PaneDisplayMode="LeftMinimal"
  macos:PaneDisplayMode="Left"
  win:IsPaneToggleButtonVisible="False"
  wasm:IsPaneToggleButtonVisible="False"
  skia:IsPaneToggleButtonVisible="False"
  macos:IsPaneToggleButtonVisible="False"
```

```
IsSettingsVisible="False"
ItemInvoked="MenuItemSelected">

<!-- omitted code -->
```

`</NavigationView>`

This may appear like a lot of code, but we are only modifying
`IsPaneToggleButtonVisible` (hamburger menu icon visibility) and `PaneDisplayMode`
(always open or flyout menu style). Since we need to customize two properties for many
platforms, the code ends up being quite verbose.

Next, let's define the `PaneCustomContent` area, which is a header that renders above
the `MenuItems`. In our application we are going to use this to display the user's name and
email address. We stubbed this out earlier when we built the basic structure. This control
is a simple `UIElement`, which makes it easy for us to add any type of `UIElement` control
such as a page or in our case a `StackPanel` to it. Update the `PaneCustomContent` to match
the code snippet in Listing 6-7.

Listing 6-7. Dashboard.xaml – NavigationView PaneCustomContent
implementation that renders at the top of the pane

```
<NavigationView.PaneCustomContent>
  <StackPanel Margin="5, 0, 5, 0" Spacing="10">
    <TextBlock
      Text="John Smith"
      FontSize="20"
      HorizontalTextAlignment="Center" />
    <TextBlock
      Text="john.smith@myemail.com"
      FontSize="18"
      HorizontalTextAlignment="Center" />

    <Border
      Height="1"
      Background="Black"
      Margin="10, 0" />
  </StackPanel>
</NavigationView.PaneCustomContent>
```

The code in Listing 6-7 displays the user's name and email and a horizontal line to separate the header section from the MenuItems section. Currently we are hard-coding the name and email address, but in future chapters when we connect to the Microsoft Graph, we will be using the logged-in user's information.

Next, we are going to implement the MenuItems, which control all the available options the user can select in the flyout menu. This container accepts a special menu item control called NavigationViewItem. This control defines an icon and content or text to display. Let's update our stubbed-out section to match the snippet in Listing 6-8.

Listing 6-8. Dashboard.xaml – NavigationViewItems

```
<NavigationView.MenuItems>
  <NavigationViewItem
    x:Name="myFiles"
    Icon="Play"
    Content="My Files"
    IsSelected="True" />
  <NavigationViewItem
    x:Name="recentFiles"
    Icon="Save"
    Content="Recent" />
  <NavigationViewItem
    x:Name="sharedFiles"
    Icon="Refresh"
    Content="Shared" />
  <NavigationViewItem
    x:Name="signOut"
    Icon="ClosePane"
    Content="Sign Out" />
</NavigationView.MenuItems>
```

The Icon property uses the standard Windows Segoe MDL2 font. It is easiest to use the official Microsoft documentation to see what the icons look like:

- https://docs.microsoft.com/en-us/windows/apps/design/
  style/segoe-ui-symbol-font

Depending on the version of Uno Platform, you may need to download the font file and add it to your various platform targets. Custom fonts are covered in Chapter 7.

Notice that each `NavigationViewItem` has a special `x:Name` property to define a name. This is intentional, and when we get to the code behind portion of this chapter, we will be using the names to configure the event handler that opens the various pages.

Next, we will be adding the page header. Let's add a simple `TextBlock` control that displays the message "My Files". We will expand upon this later, but for now we are going to keep this section simple. See the code snippet in Listing 6-9.

Listing 6-9. Dashboard.xaml – NavigationView header

```
<NavigationView.Header>
  <Border>
    <TextBlock
      Text="My Files"
      HorizontalAlignment="Left"
      FontSize="22"
      FontWeight="Bold" />
  </Border>
</NavigationView.Header>
```

The final element of our `NavigationView` object is the main content area. You will add a `<Frame>` right before the closing `</NavigationView>` tag. The `NavigationView` has an implied container that allows you to specify the content anywhere within the `NavigationView`. If you choose you can use the explicit name and insert it into the `NavigationView.Content`. See the code snippet in Listing 6-10.

Listing 6-10. Dashboard.xaml – NavigationView frame content using the implicit approach

```
<NavigationView>
  <!-- omitted code -->

  <Frame x:Name="contentFrame" Padding="15, 10" />

</NavigationView>
```

If you want to be explicit about your declaration and more verbose, you can use the following XAML. Both are correct. See the code snippet in Listing 6-11.

Listing 6-11. Dashboard.xaml – NavigationView frame content using the explicit approach

```
<NavigationView>
  <!-- omitted code -->

  <NavigationView.Content>
    <Frame x:Name="contentFrame" Padding="15, 10" />
  </NavigationView.Content>

</NavigationView>
```

The choice is yours on how you want to use the control. We are going to use the implicit approach from Listing 6-10 as it generates less verbose XAML.

The XAML of our dashboard is complete. See completed XAML in Listing 6-12.

Listing 6-12. Dashboard.xaml completed XAML

```
<Page>

  <NavigationView
    x:Name="menu"
    IsBackButtonVisible="Collapsed"
    IsPaneOpen="False"
    win:PaneDisplayMode="Left"
    wasm:PaneDisplayMode="Left"
    skia:PaneDisplayMode="Left"
    android:PaneDisplayMode="LeftMinimal"
    ios:PaneDisplayMode="LeftMinimal"
    macos:PaneDisplayMode="Left"
    win:IsPaneToggleButtonVisible="False"
    wasm:IsPaneToggleButtonVisible="False"
    skia:IsPaneToggleButtonVisible="False"
    macos:IsPaneToggleButtonVisible="False"
    IsSettingsVisible="False"
    ItemInvoked="MenuItemSelected">

    <NavigationView.PaneCustomContent>
      <StackPanel Margin="5, 0, 5, 0" Spacing="10">
```

```xml
      <TextBlock
        Text="John Smith"
        FontSize="20"
        HorizontalTextAlignment="Center" />
      <TextBlock
        Text="john.smith@myemail.com"
        FontSize="18"
        HorizontalTextAlignment="Center" />
      <Frame
        Height="1"
        Background="Black"
        Margin="10, 0" />
    </StackPanel>
  </NavigationView.PaneCustomContent>

  <NavigationView.MenuItems>
    <NavigationViewItem
      x:Name="myFiles"
      Icon="Play"
      Content="My Files"
      IsSelected="True" />
    <NavigationViewItem
      x:Name="recentFiles"
      Icon="Save"
      Content="Recent" />
    <NavigationViewItem
      x:Name="sharedFiles"
      Icon="Refresh"
      Content="Shared" />
    <NavigationViewItem
      x:Name="signOut"
      Icon="ClosePane"
      Content="Sign Out" />
  </NavigationView.MenuItems>

  <NavigationView.Header>
```

```
    <Frame>
      <TextBlock Text="My Files" />
    </Frame>
  </NavigationView.Header>

  <Frame x:Name="contentFrame" Padding="15, 10" />

</NavigationView>

</Page>
```

The application should compile and run at this point, but before we go and test it, let's configure our default page to load. Make the My Files page be your default page by adding the code in Listing 6-13 to your constructor in the code behind in Dashboard. xaml.cs.

Listing 6-13. Dashboard.xaml.cs – constructor initialization

```
public Dashboard()
{
  InitializeComponent();

  contentFrame.Navigate(
    typeof(MyFilesPage),
    null,
    new SuppressNavigationTransitionInfo());
}
```

Note   In the navigation code from Listing 6-13, we explicitly pass the SuppressNavigationTransitionInfo, which tells the navigation system to not render any animation behavior. There are several different options to provide in the Navigate() method to render rich animations.

Now we can run the application across the various platforms and figure out if we need to make any platform-specific code changes. See the running application in Figure 6-3 for Windows, Figure 6-4 for WASM, Figure 6-5 for Android, and Figure 6-6 for iOS.

Windows

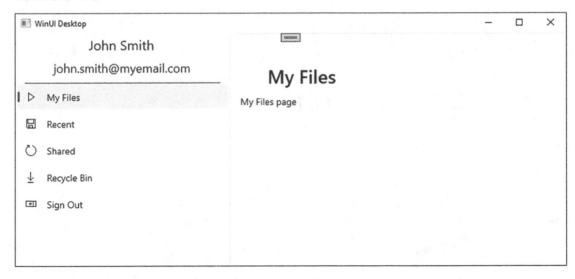

Figure 6-3. *Windows application with the flyout menu*

Note   The header object that reads "My Files" is pushed to the right, which is by design of the WinUI control we are using. This behavior will be consistent across the various platforms. As you get more content in the pages, it will look better. If you need to have the control left-aligned, you will need to add some custom styles to apply a negative margin or create your own control template.

WASM

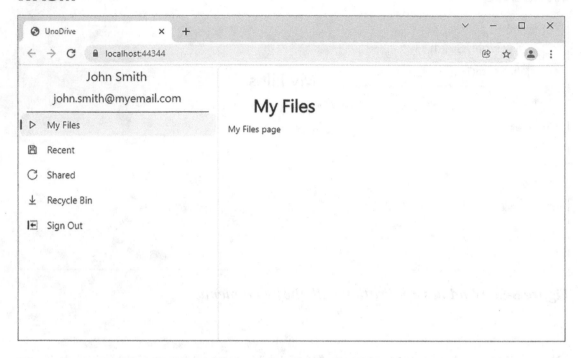

Figure 6-4. *WebAssembly application with the flyout menu*

Android

In the following we have two screenshots, one for the flyout closed and one for it opened.

Figure 6-5. *Android application with the flyout menu*

iOS

Figure 6-6. *iOS application with the flyout menu in the top bar outside of the safe zone*

Once you launch the application, you may notice that the flyout menu doesn't work as the menu icon is in the top bar of the phone. This isn't appealing for our design, and it is not functional, and the menu won't open.

In this instance we will need to add an iOS-specific top margin to move the entire NavigationView down and into the safe zone of the phone.

> **Note**   The *safe zone* is a mobile device term that was coined when iOS and Android devices started to introduce the top notch for the camera. Typically, you will want to not have any content rendered outside of the "safe zone" as you will not be able to guarantee that the user can interact with it. The "safe zone" is the area of the screen that the user can safely interact with using their touch events.

In your `Dashboard.xaml` file, add the following iOS-specific XAML for the `NavigationView` object to set a top margin. See the code snippet in Listing 6-14.

Listing 6-14. Dashboard.xaml – iOS-specific margin to prevent text from rendering behind the notch

```
ios:Margin="0, 45, 0, 0"
```

Your complete updated `NavigationView` XAML can be seen in Listing 6-15.

Listing 6-15. Dashboard.xaml – complete NavigationView property declarations

```
<NavigationView
  x:Name="menu"
  ios:Margin="0, 45, 0, 0"
  IsBackButtonVisible="Collapsed"
  IsPaneOpen="False"
  win:PaneDisplayMode="Left"
  wasm:PaneDisplayMode="Left"
  skia:PaneDisplayMode="Left"
  android:PaneDisplayMode="LeftMinimal"
  ios:PaneDisplayMode="LeftMinimal"
  macos:PaneDisplayMode="Left"
  win:IsPaneToggleButtonVisible="False"
  wasm:IsPaneToggleButtonVisible="False"
  skia:IsPaneToggleButtonVisible="False"
  macos:IsPaneToggleButtonVisible="False"
  IsSettingsVisible="False"
  ItemInvoked="MenuItemSelected">
```

You may want to adjust the margin to a different value, but we are going to use 45 as that gives us enough space between the top bar content and where we want our content to render. Launching the application again for iOS, you will now be able to interact with the flyout menu and open it up. See screenshot of iOS application in Figure 6-7.

Figure 6-7. *iOS application with the added top margin and opened flyout menu*

macOS

The macOS platform uses a very similar UI toolkit as iOS, which means behaviors on the iPhone will work on macOS. There is no notch on macOS, so we don't need to handle the safe zone. We get all the screen space as we would with any other desktop app. See screenshot of macOS application in Figure 6-8.

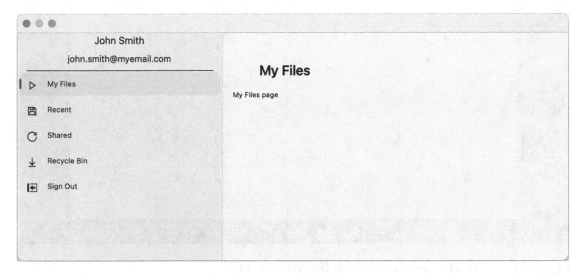

Figure 6-8. *macOS application with the flyout menu*

Linux

In Linux the page renders almost exactly how we want it. The only problem is the default fonts are not loading correctly. We aren't going to worry about this too much right now and will fix it in the next chapter, which will be a deep dive into custom fonts. See screenshot of Linux application in Figure 6-9.

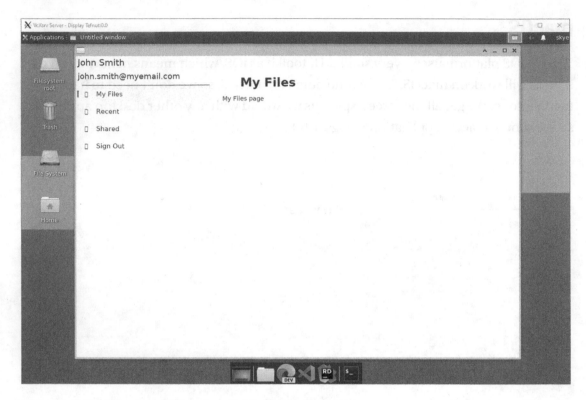

Figure 6-9.   *Linux application with the flyout menu*

WPF

The WPF platform uses the same Skia engine as the Linux target. Everything renders as we expect, and there are no additional changes needed. See screenshot of WPF application in Figure 6-10.

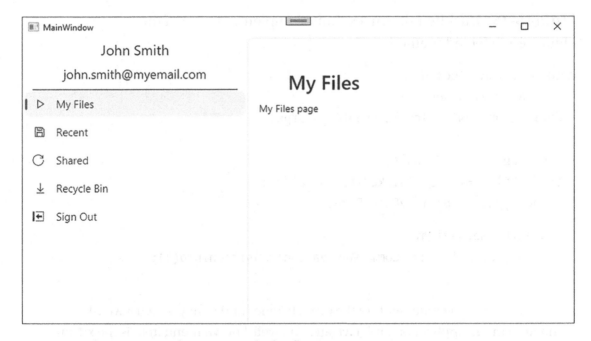

Figure 6-10. *WPF application with the flyout menu*

Menu Navigation

At this point you should have your application rendering correctly for the left menu and flyout menu depending on the platform you are running it on. Let's start adding some code in the code behind in `Dashboard.xaml.cs` that properly updates the main content area when selecting a menu option on the left.

In the last section, we defined the `MenuItems,` and each item in that collection had a unique name:

- *My Files*: myFiles

- *Recent*: recentFiles

- *Shared*: sharedFiles

- *Recycle Bin*: recycleBin

We will need to create an event handler that is triggered when a menu item is selected. This is built into the `NavigationView` using the `ItemInvoked` event. Earlier in the chapter, we stubbed out the method `MenuItemSelected` and added it to the `NavigationView` as an event listener. Since all the configuration is done, let's add our first navigation. See the code snippet in Listing 6-16.

Listing 6-16. Dashboard.xaml.cs – initial implementation of the MenuItemSelected method

```
void MenuItemSelected(
  NavigationView sender,
  NavigationViewItemInvokedEventArgs args)
{
  Type pageType = default;
  if (myFiles == args.InvokedItemContainer)
    pageType = typeof(MyFilesPage);

  contentFrame.Navigate(
    pageType, null, new CommonNavigationTransitionInfo());
}
```

We can check the arguments of the event listener and if they match a well-known menu item in the application and navigate. The well-known menu item is the x:Name property that we defined earlier in the XAML. This makes it easier to check in the event listener for navigation. Once we have identified the page type we want to navigate to, we can tell the contentFrame to navigate to the new page.

Implement the rest of the navigation items as seen in Listing 6-17.

Listing 6-17. Dashboard.xaml.cs – implementation of MenuItemSelected

```
void MenuItemSelected(
  NavigationView sender,
  NavigationViewItemInvokedEventArgs args)
{
  Type pageType = default;
  if (myFiles == args.InvokedItemContainer)
    pageType = typeof(MyFilesPage);
  else if (recentFiles == args.InvokedItemContainer)
    pageType = typeof(RecentFilesPage);
  else if (sharedFiles == args.InvokedItemContainer)
    pageType = typeof(SharedFilesPage);
```

```
  else if (recycleBin == args.InvokedItemContainer)
    pageType = typeof(RecycleBinPage);

  contentFrame.Navigate(
    pageType, null, new CommonNavigationTransitionInfo());
}
```

This will finish implementing the menu items that open a page, but it won't complete all menu items. We need to add a special implementation for "Sign Out" as that will log the user out of OneDrive. Since we haven't connected to the Microsoft Graph yet, this case will just return and do nothing.

Add the special "Sign Out" rules before all the other rules we implemented so far. See the code snippet in Listing 6-18.

Listing 6-18. Dashboard.xaml.cs – MenuItemSelected snippet for sign-out logic

```
// Signout is not implemented
if (signOut == args.InvokedItemContainer)
  return;
```

See completed code for `MenuItemSelected` in Listing 6-19.

Listing 6-19. Dashboard.xaml.cs – complete implementation of MenuItemSelected

```
void MenuItemSelected(
  NavigationView sender,
  NavigationViewItemInvokedEventArgs args)
{
  // Signout is not implemented
  if (signOut == args.InvokedItemContainer)
    return;

  Type pageType = default;
  if (myFiles == args.InvokedItemContainer)
    pageType = typeof(MyFilesPage);
  else if (recentFiles == args.InvokedItemContainer)
    pageType = typeof(RecentFilesPage);
  else if (sharedFiles == args.InvokedItemContainer)
```

```
    pageType = typeof(SharedFilesPage);
  else if (recycleBin == args.InvokedItemContainer)
    pageType = typeof(RecycleBinPage);
  else
    return;

contentFrame.Navigate(
    pageType, null, new CommonNavigationTransitionInfo());
}
```

Now if you run the application, you will be able to click the menu items, and the pages will update. There was no need to add any special platform-specific code in this section as we only configured navigation rules.

Page Header

The page header as implemented is a simple Border control and is included in the main Dashboard page. As the application complexity expands, we are going to want to add additional rules to the page header such as adding new files. Let's convert this to use a custom UserControl and decouple the XAML and code from the Dashboard page.

It is a good idea to keep your code organized. Let's create a new top-level folder in the shared project called "Controls." In this folder we will put our new page header UserControl. See Visual Studio Solution Explorer screenshot with new "Controls" folder in Figure 6-11.

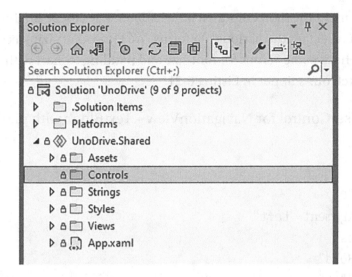

Figure 6-11. *Visual Studio Solution Explorer with the new Controls folder*

Add a new `UserControl` named `HeaderControl` to the "Controls" folder so we can begin the basic design. Let's start with a horizontal `Grid` that will have a left column and a right column. The header title will be left-aligned, and the right column will contain buttons that are right-aligned. For now, let's just add the title. See the code snippet in Listing 6-20.

Listing 6-20. UserControl for the NavigationView header

```
<UserControl>
  <Grid>
    <Grid.ColumnDefinitions>
      <ColumnDefinition Width="*" />
      <ColumnDefinition Width="*" />
    </Grid.ColumnDefinitions>

    <TextBlock
      Grid.Column="0 "
      HorizontalAlignment="Left"
      Text="My Files"
      FontWeight="Bold" />
  </Grid>
</UserControl>
```

We can implement the right column a little bit later. Let's focus on the TextBlock and get the style correct for the various platforms. We know that sizing is going to be different, and we have some values for font size and padding to start with. Update the TextBlock to match our snippet in Listing 6-21.

Listing 6-21. UserControl for NavigationView – TextBlock with platform-specific XAML

```
<TextBlock
  Grid.Column="0"
  HorizontalAlignment="Left"
  Text="My Files"
  FontWeight="Bold"
  win:FontSize="22"
  skia:FontSize="22"
  wasm:FontSize="22"
  android:FontSize="16"
  macos:FontSize="22"
  ios:FontSize="20"
  android:Padding="0, 4" />
```

We have not added any platform-specific customization for iOS, macOS, or Skia, so we may need to add additional properties for those platforms when we look at the running application. We have our basic UserControl implemented, so we can edit the Dashboard.xaml to include it.

We have been using the NavigationView.Header, but the control pushes our header content to a position that we don't want. Our goal is to make the header line up with the menu icon on mobile and be top left on desktop.

Let's remove the NavigationView.Header block and merge it with our Frame content. We will do this by creating a Grid and adding the new HeaderControl as the first item and the existing Frame as the second item.

If you haven't done so already, add a new xmlns definition that maps to the new control namespace. See the xmlns snippet in Listing 6-22.

Listing 6-22. xmlns definition for UnoDrive.Controls

```
xmlns:c="using:UnoDrive.Controls"
```

Then you can add our new `HeaderControl` to the `Grid` in the `Dashboard.xaml`. See the code snippet in Listing 6-23.

Listing 6-23. Dashboard.xaml – NavigationView content Grid that wraps the HeaderControl and the Frame

```
<Grid>
  <Grid.RowDefinitions>
    <RowDefinition Height="Auto" />
    <RowDefinition Height="*"
  </Grid.RowDefinitions>
  <c:HeaderControl Grid.Row="0" />
  <Frame Grid.Row="1" x:Name="contentFrame" />
</Grid>
```

This new XAML will place all the content starting at the top leftmost point. We need to add a little bit of padding and spacing to get our look and feel just right.

Update the `Grid` as seen in Listing 6-24.

Listing 6-24. Dashboard.xaml – NavigationView content Grid Padding and RowSpacing

```
<Grid Padding="15, 10" RowSpacing="10">
```

This change will cause the `HeaderControl` to overlap the menu icon in smaller displays for Android and iOS. When we review the screenshots, we will make changes to push the text to the right slightly.

Let's run the application and test all the platforms to make sure everything looks correct for the `TextBlock`. See screenshots of running application in Figure 6-12 for Windows, and Figure 6-13 for WASM, Figure 6-14 and Figure 6-15 for Android, Figure 6-16 and Figure 6-17 for iOS, Figure 6-18 for macOS, Figure 6-19 for Linux, and Figure 6-20 for WPF.

Windows

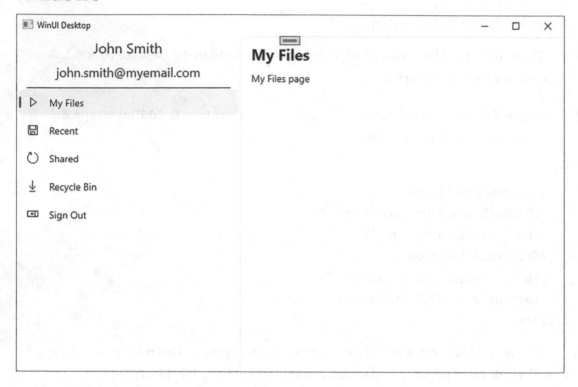

Figure 6-12. *Windows application with the new HeaderControl*

WASM

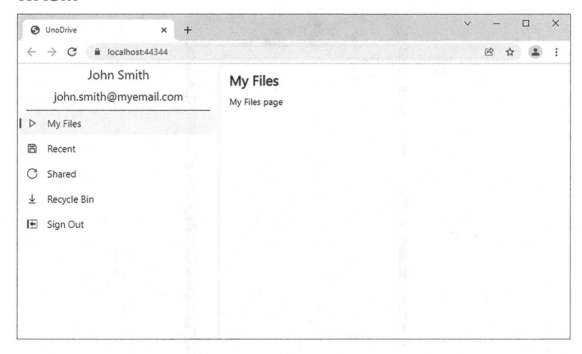

Figure 6-13. *The WebAssembly application with the new HeaderControl*

Android

Figure 6-14. *Android application with HeaderControl overlapping the menu icon*

The new design for the `HeaderControl` overlaps the menu icon, which renders an undesirable result. To solve this, we will add a special padding to push the entire header to the right. See the code snippet in Listing 6-25.

Listing 6-25. HeaderControl padding for Android

```
<c:HeaderControl android:Padding="30, 0, 0, 0" />
```

The completed XAML for this section can be seen in Listing 6-26.

Listing 6-26. Completed header main content code

```
<Grid Padding="15, 10" Spacing="10">
  <Grid.RowDefinitions>
    <RowDefinition Height="Auto" />
    <RowDefinition Height="*"
  </Grid.RowDefinitions>

  <c:HeaderControl
    Grid.Row="0"
    android:Padding="30, 0, 0, 0" />
  <Frame Grid.Row="1" x:Name="contentFrame" />
</Grid>
```

Now if you run the Android application again, you will see the header content is pushed to the right, leaving enough space for the menu icon.

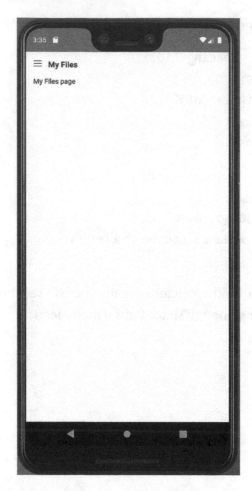

Figure 6-15. *Android application with left padding*

iOS

Figure 6-16. *iOS application with header overlapping the menu icon*

The iOS application has the same problem as Android where the header text now overlaps the menu icon. Since the padding we added for Android was specific to that platform, we will apply an iOS-specific one. See the code snippet in Listing 6-27.

```
<c:HeaderControl
  android:Padding="30, 0, 0, 0"
  ios:Padding="30, 0, 0, 0" />
```

See the completed `NavigationView` main content Grid in Listing 6-27.

Listing 6-27. Dashboard.xaml – NavigationView main content Grid complete code

```
<Grid Padding="15, 10" Spacing="10">
  <Grid.RowDefinitions>
    <RowDefinition Height="Auto" />
    <RowDefinition Height="*"
  </Grid.RowDefinitions>
  <c:HeaderControl
    Grid.Row="0"
    android:Padding="30, 0, 0, 0" />
    ios:Padding="30, 0, 0, 0" />
  <Frame Grid.Row="1" x:Name="contentFrame" />
</Grid>
```

Run the application again, and you should see the header text pushed to the right of the menu icon.

Figure 6-17. *iOS application with header text pushed to the right by left padding*

macOS

Figure 6-18. *macOS application with new HeaderControl*

Linux

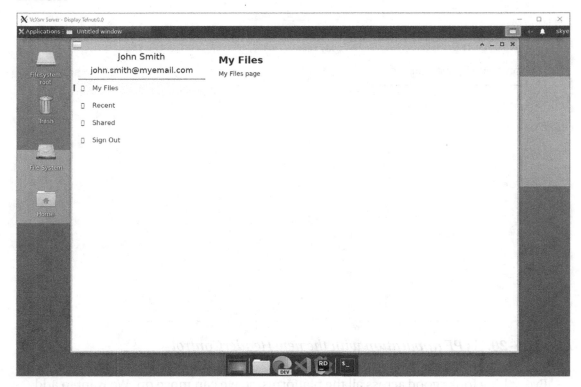

Figure 6-19. *Linux application with the new HeaderControl*

WPF

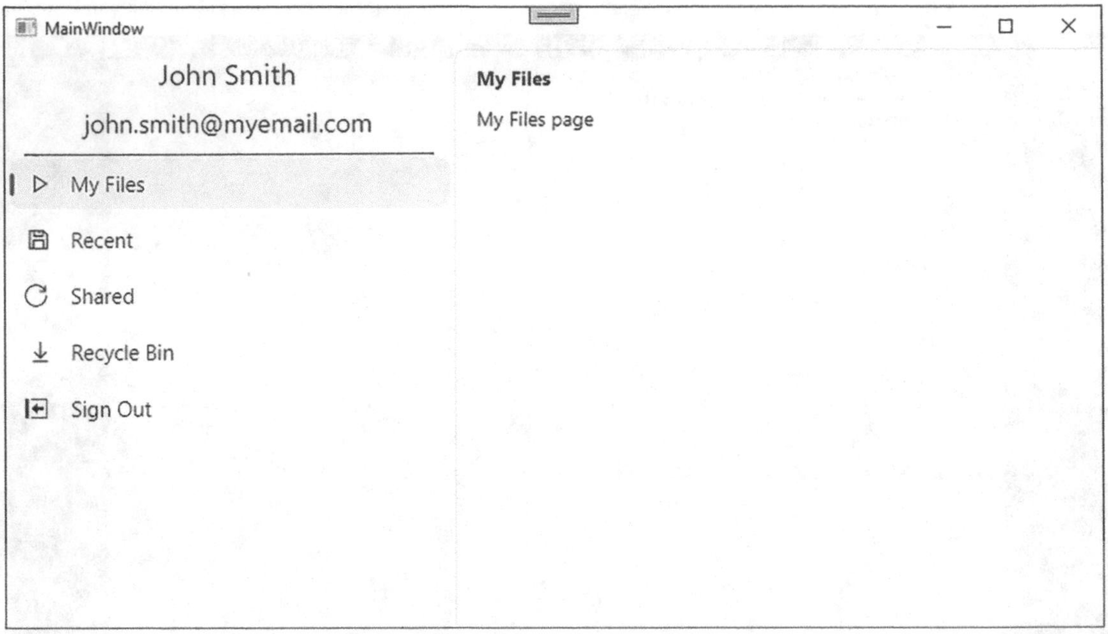

```
MainWindow                                                    —    □    ×

                John Smith                      My Files
          john.smith@myemail.com               My Files page

    ▷   My Files

    🖫   Recent

    C   Shared

    ↓   Recycle Bin

    ⬅   Sign Out
```

Figure 6-20. *WPF application with the new HeaderControl*

Everything looks good across all the platforms, so we can move on. We want to add a right column, which will display buttons to perform actions. Let's add a horizontal StackPanel that is aligned to the right of the page that wraps all content inside the PaneCustomContent. This will be our button group container to provide primary and secondary actions. For now, we are going to hard-code two buttons, New and Upload. See the code snippet in Listing 6-28.

Listing 6-28. Dashboard.xaml – NavigationView PaneCustomContent two buttons

```
<StackPanel
  Grid.Column="1"
  Orientation="Horizontal"
  HorizontalAlignment="Right"
  Spacing="10">

  <Button
    Background="#0078D4"
```

```
    Foreground="#FFFFFF"
    Content="New" />

  <Button Content="Upload" />

</StackPanel>
```

This will render the basic concept, but we want to use icons to help our user quickly identify what actions the buttons perform. In Uno Platform you can include powerful view containers inside the Button control's Content property. Let's update both buttons to display an icon prior to the text. See code for the first button in Listing 6-29 and code for the second button in Listing 6-30.

Listing 6-29. Dashboard.xaml – NavigationView PaneCustomContent first button (New) content

```
<Button
  Background="#0078D4"
  Foreground="#FFFFFF">

  <Button.Content>
    <StackPanel
      Orientation="Horizontal"
      Spacing="10"
      Margin="5, 2">

      <FontIcon
        FontFamily="Segoe MDL2 Assets"
        Glpyh="&#xE109;"
        win:FontSize="14"
        skia:FontSize="14"
        wasm:FontSize="14"
        android:FontSize="18"
        macos:FontSize="14"
        ios:FontSize="18" />

      <TextBlock
        Text="New"
        win:FontSize="16"
```

```
        skia:FontSize="16"
        wasm:FontSize="16"
        android:Fontsize="12"
        macos:FontSize="16"
        ios:FontSize="16" />

    </StackPanel>
  <Button.Content>

</Button>
```

Listing 6-30. Dashboard.xaml – NavigationView PaneCustomContent second button (Upload) content

```
<Button>

  <Button.Content>
    <StackPanel
      Orientation="Horizontal"
      Spacing="10"
      Margin="5, 2">

      <FontIcon
        FontFamily="Segoe MDL2 Assets"
        Glpyh="&#xE11C;"
        win:FontSize="14"
        skia:FontSize="14"
        wasm:FontSize="14"
        android:FontSize="18"
        macos:FontSize="14"
        ios:FontSize="18" />

      <TextBlock
        Text="Upload"
        win:FontSize="16"
        skia:FontSize="16"
        wasm:FontSize="16"
        android:Fontsize="12"
```

```
    macos:FontSize="16"
    ios:FontSize="16" />

  </StackPanel>
<Button.Content>

</Button>
```

Now let's run the application and see how the right column looks and if there are any changes we need to make to any of the platforms. See Figure 6-21 for Windows, Figure 6-22 for WASM, Figure 6-23 for Android, Figure 6-24 and Figure 6-25 for iOS, Figure 6-26 for macOS, Figure 6-27 for Linux, and Figure 6-28 for WPF.

Windows

Figure 6-21. Windows application with header buttons

WASM

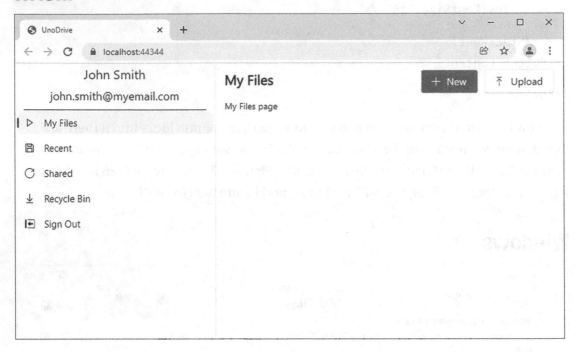

Figure 6-22. *WebAssembly application with header buttons*

Android

Figure 6-23. *Android application with header buttons*

Note   The assets were not loaded correctly for Android. This is expected as the Segoe MDL2 Assets are only available on Windows by default. We will need to explicitly add these for Android.

We will be fixing this in the next chapter.

---

iOS

Figure 6-24. *iOS application with header buttons off the screen*

The iOS application draws the buttons as expected, but they are drawn outside the bounds of the screen, making it difficult to use the "Upload" button. In our `Grid` design we defined each column to take exactly 50% of screen width as seen in the code snippet in Listing 6-31.

Listing 6-31. HeaderControl.xaml – grid column definitions

```
<ColumnDefinition Width="*" />
<ColumnDefinition Width="*" />
```

Looking at our screen, we can see the header text or the first column doesn't need exactly 50% of screen width and it can use up less. Let's update the first column to use the keyword Star that uses up the remaining space and the second column to use Auto. This will give the necessary space for both buttons:

```
<ColumnDefinition Width="*" />
<ColumnDefinition Width="Auto" />
```

When we run the application again on iOS, both buttons will be in the bounds of the screen.

Figure 6-25. *iOS application with header buttons*

> **Note**   The iOS application does not have the font icons loaded correctly as the Segoe MDL2 Assets are only included in Windows by default. We will need to add the assets to the iOS project for them to show up correctly.
>
> This will be explained in detail in the next chapter.

macOS

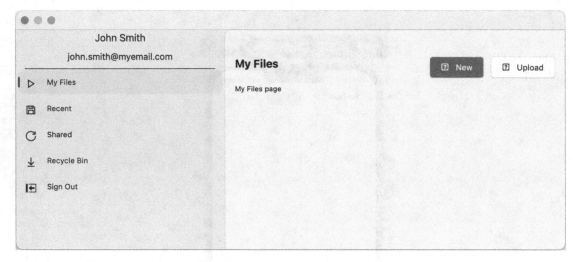

Figure 6-26.   macOS application with header buttons

The Segoe MDL2 Assets are not included by default for macOS. We will need to add them to the project.

This will be explained in the next chapter.

Linux

Figure 6-27. *Linux application with header buttons*

Note   Just like iOS and macOS, the Linux application does not have the Segoe MDL2 Assets. For this platform it is considered a custom font and needs to be added to the project.

This will be explained in the next chapter.

WPF

Figure 6-28. *WPF application with header buttons*

Even though the WPF project uses the same Skia rendering engine as Linux, since it is on Windows, it has the Segoe MDL2 Assets. There's no need to explicitly add them to the WPF project.

We are going to conclude with the fonts not working on all platforms. In the next chapter, we are going to fix this by adding custom fonts.

Conclusion

In this chapter we covered the fundamental navigation strategy of a dashboard page using a left menu or flyout menu depending on the target platform. We also added navigation for the various stubbed pages we added.

In the next chapter we are going to pick up where we left off by adding custom fonts to all the projects, so the icons look identical between the platforms. If you had any trouble following the code in this chapter, you can download the code for Chapter 6 at https://github.com/SkyeHoefling/UnoDrive/tree/main/Chapter%206.

CHAPTER 7

Custom Fonts

In the previous chapter, we added a new dashboard menu, which contained a custom header control with buttons in the top-right portion of the page. These buttons had icons that only worked on Windows using either the Windows or WPF target project. That is because all the other platforms do not have the right font files loaded into the projects. In this chapter we are going to finish that work by adding the custom font file and ensuring everything is rendered correctly.

Note   The concepts applied for icon fonts can be used for any font file you want to add to your application.

Custom fonts can be used in your application to give it the unique look and feel you are looking for. They can also provide an easy way to add various icons to your application without needing to load in hundreds of images. In this chapter we are going to review the best practices in Uno Platform for adding asset fonts to your application.

Download Material Icons

We are going to be using Microsoft's Material Icons for our icons, which are popular free permission icons made by Google using Material Design. The best place to download the required font file .ttf is from the official Material Design Icons repository on GitHub:

- `https://github.com/google/material-design-icons/`

© Skye Hoefling 2022
S. Hoefling, *Getting Started with the Uno Platform and WinUI 3*,
https://doi.org/10.1007/978-1-4842-8248-9_7

Add Font Styles

Once you have the font downloaded, we can start adding it to each platform and looking at the result. In the previous chapter, we implemented two buttons in the page content header, and on non-Windows platforms, instead of the icons there was a white rectangle or random emoji. We are expecting this to show the correct icons after making changes in this chapter.

Before we start adding the font, we need to add a little bit of code and configuration. In our application styles, let's create a new XAML file to contain application-wide font information.

Create a new `Fonts.xaml` file under the `Styles/Application` directory. See screenshot of Visual Studio Solution Explorer with new file in Figure 7-1.

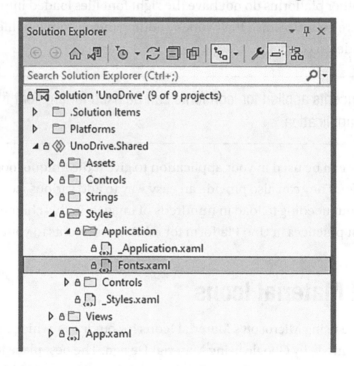

Figure 7-1. *Visual Studio Solution Explorer – Fonts.xaml*

Add the following code to `Fonts.xaml` as seen in Listing 7-1.

Listing 7-1. Fonts.xaml – add Windows FontFamily

```
<ResourceDictionary
  xmlns="http://schemas.microsoft.com/winfx/2006/xaml/presentation"
  xmlns:x="http://schemas.microsoft.com/winfx/2006/xaml"
```

```
xmlns:win="http://schemas.microsoft.com/winfx/2006/xaml/presentation"
mc:Ignorable=" ">

<win:FontFamily x:Key="MaterialIcons">ms-appx:///Fonts/MaterialIcons-
Regular.ttf#Material Icons</win:FontFamily>

</ResourceDictionary>
```

The important line of XAML is the declaration that sets the FontFamily. This is a special property that can be applied as a StaticResource in the control. We explicitly added the win: prefix so it doesn't affect any other target platforms that we will be implementing later in this chapter. See the code snippet in Listing 7-2.

Listing 7-2. Windows-specific FontFamily XAML

```
<win:FontFamily x:Key="MaterialIcons">ms-appx:///Fonts/MaterialIcons-
Regular.ttf#Material Icons</win:FontFamily>
```

Next, we need to update the _Application.xaml file to reference our new Fonts. xaml file. This will make sure that the font is loaded into memory and can be used in other pages and controls. See code ResourceDictionary addition in Listing 7-3 and complete code for _Application.xaml in Listing 7-4.

Listing 7-3. _Application.xaml – add ResourceDictionary for Fonts.xaml

```
<ResourceDictionary Source="Fonts.xaml" />
```

Listing 7-4. _Application.xaml – complete XAML code

```
<ResourceDictionary
  xmlns="http://schemas.microsoft.com/winfx/2006/xaml/presentation"
  xmlns:x="http://schemas.microsoft.com/winfx/2006/xaml">

  <ResourceDictionary.MergedDictionaries>
    <XamlControlsResources xmlns="using:Microsoft.UI.Xaml.Controls" />
    <ResourceDictionary Source="Fonts.xaml" />
  </ResourceDictionary.MergedDictionaries>

</ResourceDictionary>
```

Update the Header Control

With the font set as a `FontFamily` element, we can reference it in our `HeaderControl.xaml` file. Let's go and update the `FontFamily` property on both `FontIcon` elements. See the code snippet in Listing 7-5 for updates to the New button and Listing 7-6 for updates to the Upload button.

Listing 7-5. HeaderControl.xaml – updates the New button to use FontFamily from styles

```
<FontIcon
  FontFamily="{StaticResource MaterialIcons}"
  Glyph="&#xE145;"
  win:FontSize="14"
  skia:FontSize="14"
  wasm:FontSize="14"
  android:FontSize="10"
  macos:FontSize="14"
  ios:FontSize="14" />
```

Listing 7-6. HeaderControl.xaml – updates the Upload button to use FontFamily from styles

```
<FontIcon
  FontFamily="{StaticResource SegoeMDL2Assets}"
  Glyph="&#xF09B;"
  win:FontSize="14"
  skia:FontSize="14"
  wasm:FontSize="14"
  android:FontSize="10"
  macos:FontSize="14"
  ios:FontSize="14" />
```

All the configuration is done, and we can start adding the fonts to the various target platforms. At this point if you run the application, it will not work on any platform as we need to add the font files. This includes the Windows project that we just configured.

Add Font Files to Projects

There is a shared project that is used by all projects, and this is useful for adding images and other shared assets. It does not work with fonts, and the fonts must be stored in the correct location for the various target projects. The rest of the chapter will detail how to do this for all the platforms we are supporting.

It is always useful to refer to the official Uno Platform documentation on adding fonts:

- `https://platform.uno/docs/articles/features/custom-fonts.html`

Windows

To add the font file to Windows, start by creating a new folder in the UnoDrive.Windows project at the root of the project named `Fonts`. Then copy the MaterialIcons-Regular. ttf file into that new folder and ensure it is using the build action `Content`. If you do not set the build action, the Windows app will not be able to load the font file correctly. See Figure 7-2 for a screenshot of the Visual Studio Solution Explorer.

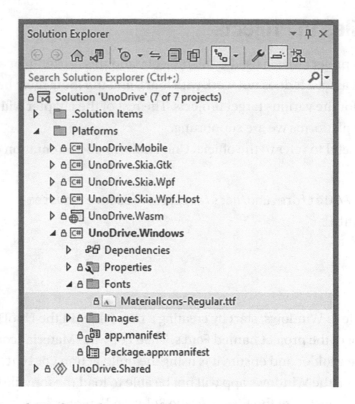

Figure 7-2. *Visual Studio Solution Explorer – Windows font*

We already added the necessary font code in the previous section. Now you can run the application on Windows, and you will see the Material Icons being used in the buttons on the top right of the screen.

Android

To add the font to Android, start by copying the MaterialIcons-Regular.ttf file into the Android ➤ Assets ➤ Fonts folder of the mobile project. The multi-targeted mobile project will automatically build this file as an AndroidAsset. To double-check, you can right-click and select Properties. The build action should be AndroidAsset. See screenshot of Visual Studio Solution Explorer Android fonts in Figure 7-3.

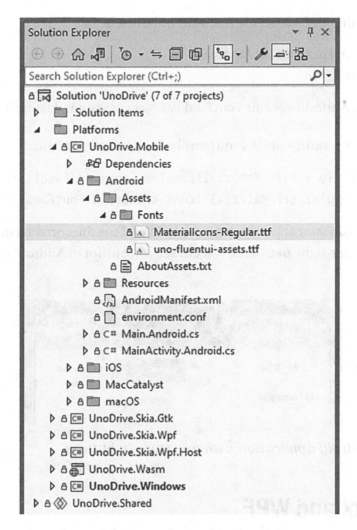

Figure 7-3. *Visual Studio Solution Explorer – Android font*

Note   You may see the font file uno-fluentui-assets.ttf depending on how you generated your project. It is included in some of the Uno Platform templates and is a free permission font using some of the icons from Fluent Design.

Once this is completed, we can update our Fonts.xaml file to include the necessary Android code. Add the Android xmlns definition to specify platform-specific XAML. When adding platform-specific xmlns definitions, you will need to add non-Windows items to the ignorable. See the xmlns definition for Android in Listing 7-7.

Listing 7-7. xmlns definition for Android in Fonts.xaml

```
xmlns:android="http://uno.ui/android"
mc:Ignorable="android"
```

Then add the Android-specific `FontFamily` object as seen in Listing 7-8.

Listing 7-8. Fonts.xaml – adds FontFamily declaration for Android

```
<android:FontFamily x:Key="MaterialIcons">ms-appx:///Assets/Fonts/
MaterialIcons-Regular.ttf#Material Icons </android:FontFamily>
```

You can now run your application for Android and see the correct icons in the buttons in the upper-right area of the screen. See screenshot of Android application in Figure 7-4.

Figure 7-4. *Android application with font icons in buttons*

Skia: Linux and WPF

Both Linux and WPF use Skia to create a rendered user interface. This means we can implement the custom code for these platforms together. Start by updating the `Fonts.xaml` to include a Skia target platform. See the xmlns definition for Skia in Listing 7-9.

Listing 7-9. xmlns definition for Skia in Fonts.xaml

```
xmlns:skia="http://uno.ui/skia"
mc:Ignorable="android skia"
```

Then add the Skia-specific `FontFamily` object as seen in Listing 7-10.

Listing 7-10. Fonts.xaml – adds FontFamily declaration for Skia

```
<skia:FontFamily x:Key="MaterialIcons">ms-appx:///Assets/Fonts/
MaterialIcons-Regular.ttf#Material Icons </skia:FontFamily>
```

Now we can start adding the font file to both the Linux and WPF projects.

Linux

In the Linux project, add the font file to the `Assets` ➤ `Fonts` directory. Once it is included in the project, ensure it has the build action of `Content`. See screenshot of Visual Studio Solution Explorer GTK fonts in Figure 7-5.

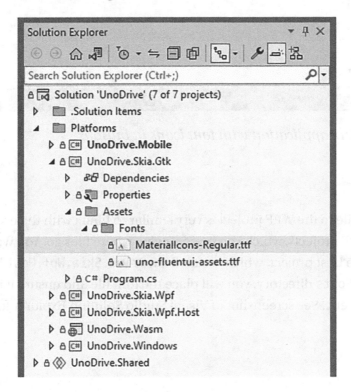

Figure 7-5. *Visual Studio Solution Explorer – GTK font*

You can now launch your GTK project, and you will see the buttons are using the correct icons. See running Linux application in Figure 7-6.

Figure 7-6. *Linux application with font icons in buttons*

WPF

Adding the font file to the WPF project is very similar to Linux with the exception that there are two WPF projects, which can be confusing where files go. You will need to add the font file to the host project, which is called `UnoDrive.Skia.Wpf.Host` in our solution. In the `Assets` ➤ `Fonts` directory, you will place the font file and ensure it is being compiled as `Content`. See screenshot of Visual Studio Solution Explorer for WPF fonts in Figure 7-7.

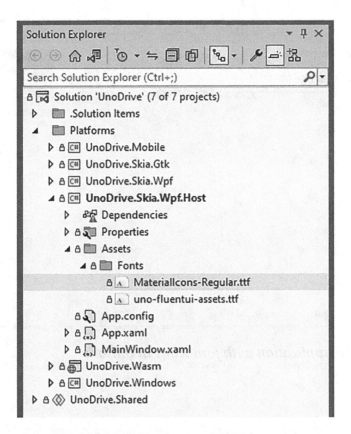

Figure 7-7. *Visual Studio Solution Explorer – WPF font*

You can now launch the application as a WPF project, and you will see the buttons are using the correct icons. See running WPF application in Figure 7-8.

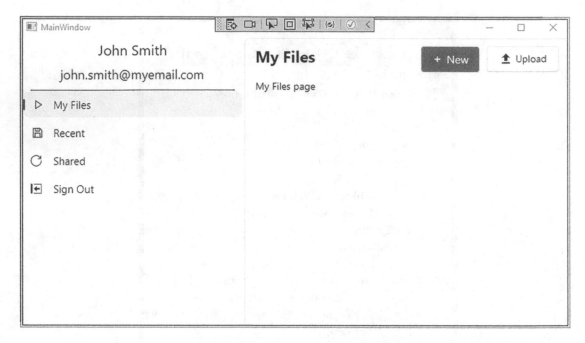

Figure 7-8. *WPF application with font icons in buttons*

iOS

To add the custom font to iOS, you will need to add the font file to the iOS ➤ Resources ➤ Fonts directory in the mobile project. The multi-targeted project will automatically build the file as a BundleResource. You can verify this by right-clicking the font file and selecting Properties. See screenshot of Visual Studio Solution Explorer for iOS fonts in Figure 7-9.

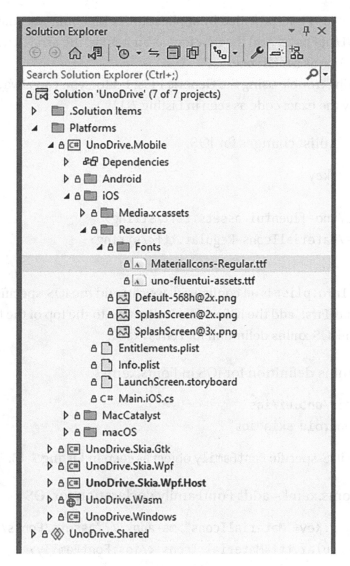

Figure 7-9. Visual Studio Solution Explorer – iOS font

You will need to update the Info.plist file to include your font. If you are using Visual Studio on Windows, it will be easiest to open this file via right-clicking and selecting Open With. Select the Generic PList Editor, which gives you a similar editing experience as Visual Studio for Mac. It makes it easier to see the custom attribute and add a new row of data.

Add a new row to "Fonts provided by application," which may use that title or the technical key of UIAppFonts. Add the new font as an item in the array. There should be an existing one to use as a reference.

If you are having trouble using the Generic PList Editor, you can always open it as an XML file and copy the exact code as seen in Listing 7-11.

Listing 7-11. Info.plist changes for iOS

```
<key>UIAppFonts</key>
<array>
  <string>Fonts/uno-fluentui-assets.ttf</string>
  <string>Fonts/MaterialIcons-Regular.ttf</string>
</array>
```

Now that the Info.plist is all configured, we can add the iOS-specific font styles to the Fonts.xaml file. First, add the iOS xmlns declaration to the top of the file. See Listing 7-12 for the iOS xmlns definition for Fonts.xaml.

Listing 7-12. xmlns definition for iOS in Fonts.xaml

```
xmlns:ios="http://uno.ui/ios"
mc:Ignorable="android skia ios"
```

Then add the iOS-specific FontFamily object as seen in Listing 7-13.

Listing 7-13. Fonts.xaml – adds FontFamily declaration for iOS

```
<ios:FontFamily x:Key="MaterialIcons">ms-appx:///Assets/Fonts/
MaterialIcons-Regular.ttf#Material Icons </ios:FontFamily>
```

Once the style is added, you can go ahead and test your application. Run your iOS application and verify that the icons are displaying correctly in the buttons in the header control. See running iOS application in Figure 7-10.

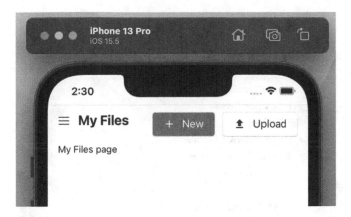

Figure 7-10. *iOS application with font icons in buttons*

macOS

Adding the font to macOS is very similar to iOS except there are some differences in how you edit the Info.plist file. Start by adding the font file to the project under the directory macOS ➤ Resources ➤ Fonts. Since we are using a multi-targeted project, the newly added font file will use the build action BundleResource. You can double-check this by right-clicking the font file and selecting Properties. See screenshot of Visual Studio Solution Explorer for macOS fonts in Figure 7-11.

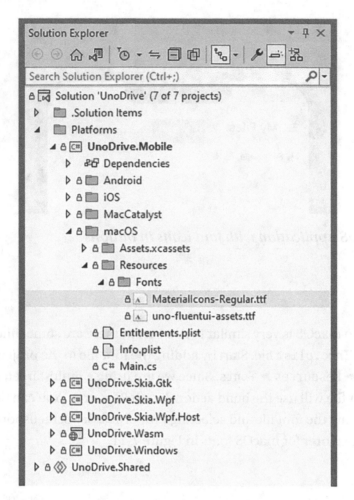

Figure 7-11. *Visual Studio Solution Explorer – macOS font*

With the font file correctly added to your project, you can edit the Info.plist file. As we did before, right-click this file and select Open With and then select the Generic PList Editor. This will give you the closest editing experience to Visual Studio for Mac.

Update the key ATSApplicationFontPath to the directory where the fonts are stored. The full path is not needed as the Resources directory is implied; all you need to do is edit this value to be Fonts. If you are having trouble with the Generic PList Editor, you can always edit the file as XML and use the exact code as seen in Listing 7-14.

Listing 7-14. Info.plist changes for macOS

```
<key>ATSApplicationFontsPath</key>
<string>Fonts</string>
```

There is no need to specify every single font file in the `Fonts` directory like you did on the iOS target. You only need to specify where the fonts are, and the macOS target loads them correctly.

Once you have updated the `Info.plist`, we can update the `Fonts.xaml` in the shared code project to specify the macOS-specific font styles. Start by adding the macOS-specific xmlns declarations to the top of the file. See the code snippet in Listing 7-15 for the xmlns definition in the `Fonts.xaml`.

Listing 7-15. xmlns definition for macOS in Fonts.xaml

```
xmlns:macos="http://uno.ui/macos"
mc:Ignorable="android skia ios macos"
```

Then add the macOS `FontFamily` object as seen in Listing 7-16.

Listing 7-16. Fonts.xaml – adds FontFamily declaration for macOS

```
<macos:FontFamily x:Key="MaterialIcons">ms-appx:///Assets/Fonts/
MaterialIcons-Regular.ttf#Material Icons </macos:FontFamily>
```

Once the `Fonts.xaml` file is updated, you can launch the macOS application to verify that the icons are displaying correctly in the header control. See running macOS application in Figure 7-12.

Figure 7-12. *macOS application with font icons in buttons*

WASM

The last target platform is WASM, and this one is set up a little bit differently than the rest of the projects. There is no direct need to include the font file in the project, and you can include it as part of the CSS file using a base64 string. There are several examples already included in our WASM project of web fonts. If you open the WasmCSS ➤ fonts.css file, you will see several declarations of @font-face. In the CSS file, the font-family attribute maps to the name you will need to use in your XAML.

You will need to convert the SegMDL2.ttf file to a base64 string. You can use any tool you prefer or write your own application. There are also many free file converters online. If you are unsure how to convert the file, you can reference the code sample with this chapter. See code in Listing 7-17 for a quick way to convert a file to base64.

Listing 7-17. Quick way to convert a file to a base64 string

```
byte[] bytes = File.ReadAllBytes("path\\to\\file");
string base64 = Convert.ToBase64String(bytes, 0, bytes.Length);
```

Once converted to base64, you can add the following CSS. Swap out the *** for your actual base64 string. See the code snippet in Listing 7-18.

Listing 7-18. CSS for font in WASM

```
@font-face {
  font-family: "Material Icons";
  src: url(data-application:x-font-ttf;charset:utf-8;base64,***)
format('truetype');
}
```

Now that you have successfully added the font to your WASM project, you can edit the Fonts.xaml file. First, add the WASM xmlns to the top of the file. See Listing 7-19 for the xmlns definition in the Fonts.xaml.

Listing 7-19. xmlns definition for WASM in Fonts.xaml

```
xmlns:wasm="http://uno.ui/wasm"
mc:Ignorable="android skia ios macos wasm"
```

Then add the WASM `FontFamily` object as seen in Listing 7-20.

Listing 7-20. Fonts.xaml – adds FontFamily declaration for WASM

```
<wasm:FontFamily x:Key="MaterialIcons">ms-appx:///Assets/Fonts/
MaterialIcons-Regular.ttf#Material Icons </wasm:FontFamily>
```

Once you have finished editing the `Fonts.xaml` file, you can test the application. Launch your WASM target and open the web browser, so you can verify that the header control buttons are using the correct icons. See running WASM application in Figure 7-13.

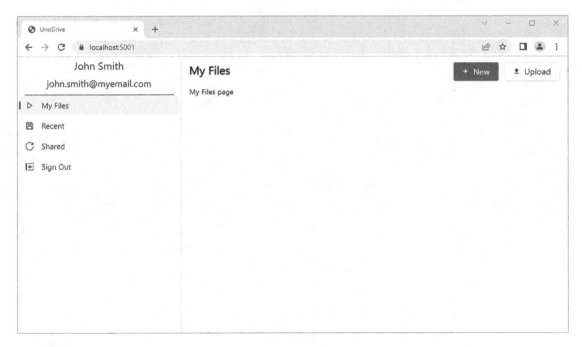

Figure 7-13. *WebAssembly application with font icons in buttons*

Conclusion

In this chapter we finished work from the previous chapter by adding the Segoe MDL2 Assets font file to all the target platforms that are not Windows. You can even add this file to your UWP application to ensure it is using the latest assets.

The techniques covered here also apply to any custom font you may want to use whether it is icons or a standard text font to use in `TextBlock` and similar controls.

If you had any trouble following along, you can find the completed code for Chapter 7 on the GitHub repository:

- `https://github.com/SkyeHoefling/UnoDrive/tree/main/`
  `Chapter%207`

CHAPTER 8

Model-View-ViewModel (MVVM)

In the last few chapters, we have been building our main application dashboard and login page. We are now ready to start architecting our application to support scalable design patterns that separate the user interface code from business rules and code that communicates with the Microsoft Graph for OneDrive APIs.

The most common application architecture for Uno Platform is Model-View-ViewModel or MVVM, which is used in various application platforms such as WPF, UWP, Xamarin.Forms, and more. There are many open source libraries that implement their own MVVM framework available in the .NET ecosystem. The concept of MVVM can be as simple or complicated as you choose to make it, and we are going to try and find a middle ground between those. This should help our application scale, separating concerns without making it too complicated to maintain.

What Is MVVM?

Before we start writing any code, let's understand the concept of MVVM and how a basic implementation may look. By definition MVVM is Model-View-ViewModel, which has the main goal of separating our user interface code from any business rules that are not controlling the presentation layer:

- Model
- View
- ViewModel

The View and ViewModel are connected via the data binding technique. This provides multiple transport scenarios to update the user interface from the ViewModel.

© Skye Hoefling 2022
S. Hoefling, *Getting Started with the Uno Platform and WinUI 3*,
https://doi.org/10.1007/978-1-4842-8248-9_8

The data binding is our communication bridge and what allows us to have the two concepts isolated.

Note   In a well-built MVVM application, you should be able to swap out any View without changing the code in the ViewModel. This is because of the isolation of the ViewModel and the View. They should only be communicating through the decoupled data binding communication layer.

Let's flip the acronym and explain it out of order: View, Model, and ViewModel.

View

The presentation layer or the user interface is the View. In Uno Platform this is your XAML page where you are placing controls on the controls. It is also the code behind where you may be configuring animations or other complex presentation layer effects.

Model

The View sometimes needs more information about the objects in the presentation layer. A Model can define these properties to help with the data binding. Consider you are building a list of people and you want each person to have a name and email property. You may create a Person model that defines these items so you can directly bind the data.

ViewModel

The business rules are stored in the ViewModel. This is where all of your other code lives or starts from. The ViewModel can start communicating with a database or API service to get data for the presentation layer. It will use data binding to send that data to the View or to have actions from the View start a business method.

Tip   ViewModels can be as complicated or simple as you make them. It should focus on business rules and not user interface operations such as animations. When you implement a ViewModel, you should keep the code as simple as

---

possible. When a ViewModel starts getting very complex, some of the code may need to be moved into other classes that are invoked from the ViewModel.

MVVM Example

Let's try putting the concepts to use and seeing a simple example of MVVM before we open up our UnoDrive application. Earlier we learned that MVVM is broken into three main categories: Model, View, and ViewModel. Let's see what some code looks like.

Consider you have a `MainPage.xaml` file that renders "Hello World!". See code snippet in Listing 8-1.

Listing 8-1. MainPage.xaml code displaying Hello World!

```
<Page>
  <Grid>
    <TextBlock Text="Hello World!" />
  </Grid>
</Page>
```

Instead of hard-coding the text in the View, we want to pull this data from a ViewModel.

Note   A real-world example for this is processing application localization. The text may need to go through a special localization method that gets the correct content for the language selected by the user. If we hard-code our application to English, it won't be usable by people who aren't familiar with English. The ViewModel can orchestrate this and decouple the localization function from the View.

Let's create a `MainViewModel` that displays "Hello World!" in a property called Message. See code snippet in Listing 8-2.

Listing 8-2. MainViewModel.cs that contains the necessary properties for the View

```
public class MainViewModel
{
  public string Message => "Hello World!";
}
```

Now we have all the pieces put together, we need to go back to the MainPage.xaml and connect it to the MainViewModel. Then we will add the data binding to render the message correctly on the page.

In Uno Platform all the View objects have a special property called DataContext. This allows you to use data binding to communicate between the View and the ViewModel. It supports various types of binding, but for this example we are going to use simple data binding.

Update the MainPage.xaml.cs to set the DataContext to our new ViewModel, the MainViewModel. See code snippet in Listing 8-3.

Listing 8-3. MainPage.xaml.cs (code behind) setting the DataContext for the ViewModel and Message property

```
public sealed partial class MainPage : Page
{
  public MainPage()
  {
    InitializeComponent();
    DataContext = new MainViewModel();
  }
  public string Message => ""Hello World!";
}
```

Update the MainPage.xaml.cs to use data binding to use the message from the MainViewModel. The syntax uses a markup extension, which is denoted by curly braces {}. When performing a binding operation, you have access to all public properties on the ViewModel. See code snippet in Listing 8-4.

Listing 8-4. Data binding code

```
{Binding Message}
```

Take this code and plug it into the Text property in the TextBlock of our MainPage.xaml.cs. See code snippet in Listing 8-5.

Listing 8-5. Completed MainPage.xaml.cs code with data binding to ViewModel

```
<Page>
  <Grid>
    <TextBlock Text="{Binding Message}" />
  </Grid>
</Page>
```

That's it! We have now implemented the basics of the MVVM architecture. Not all applications require a large MVVM framework or advanced concepts. You may want to just set your `DataContext` manually in the code behind. It just means you won't get some of the advanced features such as Dependency Injection, which is covered in Chapter 9.

MVVM in UnoDrive

We now have a basic understanding of MVVM and how it works. We can start adding it to our UnoDrive application to see it in real-world scenarios. The preceding example is to just get us started with MVVM, and we are going to be expanding on those concepts in this section. Instead of instantiating our ViewModels in the code behind, we are going to use a `ViewModelLocator` to find our ViewModel and set the `DataContext` for us.

ViewModelLocator

A `ViewModelLocator` is a concept in MVVM where your View automatically searches for the correct ViewModel and sets it to the `DataContext`. You can configure this to be the default on all Views using a parent class on your Views or manually set it each time. In UnoDrive we are going to explicitly set the `ViewModelLocator` in each View.

Let's get started by adding ViewModels for all of our pages in the application. In the shared project, create a new folder called ViewModels and add a new ViewModel for each page we have already created. Swap out the keyword "Page" for "ViewModel." If your page doesn't have the "Page" keyword, just append the keyword "ViewModel" to it. You should have the following ViewModels or by referencing the Visual Studio Solution Explorer screenshot in Figure 8-1.

- DashboardViewModel
- LoginViewModel

- MyFilesViewModel

- RecentFilesViewModel

- RecycleBinViewModel

- SharedFilesViewModel

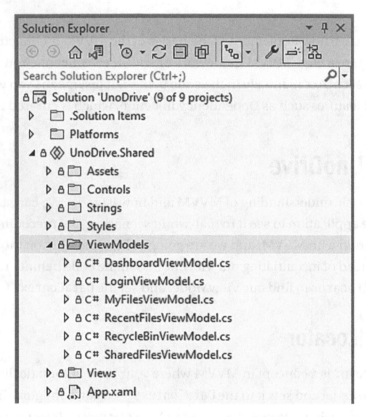

Figure 8-1. *Visual Studio Solution Explorer – ViewModels folder*

Each of the ViewModel files will be an empty public class, and it doesn't need to inherit from any parent class. See the code sample in Listing 8-6, which can be used for all the ViewModels at this point.

Listing 8-6. Empty class for DashboardViewModel

```
public class DashboardViewModel
{
}
```

With all the ViewModels created, we can start building our `ViewModelLocator`. This is a MVVM-specific object and isn't part of the ViewModels namespace we have just created. Let's create a new folder called Mvvm and create a new empty class called `ViewModelLocator.cs`. See screenshot of Visual Studio Solution Explorer with new folder and file in Figure 8-2.

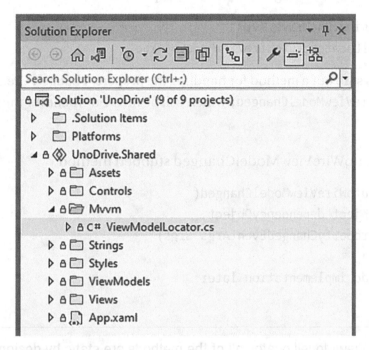

Figure 8-2. *Visual Studio Solution Explorer – ViewModelLocator*

The `ViewModelLocator` is where we will be configuring the automatic ViewModel searching. Let's start by adding an attached property so we can configure this setting on each individual View. An attached property is a technique in XAML applications to extend functionality in the XAML specification that may not be there out of the box.

Note   Many developers are using attached properties without knowing it. The most common one is specific, the `Grid.Row` or `Grid.Column` on any control that exists inside of a `Grid` control.

Before we get into the implementation of our `ViewModelLocator,` let's focus on the usage of it. That will help us better understand how it works before we implement it. In any page that you want to enable the ViewModelLocator to automatically search for the correct ViewModel, you will add the code in Listing 8-7.

Listing 8-7. xmlns for using the attached property from ViewModelLocator

```
xmlns:mvvm="using:UnoDrive.Mvvm"
mvvm:ViewModelLocator.AutoWireViewModel="True"
```

To start let's stub out a method for handling the property changes. Create a static method `AutoWireViewModelChanged,` which will be invoked whenever the property is changed.

Listing 8-8. AutoWireViewModelChanged stubbed method

```
static void AutoWireViewModelChanged(
  DependencyObject dependencyObject,
  DependencyPropertyChangedEventArgs args)
{
  // TODO - Add implementation later
}
```

Note   In the ViewModelLocator, all of the methods are static by design as they will not have an instance to access. This is part of how we implement the attached property pattern.

Next, you will add the `DependencyProperty` – see Listing 8-8. When creating the `DependencyProperty,` you need to specify the return type, encapsulated class, and what code to invoke when changed. We will map the method we created earlier in the `DependencyProperty.`

Listing 8-9. DependencyProperty implementation

```
public static DependencyProperty AutoWireViewModelProperty =
  DependencyProperty.RegisterAttached(
    "AutoWireViewModel",
    typeof(bool),
    typeof(ViewModelLocator),
    new PropertyMetadata(false, AutoWireViewModelChanged));
```

Next, we will create the accessor (getters) and mutators (setters) for the attached property – see Listing 8-9. Since the attached property always returns object, which isn't very useful, we will need to cast it to the desired type, which is bool. See code snippet in Listing 8-10.

Listing 8-10. Accessor and mutators for the attached property

```
public static bool GetAutoWireViewModel(UIElement element)
{
  return (bool)element.GetValue(AutoWireViewModelProperty);
}

public static void SetAutoWireViewModel(
  UIElement element,
  bool value)
{
  element.SetValue(AutoWireViewModelProperty, value);
}
```

The attached property is all implemented. You can use it as we demonstrated earlier in Listing 8-7 and Listing 8-8.

We will be updating all of our Views later as we need to finish implementing the ViewModelLocator. The attached property is complete, and now we need to implement the method that searches for the correct ViewModel and sets it to the DataContext on the View.

In the ViewModelLocator.cs create a new method stub named FindViewModel – see Listing 8-11.

Listing 8-11. FindViewModel method stub

```
static Type FindViewModel(Type viewType)
{
}
```

The goal of `FindViewModel` is to retrieve the ViewModel type, and then we will instantiate that type and set it to the `DataContext` in another method. The searching is convention based that will search for all Views that have a suffix of "Page" or are part of the "Views" namespace. This handles pages like the `Dashboard.xaml,` which don't explicitly have a suffix of "Page."

Caution   The `ViewModelLocator` typically uses reflection, and depending on your target platform, you may need to add instructions to the linker to prevent your ViewModels from being removed at compile time for release modes.

This is one of the only times where it is okay to use reflection in the application.

Let's look at what our algorithm will do in steps:

1. Using the supplied View, determine if it is a page by checking the class name for a suffix of "Page" or if it is part of the "UnoDrive. Views" namespace.

2. Update the View name to remove and replace the keyword of "Page" and the namespace of "Views" with "ViewModel."

3. Retrieve the ViewModel using the new name and return the Type.

See the implemented algorithm in Listing 8-12.

Listing 8-12. Implemented FindViewModel in the ViewModelLocator

```
static Type FindViewModel(Type viewType)
{
  string viewName = string.Empty;

  if (viewType.FullName.EndsWith("Page") ||
      viewType.FullName.StartsWith("UnoDrive.Views"))
  {
```

```
  viewName = viewType.FullName
    .Replace("Page", string.Empty)
    .Replace("Views", "ViewModels");
}

string viewASsemblyName = viewType
  .GetTypeInfo()
  .Assembly
  .FullName;

string viewModelName = string.Format(
  CultureInfo.InvariantCulture,
  "{0}ViewModel, {1}",
  viewName,
  viewAssemblyName);

  return Type.GetType(viewModelName);
}
```

To complete our ViewModelLocator implementation, we now need to connect
the attached property of AutoWireViewModel to the FindViewModel method when the
property is changed. Earlier we created a stub for AutoWireViewModelChanged
(Listing 8-8), which we will be using to complete the ViewModelLocator. See the updated
implementation in Listing 8-13.

Listing 8-13. Updated AutoWireViewModelChanged to perform binding
operation

```
static void AutoWireViewModelChanged(
  DependencyObject dependencyObject,
  DependencyPropertyChangedEventArgs args)
{
  if (args.NewValue is bool autoWireEnabled &&
    autoWireEnabled)
  {
    Bind(dependencyObject);
  }
}
```

Next, we will implement the Bind method, which will instantiate the ViewModel and set it to the DataContext property on the View. See Listing 8-14 for Bind implementation.

Listing 8-14. Bind method for instantiating the ViewModel and setting it to the DataContext

```
static void Bind(DependencyObject view)
{
  if (view is FrameworkElement frameworkElement)
  {
    Type viewModelType =
      FindViewModel(frameworkElement.GetType());

    frameworkElement.DataContext =
      Activator.CreateInstance(viewModelType);
  }
}
```

Caution   The Bind method also uses reflection for the instantiation of the object. This may cause linker issues on some target platforms.

The ViewModelLocator is completed. When in use it will search by convention for an associated ViewModel and automatically set it to the correct DataContext property on the View. See completed ViewModelLocator code in Listing 8-15.

Listing 8-15. Completed ViewModelLocator

```
public class ViewModelLocator
{
  public static DependencyProperty AutoWireViewModelProperty =
    DependencyProperty.RegisterAttached(
      "AutoWireViewModel",
      typeof(bool),
      typeof(ViewModelLocator),
      new PropertyMetadata(false, AutoWireViewModelChanged));

  public static bool GetAutoWireViewModel(UIElement element)
```

```
{
  return (bool)element.GetValue(AutoWireViewModelProperty);
}

public static void SetAutoWireViewModel(
  UIElement element,
  bool value)
{
  element.SetValue(AutoWireViewModelProperty, value);
}

static void AutoWireViewModelChanged(
  DependencyObject dependencyObject,
  DependencyPropertyChangedEventArgs args)
{
  if ((bool)args.NewValue)
  {
    Bind(dependencyObject);
  }
}

static void Bind(DependencyObject view)
{
  if (view is FrameworkElement frameworkElement)
  {
    Type viewModelType =
      FindViewModel(frameworkElement.GetType());

    frameworkElement.DataContext =
      Activator.CreateInstance(viewModelType);
  }
}

static Type FindViewModel(Type viewType)
{
  string viewName = string.Empty;

  if (viewType.FullName.EndsWith("Page") ||
```

```
            viewType.FullName.StartsWith("UnoDrive.Views"))
  {
    viewName = viewType.FullName
      .Replace("Page", string.Empty)
      .Replace("Views", "ViewModels");
  }

  string viewASsemblyName = viewType
    .GetTypeInfo()
    .Assembly
    .FullName;

  string viewModelName = string.Format(
    CultureInfo.InvariantCulture,
    "{0}ViewModel, {1}",
    viewName,
    viewAssemblyName);

  return Type.GetType(viewModelName);
  }
}
```

Set AutoWireViewModel

When we build the ViewModelLocator, we create a special attached property to communicate to the Views that we want to automatically find the ViewModel and set it to the View's DataContext property. Now that all of this code is completed, we can start going through each View and updating the top xmlns to define this.

In each View at the top <Page> element, add the XAML from Listing 8-16.

Listing 8-16. Configure AutoWireViewModel

```
xmlns:mvvm="using:UnoDrive.Mvvm"
mvvm:ViewModelLocator.AutoWireViewModel="True"
```

You will want to add this to all of the XAML files in your "Views" folder:

- Dashboard

- LoginPage

- MyFilesPage

- RecentFilesPage

- RecycleBinPage

- SharedFilesPage

At this point you should be able to launch the application, and everything will run like it did before. We haven't made any functional changes to the application yet as we have just implemented our MVVM architecture.

Use LoginViewModel

The LoginPage is currently using hard-coded strings for all the TextBlock controls on the page. We are going to update these to be in the LoginViewModel and use data binding to render them on the page. This is very similar to our simple MVVM example we did at the beginning of the chapter, but we are using it on our UnoDrive application.

First, let's take all the strings from the LoginPage and add them to the LoginViewModel with the following properties: Title, Header, ButtonText. See Listing 8-17 for completed LoginViewModel code.

Listing 8-17. Completed LoginViewModel code

```
public class LoginViewModel
{
  public string Title => "Welcome to UnoDrive!";
  public string Header => "Uno Platform ♥ OneDrive = UnoDrive";
  public string ButtonText => "Login to UnoDrive";
}
```

Next, let's update the LoginPage using the simple data binding we learned earlier to update all the TextBlock controls to bind to the LoginViewModel. See Listing 8-18.

Listing 8-18. Completed LoginPage code. This snippet omits everything except the Grid and children

```
<Grid>
  <Grid.RowDefinitions>
    <RowDefinition Height="*" />
```

```xml
    <RowDefinition Height="*" />
  </Grid.RowDefinitions>

  <StackPanel Grid.Row="0">
    <TextBlock
      Text="{Binding Title}"
      Style="{StaticResource Header}" />
    <TextBlock
      Text="{Binding Header}"
      Style="{StaticResource SubHeader}" />
  </StackPanel>

  <StackPanel Grid.Row="0" Grid.RowSpan="2">
    <Button
      Content="{Binding ButtonText}"
      Style="{StaticResource LoginButton}"
      Click="OnLoginClick"/>
  </StackPanel>

</Grid>
```

Now you can run the application, and everything will still work as before, but the data is being used from the `LoginViewModel` instead of the `LoginPage`.

Conclusion

In this chapter we covered the basics of configuring the MVVM architecture in your Uno Platform application without using any third-party frameworks. We are going to be building upon these concepts in the next chapter as we expand our MVVM implementation to support Dependency Injection.

If you had any trouble following along with the code, it is all available on the GitHub repository: https://github.com/SkyeHoefling/UnoDrive/tree/main/Chapter%208.

CHAPTER 9

Dependency Injection and Logging

In the previous chapter, we learned about building our Model-View-ViewModel (MVVM) application architecture and how all the pieces fit together in our application. MVVM applications thrive when they use Dependency Injection, which decouples the deeper business rules from the ViewModels. We are going to continue building up our MVVM library by adding Dependency Injection into it and configure our logging so we can use a simple ILogger interface in any class.

What Is Dependency Injection?

Dependency Injection is when your class automatically resolves dependencies as they are required. There are several ways to inject your dependencies depending on the toolkit you are using, but the most common solution is using constructor injection.

The idea is to create a mapping between an interface and a concrete implementation of that interface. In theory you will be able to change your concrete implementation without changing the interface. In practice that doesn't always work as well as we would hope. You do not have to always have an interface if it doesn't make sense for your solution. It is also a valid solution to just have concrete objects that are injected instead of interfaces.

Note   Dependency Injection is a popular technique as you can create an interface for every registered object in your Dependency Injection system. This makes it much easier to test complex code as you can create mock instances or test objects for your interfaces instead of using real implementation.

© Skye Hoefling 2022
S. Hoefling, *Getting Started with the Uno Platform and WinUI 3*,
https://doi.org/10.1007/978-1-4842-8248-9_9

Dependency Injection is important when building MVVM applications because any ViewModel can start having many dependencies on various objects, which can have their own dependencies. The Dependency Injection system will keep all of this configured for us, so all we need to know is what object will be performing the actions for us.

Parts of the System

The concept of Dependency Injection has four main categories:

- Container
- Registration
- Retrieval or injection
- Lifetime

Container

The Dependency Injection container is the most important part of Dependency Injection and can be hard to see or explain as it isn't seen in the standard usage. The container is the object that stores all the registrations and mappings of objects to resolve. This can include how to resolve the objects, whether it should create a new one every time or use a cached object. The container is sometimes leveraged in library code when performing advanced Dependency Injection features, which we will see later when we add it to our UnoDrive application.

Registration

The registration part of Dependency Injection is the bit of code or configuration files that create your mapping for the various objects including their lifetime constraints. The lifetime constraints communicate how the object should be instantiated into the system or if it should use a cached value. Dependency Injection registration code should be invoked as early as possible in the application lifecycle so it can be used right away. Some Dependency Injection libraries will use a configuration file instead of mapping by code, and just like the code solution, this should be invoked as early as possible in the application lifecycle.

> **Note**   Registering objects for Dependency Injection does not mean they are instantiated and ready to be used. Most objects are instantiated when they are resolved. This is configured at registration time. See Table 9-1 for detailed lifetime descriptions.

Retrieval

The standard usage of Dependency Injection is the act of resolving an object from the container. In the case of constructor injection, the process of resolving arguments is typically handled by the Dependency Injection container as part of resolving an object. When the object is requested, the container will find it and determine how to create it depending on the configured lifecycle.

Lifetime

The lifetime or lifecycle defines how the registered object will be instantiated by the container. You can configure it to generate a new object upon every retrieval or use a cached value. Microsoft's latest Dependency Injection library is called `Microsoft.Extensions.DependencyInjection,` and you can see the lifetimes in Table 9-1.

Table 9-1. *Microsoft.Extensions Dependency Injection Available Lifetimes*

Lifetime	Description
Transient	Always create a new object upon retrieval. This can be a greedy operation especially if there are many dependencies. It is still one of the most common lifetimes to use.
Scoped	Most useful in web applications as it caches the object for the duration of a request.
Singleton	Creates one instance of the object the first time it is requested. All following requests will use that same object.

Example

Before we start adding any code to our UnoDrive application, it will be useful to understand the concepts in code to see how it would work. Let's look at a simple example that uses Dependency Injection for printing "Hello World!" to the console. Consider the starter code in Listing 9-1.

Listing 9-1. Dependency Injection example starter code

```
public class Main
{
  public Main()
  {
    Console.WriteLine("Hello World!");
  }
}
```

This code snippet will print the message "Hello World!" to the console when the Main object is instantiated. The goal of this example will be to use constructor injection to offload that API to another class. We will accomplish this by following these steps:

1. Create a MessageService with a Write method.

2. Register the MessageService with the Dependency Injection container.

3. Inject the MessageService into the Main class and use the Write method to print "Hello World!"

Create an IMessageService interface to define the contract we want to implement in the MessageService – see Listing 9-2.

Tip   It is always a good idea in Dependency Injection systems to have an interface for any concrete implementation you build. While you may not need to swap out the implementation, it helps you organize your contract on how the consuming code will integrate with your registered object. Using interfaces makes the code easier to test as things can be mocked out.

Listing 9-2. IMessageService interface for the Dependency Injection example

```
public interface IMessageService
{
  void WriteLine(string message);
}
```

Next, we can create our implementation of the IMessageService in a concrete class called MessageService. This class will implement the contract and print the message – see Listing 9-3.

Listing 9-3. MessageService implementation for the Dependency Injection example

```
public class MessageService : IMessageService
{
  public void WriteLine(string message)
  {
    Console.WriteLine(message);
  }
}
```

Now that we have both the interface and implementation completed, we will need to register this with our Dependency Injection container. Since we have both an interface and implementation, let's map them to resolve the implementation when the interface is requested – see Listing 9-4.

Note   This example doesn't go into how you will start the registration process and covers just the act of registration. The startup process will be covered later in the chapter.

Listing 9-4. Container registration of IMessageService for the Dependency Injection example

```
public void RegisterServices(IServiceCollection services)
{
  Services.AddTransient<IMessageService, MessageService>();
}
```

We are going to use a transient lifetime manager as it will create a new instance every time it is requested. This will help the garbage collector remove this object when it is no longer needed.

The Dependency Injection system is all configured. The last thing to do is update the Main class and use constructor injection. Once we have the IMessageService injected, we can update the Console.WriteLine API to use the IMessageService.WriteLine API – see Listing 9-5.

Listing 9-5. Main class using constructor injection for the Dependency Injection example

```
public class Main
{
  public Main(IMessageService messageService)
  {
    messageService.WriteLine("Hello World!");
  }
}
```

A way to expand upon this example is using the MessageService implementation to write messages to other places other than just the console. You could add code to determine if you are in production and write the message to a logging tool or if you are in debug mode and write it to the console.

Dependency Injection in UnoDrive

Now that we have a basic understanding of Dependency Injection, let's expand on this topic to add it to our application. In the preceding example, we didn't go into detail about how the container registration process is started. We will start by orchestrating that in our UnoDrive application.

We will be using the latest Microsoft Dependency Injection library from the Extensions project, Microsoft.Extensions.DependencyInjection. The current Uno Platform templates have a dependency on Microsoft.Extensions. DependencyInjection, which is Microsoft's latest Dependency Injection library. It is used throughout the .NET ecosystem, and many third-party libraries support the abstractions to interop with their systems. To ensure there are no issues with NuGet packages, we are going to manually add the Dependency Injection library to our projects. In all the target head projects, add the PackageReference code snippet in Listing 9-6.

Listing 9-6. PackageReference for Microsoft.Extensions.DependencyInjection

```
<PackageReference
  Include="Microsoft.Extensions.DependencyInjection"
  Version="6.0.0" />
```

MVVM thrives best with Dependency Injection, so we will be adding some of our Dependency Injection code to the UnoDrive.Mvvm folder. Create a new class in the Mvvm folder called MvvmApplication, which will be a new parent class for the entry point of the Uno Platform application. See screenshot of Visual Studio Solution Explorer in Figure 9-1.

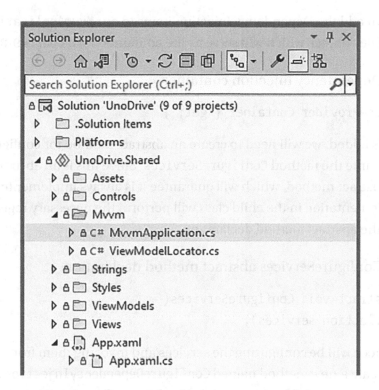

Figure 9-1. *Visual Studio Solution Explorer – MvvmApplication.cs*

Start by creating the basic class and adding a Current property that replaces the existing one in the Application object. We can do this by using the new keyword, which will be available only when using the MvvmApplication directly. See Listing 9-7 for the MVVM part of the code.

Listing 9-7. Initial implementation of MvvmApplication

```
public abstract class MvvmApplication : Application
{
  public MvvmApplication()
  {
    Current = this;
  }

  public static new MvvmApplication Current { get; private set; }
}
```

Next, we can add the Dependency Injection items to our MvvmApplication. Add an IServiceProvider object, which will serve as the container – see Listing 9-8.

Listing 9-8. Dependency Injection container

```
public IServiceProvider Container { get; }
```

Once that is added, we will need to create an abstract method for configuring the services. Let's name the method ConfigureServices. Since this is an abstract class, we can make an abstract method, which will guarantee it is always implemented in the child class. The implementation in the child class will perform the necessary registrations. See Listing 9-9 for the abstract method declaration.

Listing 9-9. ConfigureServices abstract method declaration

```
protected abstract void ConfigureServices(
  IServiceCollection services);
```

The final piece will be configuring the services and invoking them from the constructor. Create a new method named ConfigureDependencyInjection, which will create a new ServiceCollection and then configure the services and build the container. See Listing 9-10 for the ConfigureDependencyInjection method implementation.

Listing 9-10. ConfigureDependencyInjection method implementation

```
IServiceProvider ConfigureDependencyInjection()
{
  ServiceCollection services = new ServiceCollection();
  ConfigureServices(services);
  return services.BuildServiceProvider();
}
```

See Listing 9-11 for the completed MvvmApplication code, which creates the Dependency Injection entry point.

Listing 9-11. MvvmApplication completed code

```
public abstract class MvvmApplication : Application
{
  public MvvmApplication()
  {
    Current = this;
    Container = ConfigureDependencyInjection();
  }

  public static new MvvmApplication Current { get; private set; }

  public IServiceProvider Container { get; }

  IServiceProvider ConfigureDependencyInjection()
  {
    ServiceCollection services = new ServiceCollection();
    ConfigureServices(services);
    return services.BuildServiceProvider();
  }

  protected abstract void ConfigureServices(
    IServiceCollection services);
}
```

With our new MvvmApplication class completed, we can update the App.xaml and App.xaml.cs. Both files must be updated to use the new MvvmApplication. Start by editing the App.xaml.cs and changing the parent class from Application to MvvmApplication. Then add the override for the ConfigureServices method. See Listing 9-12, which omits all existing code and only shows the changes.

Listing 9-12. App.xaml.cs updates to use the new MvvmApplication. This code snippet omits existing code and only shows new additions and updates

```
public sealed partial class App : MvvmApplication
{
  protected override void ConfigureServices(
    IServiceCollection services)
  {
    // TODO - Add container registrations here
  }
}
```

We are creating a special MvvmApplication in Listing 9-12 to contain our MVVM and Dependency Injection application-level code. This is allowing us to separate it from any Uno Platform code that is already in the App.xaml.cs, which will make it easier to manage.

Since this is a partial class, we need to update the XAML file App.xaml to use the same parent class. To do this you will add an xmlns to the top of the file and use that xmlns to gain access to the MvvmApplication. See Listing 9-13 for changes in App.xaml. This code snippet has items omitted and only shows the important code.

Listing 9-13. App.xaml updates to use the new MvvmApplication. This code snippet has items omitted and only shows updates

```
<mvvm:MvvmApplication
  x:Class="UnoDrive.App"
  xmlns:mvvm="using:UnoDrive.Mvvm">

</mvvm:MvvmApplication>
```

At this point you should still be able to compile your application for the various target heads and run it.

Tip   We have not changed any code or started using the Dependency Injection, but it is useful to check the progress to ensure we didn't break anything.

We would like to use constructor injection for our ViewModels. This means any dependency that is registered with the container should be resolved when a ViewModel is created. We will complete this by updating the `ViewModelLocator` that we created in the previous chapter. Currently it creates the ViewModel by using the activator. There are special utility APIs that will use the container to inject the parameters.

The Dependency Injection library we are using provides a special API that can resolve any object using the container. `ActivatorUtilities.GetServiceOrCreateInstance` is the method name, and it will try and instantiate the constructor by going through each parameter and attempting to resolve it.

In the `ViewModelLocator` find the Bind method and update it to retrieve the current container and then use `ActivatorUtilities.GetServiceOrCreateInstance` to create our ViewModel. See Listing 9-14 for the updated implementation of the `Bind` method.

Listing 9-14. Updated ViewModelLocator.Bind method using Dependency Injection

```
static void Bind(DependencyObject view)
{
  if (view is FrameworkElement frameworkElement)
  {
    Type viewModelType = FindViewModel(
      frameworkElement.GetType());

    IServiceProvider container = MvvmApplication
      .Current.Container;

    frameworkElement.DataContext = ActivatorUtilities
      .GetServiceOrCreateInstance(
        container,
        viewModelType);
  }
}
```

Caution   Switching to ActivatorUtilities still requires us to use reflection to instantiate the ViewModel. You may run into linker issues when compiling under release mode.

Note   `ActivatorUtilities.GetServiceOrCreateInstance` is a useful method that uses the provided container to resolve all parameters on an object with Dependency Injection. It first attempts to resolve object type with the container, and if it is not found, it will go through each parameter and resolve it and then inject it into the object. This provides a safe way to instantiate objects that you may not want in the container but are important for the Dependency Injection system.

We have implemented our Dependency Injection system to work with the MVVM architecture, and we are ready to start registering and injecting objects.

Add Logging to Dependency Injection

At this point our Uno Platform application has out-of-the-box logging provided by the Uno Platform template. This is nice as the standard console tools should work, but we are building a MVVM application with Dependency Injection. This means we want to decouple items and depend on interfaces when we can. In this section we will be registering the `ILogger` interface so we can inject it into any object using the Microsoft Extensions Logging library.

To get started, create a new Logging folder at the top level. We will be creating our container registration code here. We want it to be in its own folder because we will be adding variations depending on the target platform. Managing this in one place will be easier to maintain than using a series of compiler directives. Once the folder is created, you will add two classes to it: `LoggingConfiguration` and `LoggingExtensions`. See screenshot of Visual Studio Solution Explorer in Figure 9-2.

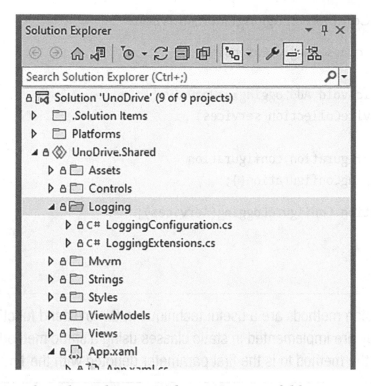

Figure 9-2. *Visual Studio Solution Explorer – Logging folder*

The LoggingExtensions will be your entry point using an extension method to create a simple API in the ConfigureServices method, whereas the LoggingConfiguration will handle the configuration of the logging. Stub out the LoggingConfiguration as seen in Listing 9-15.

Listing 9-15. LoggingConfiguration stub with method but no implementation

```
public class LoggingConfiguration
{
  public void ConfigureLogging(IServiceCollection services)
  {
  }
}
```

Next, in the LoggingExtensions we can create our extension method and implementation that uses the LoggingConfiguration. See Listing 9-16 for the completed extension method.

Listing 9-16. Completed LoggingExtensions code

```
public static class LoggingExtensions
{
  public static void AddLoggingForUnoDrive(
    this IServiceCollection services)
  {
    LoggingConfiguration configuration =
      new LoggingConfiguration();

    configuration.ConfigureLogging(services);
  }
}
```

Note   Extension methods are a useful technique in C# to extend functionality on an object. They are implemented in static classes using a static method where the object to add the method to is the first parameter denoted with the `this` keyword.

Head back to the `App.xaml.cs` file, and we can now update our `ConfigureServices` method to use the extension method to configure the logging. By using the extension method, it keeps our configuration code to one line, which makes it easier to maintain in the larger class. See Listing 9-17 for the updated `ConfigureServices` method implementation.

Listing 9-17. Updated ConfigureServices method in App.xaml.cs to include logging

```
protected override void ConfigureServices(
  IServiceCollection services)
{
  Services.AddLoggingForUnoDrive();
}
```

That completes our application startup configuration. The logging code will be registered with the container at application startup. We still need to create the implementation details in the `LoggingConfiguration`. We want to create different implementations for the various target heads. Earlier in Chapter 5, we learned about platform-specific code techniques.

We will be putting those techniques to use while we implement the various target platforms. To complete this we will need to use partial methods and partial classes. Let's update all the `csproj` files to use the C# language version 9.0.

Update all csproj files to include `<LangVersion>` in the first `<PropertyGroup>` – see Listing 9-18.

Listing 9-18. New <PropertyGroup> element for the csproj

```
<LangVersion>9.0</LangVersion>
```

You will need to update the following csproj files:

- UnoDrive.Mobile

- UnoDrive.Skia.Gtk

- UnoDrive.Skia.Wpf

- UnoDrive.Skia.Wpf.Host

- UnoDrive.Wasm

- UnoDrive.Windows

Once all the csproj files have been updated, we can head back to the `LoggingConfiguration` class and update it to be a partial class. We are also going to update the `ConfigureLogging` method to be a partial method, which is a special type of method where we can define the method in one part of the partial class and implement it in another part of the partial class. This is useful when working in cross-platform code because you can define the method signature in your shared code partial class and the implementation in each platform-specific partial class. See updated code in Listing 9-19.

Listing 9-19. Updated LoggingConfiguration to use partial class and partial method

```
public partial class LoggingConfiguration
{
  public partial void ConfigureLogging(
    IServiceCollection services);
}
```

Next, we will need to create target implementations for all the targets we want to support. Create the following files or see screenshot of files the Visual Studio Solution Explorer in Figure 9-3.

- LoggingConfiguration.android.cs

- LoggingConfiguration.gtk.cs

- LoggingConfiguration.ios.cs

- LoggingConfiguration.macos.cs

- LoggingConfiguration.wasm.cs

- LoggingConfiguration.windows.cs

- LoggingConfiguration.wpf.cs

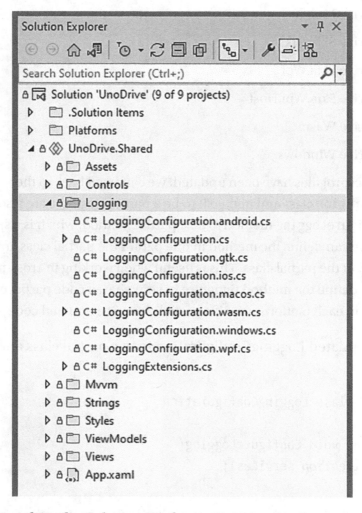

Figure 9-3. *Visual Studio Solution Explorer – LoggingConfiguration various target platforms*

When implementing all these platforms, you will need to manually add a pre-processor directive to tell the compiler to only compile for the platform of that file. Since it is a shared project, there is no special compile convention being applied.

LoginViewModel

Before we start implementing the various target platforms, we want to add some test code to the LoginViewModel so we can validate it works for each platform. Add a constructor that injects the ILogger and then prints the message "Hello logging" – see Listing 9-20.

Listing 9-20. Adds logger injection to LoginViewModel

```
public class LoginViewModel
{
  ILogger logger;
  public LoginViewModel(ILogger<LoginViewModel> logger)
  {
    this.logger = logger;
    this.logger.LogInformation("Hello logging");
  }
}
```

Windows

You may have issues with the Windows project detecting the correct directive. Our workaround to this is creating a special UnoDrive directive for the Windows project to use. These directives are stored in the <PropertyGroup> element of <DefineConstants>. Whenever you are updating this, you will need to ensure all current constants are included using the $(DefineConstants); syntax. Update the UnoDrive.Windows.csproj file to add a new constant called __UNO_DRIVE_WINDOWS__ see Listing 9-21.

Listing 9-21. New <DefineConstants> entry for UnoDrive.Windows.csproj

```
<DefineConstants>$(DefineConstants);__UNO_DRIVE_WINDOWS__</DefineConstants>
```

Back in the code, we can now edit LoggingConfiguration.windows.cs to use this new pre-processor directive to only compile the code if it is for Windows. Starting at line 1, wrap the entire file with the directive – see Listing 9-22 for the stubbed-out implementation.

Listing 9-22. LoggingConfiguration.windows.cs stub

```
#if __UNO_DRIVE_WINDOWS__
namespace UnoDrive.Logging
{
  public partial class LoggingConfiguration
  {
    public partial void ConfigureLogging(
      IServiceCollection services)
    {
    }
  }
}
#endif
```

We want our logger to print to the debug viewer and the current running console. The template already included Microsoft.Extensions.Logging.Console for console logging, and we need to add the debug logger NuGet package. Add Microsoft.Extensions.Logging.Debug by manually editing the csproj file. You will want to ensure the package version matches the other logging dependencies. Add the code seen in Listing 9-23 to the UnoDrive.Windows.csproj.

Listing 9-23. NuGet package reference for UnoDrive.Windows.csproj

```
<PackageReference
  Include="Microsoft.Extensions.Logging.Debug"
  Version="6.0.0" />
```

Tip   If you are using Visual Studio, you can add the NuGet package using the GUI, but it is safer to manually edit the csproj file's XML. If you decide to use the GUI, just be sure to always match the version of the logger that is already included in other NuGet packages.

With all the NuGet packages updated correctly, let's update the implementation details of the ConfigureLogging in the LoggingConfiguration class. See Listing 9-24 for implementation.

Listing 9-24. Updated LoggingConfiguration for Windows

```
#if __UNO_DRIVE_WINDOWS__
using Microsoft.Extensions.DependencyInjection;
using Microsoft.Extensions.Logging;

namespace UnoDrive.Logging
{
  public partial class LoggingConfiguration
  {
    public partial void ConfigureLogging(
      IServiceCollection services)
    {
      services.AddLogging(builder =>
      {
        builder
          .ClearProviders()
#if DEBUG
          .AddFilter("UnoDrive", LogLevel.Information)
#else
          .AddFilter("UnoDrive", LogLevel.Debug)
#endif
          .AddFilter("Uno", LogLevel.Debug)
          .AddFilter("Windows", LogLevel.Debug)
          .AddFilter("Microsoft", LogLevel.Debug)
          .AddDebug()
          .AddConsole();
      });
    }
  }
}
#endif
```

In the last two lines, we add both AddDebug and AddConsole logging. In our app we are adding both to help ease debugging any problems. This will force log statements to be visible in the Visual Studio debug output window as well as any console window that may be open.

We can test this by launching the Windows application, and you should see our test message available in the debug output window. See Listing 9-25 for a sample of the log output.

Listing 9-25. Windows logger output

```
UnoDrive.ViewModels.LoginViewModel: Information: Hello logging
```

WebAssembly (WASM)

To get started for the WASM target, update the LoggingConfiguration.wasm.cs file to include our empty class. You will need to add the pre-processor directive to the top of the file to ensure that it only compiles for WebAssembly – see Listing 9-26.

Listing 9-26. LoggingConfiguration.wasm.cs stub

```
#if __WASM __
namespace UnoDrive.Logging
{
  public partial class LoggingConfiguration
  {
    public partial void ConfigureLogging(
      IServiceCollection services)
    {
    }
  }
}
#endif
```

Next, you will need to add the NuGet package Microsoft.Extensions.Logging. Debug to the UnoDrive.Wasm.csproj – see Listing 9-27.

Tip   You can use the GUI in Visual Studio to add the NuGet package for you to one or all your projects. It may save time. However, we are going to include the csproj XML statements, so you can double-check how it is supposed to look.

Listing 9-27. NuGet package reference for UnoDrive.Wasm.csproj

```
<PackageReference
  Include="Microsoft.Extensions.Logging.Debug"
  Version="6.0.0" />
```

Now we can implement the ConfigureLogging method, which will look like what we have done before. The WASM target requires a special Uno Platform provider to help it write to the console: WebAssemblyConsoleLoggerProvider. See Listing 9-28 for completed WASM code.

Listing 9-28. Updated LoggingConfiguration for WASM

```
#if __WASM__
using Microsoft.Extensions.DependencyInjection;
using Microsoft.Extensions.Logging;

namespace UnoDrive.Logging
{
  public partial class LoggingConfiguration
  {
    public partial void ConfigureLogging(
      IServiceCollection services)
    {
      services.AddLogging(builder =>
      {
        builder
          .ClearProviders()
          .AddProvider(new global::Uno.Extensions.Logging
            .WebAssembly
            .WebAssemblyConsoleLoggerProvider())
```

```
#if DEBUG
        .AddFilter("UnoDrive", LogLevel.Information)
#else
        .AddFilter("UnoDrive", LogLevel.Debug)
#endif
        .AddFilter("Uno", LogLevel.Debug)
        .AddFilter("Windows", LogLevel.Debug)
        .AddFilter("Microsoft", LogLevel.Debug)
        .AddDebug()
        .AddConsole();
    });
  }
 }
}
#endif
```

That completes the WASM logging configuration. You can launch the WASM web project to test if the logging works. Once the login page loads, open the developer console in the browser of your choice and search for the output. See Listing 9-29 for logger output.

Listing 9-29. WASM logger output

```
info: UnoDrive.ViewModels.LoginViewModel[0]
      Hello logging
```

WPF

Update the LoggingConfiguration.wpf.cs to include the standard stub that we have been using. You will add the pre-processor directive HAS_UNO_SKIA_WPF to ensure the code only compiles under WPF. See Listing 9-30 for stubbed code.

Listing 9-30. LoggingConfiguration.wpf.cs stub

```
#if HAS_UNO_SKIA_WPF
namespace UnoDrive.Logging
{
  public partial class LoggingConfiguration
```

```
    {
      public partial void ConfigureLogging(
        IServiceCollection services)
      {
      }
    }
  }
}
#endif
```

The WPF project uses two projects, one for the WPF code and the host project. You will need to add the NuGet package Microsoft.Extensions.Logging.Debug to the UnoDrive.Skia.Wpf.csproj project. See Listing 9-31 for XML to add.

Listing 9-31. NuGet package reference for UnoDrive.Skia.Wpf.csproj

```
<PackageReference
  Include="Microsoft.Extensions.Logging.Debug"
  Version="6.0.0" />
```

Now update the LoggingConfiguration.wpf.cs code with the logging implementation. This will look identical to what we did for the Windows target, but the pre-processor directive will be for WPF. See Listing 9-32 for completed code.

Listing 9-32. Updated LoggingConfiguration for WPF

```
#if HAS_UNO_SKIA_WPF
using Microsoft.Extensions.DependencyInjection;
using Microsoft.Extensions.Logging;

namespace UnoDrive.Logging
{
  public partial class LoggingConfiguration
  {
    public partial void ConfigureLogging(
      IServiceCollection services)
    {
      services.AddLogging(builder =>
      {
```

```
        builder
          .ClearProviders()
#if DEBUG
          .AddFilter("UnoDrive", LogLevel.Information)
#else
          .AddFilter("UnoDrive", LogLevel.Debug)
#endif
          .AddFilter("Uno", LogLevel.Debug)
          .AddFilter("Windows", LogLevel.Debug)
          .AddFilter("Microsoft", LogLevel.Debug)
          .AddDebug()
          .AddConsole();
      });
    }
  }
}
#endif
```

That completes the configuration for WPF, and it is time to test it. When you launch the WPF application, a console application window opens automatically. You will see the logging output in both the console window and the debug output window in Visual Studio. See Listing 9-33 for the debug output and Listing 9-34 for the console output.

Listing 9-33. WPF debug logger output

```
UnoDrive.ViewModels.LoginViewModel: Information: Hello logging
```

Listing 9-34. WPF console logger output

```
info: UnoDrive.ViewModels.LoginViewModel[0]
      Hello logging
```

GTK

Update the LoggingConfiguration.gtk.cs to include the standard stub that we have been using. You will add the pre-processor directive HAS_UNO_SKIA_GTK to ensure the code only compiles under GTK. See Listing 9-35 for stubbed code.

Listing 9-35. LoggingConfiguration.gtk.cs stub

```
#if HAS_UNO_SKIA_GTK
namespace UnoDrive.Logging
{
  public partial class LoggingConfiguration
  {
    public partial void ConfigureLogging(
      IServiceCollection services)
    {
    }
  }
}
#endif
```

There are no additional NuGet packages that need to be added to the GTK project. The template already includes `Microsoft.Extensions.Logging.Console,` which will print items into the Visual Studio output window.

Go ahead and update the implementation to match the code in Listing 9-36. It is very similar to the others except there is only `AddConsole()`. We are using just `AddConsole()` because everything prints to the Visual Studio debug output window using that API. There is no need for `AddDebug()`.

Listing 9-36. Updated LoggingConfiguration for GTK

```
#if HAS_UNO_SKIA_GTK
using Microsoft.Extensions.DependencyInjection;
using Microsoft.Extensions.Logging;

namespace UnoDrive.Logging
{
  public partial class LoggingConfiguration
  {
    public partial void ConfigureLogging(
      IServiceCollection services)
    {
      services.AddLogging(builder =>
      {
```

```
        builder
            .ClearProviders()
#if DEBUG
            .AddFilter("UnoDrive", LogLevel.Information)
#else
            .AddFilter("UnoDrive", LogLevel.Debug)
#endif
            .AddFilter("Uno", LogLevel.Debug)
            .AddFilter("Windows", LogLevel.Debug)
            .AddFilter("Microsoft", LogLevel.Debug)
            .AddConsole();
    });
    }
  }
}
#endif
```

That completes the code for GTK, and it is time to test the application. Launch the application into XLaunch using WSL2 and check the Visual Studio debug output window. See Listing 9-37 for your output response.

Listing 9-37. GTK logger output

```
UnoDrive.ViewModels.LoginViewModel[0]
      Hello logging
```

Android/iOS/macOS

Using the single project means we only need to include one NuGet package for all three of the platforms. We want to add logging to the Visual Studio debug output window. Just like the other platforms, you will need to add the NuGet package `Microsoft.Extensions.Logging.Debug` to the `UnoDrive.Mobile.csproj` file. See Listing 9-38 for XML code to add.

Listing 9-38. NuGet package reference for UnoDrive.Mobile.csproj

```
<PackageReference
  Include="Microsoft.Extensions.Logging.Debug"
  Version="6.0.0" />
```

Next, we will need to stub out our code for the three platforms – see Listings 9-39 for Android, 9-40 for iOS, and 9-41 for macOS.

Listing 9-39. LoggingConfiguration.android.cs stub

```
#if __ANDROID__
namespace UnoDrive.Logging
{
  public partial class LoggingConfiguration
  {
    public partial void ConfigureLogging(
      IServiceCollection services)
    {
    }
  }
}
#endif
```

Listing 9-40. LoggingConfiguration.ios.cs stub

```
#if __IOS__
namespace UnoDrive.Logging
{
  public partial class LoggingConfiguration
  {
    public partial void ConfigureLogging(
      IServiceCollection services)
    {
    }
  }
}
#endif
```

Listing 9-41. LoggingConfiguration.macos.cs stub

```
#if __MACOS__
namespace UnoDrive.Logging
{
  public partial class LoggingConfiguration
  {
    public partial void ConfigureLogging(
      IServiceCollection services)
    {
    }
  }
}
#endif
```

Next, we will update the implementation details for each platform. We will start with Android and macOS as they don't have anything special. The code will be identical to what we have done before to configure the provider. See Listing 9-42 for Android and Listing 9-43 for macOS.

Listing 9-42. Updated LoggingConfiguration for Android

```
#if __ANDROID__
using Microsoft.Extensions.DependencyInjection;
using Microsoft.Extensions.Logging;

namespace UnoDrive.Logging
{
  public partial class LoggingConfiguration
  {
    public partial void ConfigureLogging(
      IServiceCollection services)
    {
      services.AddLogging(builder =>
      {
        builder
          .ClearProviders()
```

```
#if DEBUG
          .AddFilter("UnoDrive", LogLevel.Information)
#else
          .AddFilter("UnoDrive", LogLevel.Debug)
#endif
          .AddFilter("Uno", LogLevel.Debug)
          .AddFilter("Windows", LogLevel.Debug)
          .AddFilter("Microsoft", LogLevel.Debug)
          .AddDebug();
      });
    }
  }
}
#endif
```

Listing 9-43. Updated LoggingConfiguration for macOS

```
#if __MACOS__
using Microsoft.Extensions.DependencyInjection;
using Microsoft.Extensions.Logging;

namespace UnoDrive.Logging
{
  public partial class LoggingConfiguration
  {
    public partial void ConfigureLogging(
      IServiceCollection services)
    {
      services.AddLogging(builder =>
      {
        builder
          .ClearProviders()
#if DEBUG
          .AddFilter("UnoDrive", LogLevel.Information)
#else
          .AddFilter("UnoDrive", LogLevel.Debug)
```

```
#endif
            .AddFilter("Uno", LogLevel.Debug)
            .AddFilter("Windows", LogLevel.Debug)
            .AddFilter("Microsoft", LogLevel.Debug)
            .AddDebug();
        });
    }
  }
}
#endif
```

The iOS logging requires a special Uno Platform provider like how we implemented WebAssembly. After clearing the logging providers, you will add the OSLogLoggerProvider and then follow the configuration you have done before. See Listing 9-44 for the iOS implementation.

Listing 9-44. Updated LoggingConfiguration for iOS

```
#if __IOS__
using Microsoft.Extensions.DependencyInjection;
using Microsoft.Extensions.Logging;

namespace UnoDrive.Logging
{
  public partial class LoggingConfiguration
  {
    public partial void ConfigureLogging(
      IServiceCollection services)
    {
      services.AddLogging(builder =>
      {
        builder
          .ClearProviders()
          .AddProvider(new global::Uno.Extensions.Logging
            .OSLogLoggerProvider()
#if DEBUG
          .AddFilter("UnoDrive", LogLevel.Information)
```

```
#else
        .AddFilter("UnoDrive", LogLevel.Debug)
#endif
        .AddFilter("Uno", LogLevel.Debug)
        .AddFilter("Windows", LogLevel.Debug)
        .AddFilter("Microsoft", LogLevel.Debug)
        .AddDebug();
    });
  }
 }
}
#endif
```

Now that the mobile targets are all configured, you can run the applications, and you will see the output in the Visual Studio debug output window or Visual Studio for Mac debug output window depending on your platform. See Listings 9-45 for Android, 9-46 for iOS, and 9-47 for macOS.

Listing 9-45. Android logger output

```
[0:] UnoDrive.ViewModels.LoginViewModel: Information: Hello logging
```

Listing 9-46. iOS logger output

```
UnoDrive.iOS[1103:10807] info: UnoDrive.ViewModels.LoginViewModel[0]
Hello logging
```

Listing 9-47. macOS logger output

```
UnoDrive.ViewModels.LoginViewModel: Information: Hello logging
```

Conclusion

In this chapter we have taken our UnoDrive application and added Dependency Injection and then configured ILogger so we can inject a logger anywhere in the application to print items to the console for all platforms. This provides the fundamental building blocks for future chapters that will heavily leverage Dependency Injection and show us how we can put many concepts we have learned in this book together.

The concepts we learned in this chapter will be applied in the next chapter as we build our first complete Dependency Injection service. If you had any trouble with the code, you can download the completed code for this chapter from GitHub: `https://github.com/SkyeHoefling/UnoDrive/tree/main/Chapter%209`.

CHAPTER 10

Application Navigation

In our application we have implemented a flyout menu dashboard page to be the main landing page of the application. This required implementing dashboard-specific navigation to update the main content area. If you need a refresher on what we did, refer to Chapter 6. That was an introduction to application navigation but didn't cover it in detail. In this chapter we will be learning more about navigation in Uno Platform and how to add a navigation service to work in our MVVM architecture.

Note There are many free open source MVVM libraries in the ecosystem that have ready-to-use navigation implementations such as the Prism Library, MvvmCross, and Uno.Extensions. We are building our own lightweight solution. Pick the solution that best fits your project needs.

When building highly scalable applications using the MVVM architecture, the goal is to isolate presentation code, or user interface code, from your business rules or your view models. You can take this goal as a rule to never be broken or more of a guideline that is flexible. I recommend being flexible with this rule as it can very difficult to move all navigation code to the view models as it depends on presentation elements such as the main content area.

Tip It is okay to have some of your presentation code in XAML and some of it in the code behind. There is no perfect solution in application design, and find guidelines that work best for you and your team.

© Skye Hoefling 2022
S. Hoefling, *Getting Started with the Uno Platform and WinUI 3*,
https://doi.org/10.1007/978-1-4842-8248-9_10

Navigation in Uno Platform

Our application is already using various navigation APIs that we haven't explained yet. See the code in Listing 10-1, which is from LoginPage.xaml.cs.

Listing 10-1. OnLoginClick event handler to navigate to the dashboard

```
void OnLoginClick(object sender, RoutedEventArgs args)
{
  Window window = ((App)App.Current).Window;
  if (window.Content is Frame rootFrame)
  {
    rootFrame.Navigate(typeof(Dashboard), null);
  }
}
```

The Frame control allows you to navigate and render a Page while maintaining a view stack. In Listing 10-1 we use the rootFrame, which is retrieved from the Window object. This allows us to perform full application window navigation. The API has two overloads – see Listing 10-2 for the first overload and Listing 10-3 for the second overload.

Listing 10-2. Simple Navigate API method signature

```
bool Navigate(Type page, object parameter)
```

Listing 10-3. Navigate API method signature with transition behavior

```
bool Navigate(
  Type page,
  object parameter,
  NavigationTransitionInfo info)
```

Our LoginPage.xaml.cs as shown in Listing 10-1 uses the simple Navigate API method shown in Listing 10-2. This will render the page but does not perform any transition behavior or does not have parameters.

Optional Parameters

The navigation API provides two main optional parameters that can be added to the invocation: parameter and a transition.

Object Parameter

The object parameter is any type of object that you may need to share with the `Page` after the navigation has been completed. This can be something as simple as a string value or a complex object that has more detailed data to be used by the page. The API structure is open-ended by design to let the developer decide how they want to use it.

The object parameter can be retrieved by overriding the `OnNavigated()` method in the page that is navigated to. This allows us to pass data from one page to the next as a built-in feature of the platform.

NavigationTransitionInfo

Uno Platform implements the WinUI 3 transition behaviors when navigating from one page to another page. There are various ways to animate the page transition, and you can write your own transitions. The API ships several out of the box that you can use:

- CommonNavigationTransitionInfo
- ContinuumNavigationTransitionInfo
- DrillInNavigationTransitionInfo
- EntranceNavigationTransitionInfo
- SlideNavigationTransitionInfo
- SuppressNavigationTransitionInfo

Tip   If you want to update the `Frame` with no transition behavior, you will need to use the `SuppressNavigationTransitionInfo` explicitly. You have to pass this specific transition behavior. If you pass null, it will use the default.

Navigation Page Overrides

The implementation of navigating to a new page is useful by itself, but sometimes you need to perform additional actions while the page is first loading or pass data from one page to the next. In the previous section, we mentioned that the API supports an `object` parameter that allows anything to be passed and used in the new page.

There are three navigation method overrides on the `Page` control that can be used at various stages of the page lifecycle. See Table 10-1 for a description of each.

Table 10-1. *Navigation Method Overrides*

Method Name	Description
OnNavigatedTo	Invoked after the page has been navigated and when navigating back to a previous page. This provides direct access to the object parameter.
OnNavigatingFrom	Invoked when the current page is navigating to another page or leaving the current page. This method is invoked at the beginning of the navigation invocation. This method is cancelable to prevent the navigation from occurring.
OnNavigatedFrom	Invoked after the current page is unloaded or right after the navigation behavior completes.

In this chapter we will be learning more about `OnNavigatedTo` as it provides us the most value for the UnoDrive application we are building. This allows us to pass data from one page to another.

Navigation Example

Let's look at an example of navigating from one page to another and passing a simple string message of "Hello World". In our system we will be navigating to `MainPage` from the main `Window`. The code in Listing 10-4 shows the navigation command but doesn't contain the rest of the starting code.

Listing 10-4. Navigate to the MainPage and pass "Hello World"

```
Window window = ((App)App.Current).Window;
Window.Navigate(typeof(MainPage), "Hello World");
```

In our `MainPage` we need to handle the navigation event and do something with the message passed as a parameter. In our next code block (Listing 10-5), let's write the message to the console.

Listing 10-5. Navigation event handler in MainPage

```
protected override void OnNavigatedTo(NavigationEventArgs e)
{
  // Invoke the base functionality first
  base.OnNavigatedTo(e);

  if (e.Parameter is string message)
  {
    Console.WriteLine(message);
  }
}
```

In Listing 10-5 we need to confirm that the `Parameter` is of type `string`, and then we can perform logic on it. The standard object value isn't very useful to us until we can convert it to a type that we know.

Add Navigation to LoginViewModel

Navigation in Uno Platform is part of the presentation layer of the specification as it is tightly coupled to `Frame` controls. The goal of the MVVM architecture is to isolate presentation code from business rules. Navigation can be considered both business rules and presentation code. Throughout the application, we will be using it in both scenarios as it makes sense to do so and explaining why it is best to handle navigation using that technique.

Currently the navigation code that performs the navigation from the `LoginPage` to the `Dashboard` page is in the `LoginPage.xaml.cs` or the code behind. You can see this code in Listing 10-1. We are going to move this code to the view model as we implement the MVVM commanding pattern. In MVVM applications the command pattern is when you have a bit of code on a view model that is invoked from a command action on the view. The most basic command implementation is when a button press occurs, it uses the command pattern to communicate to the view model to run the code.

In .NET there is an interface named ICommand that can be implemented by your project or a framework to support commanding. Command implementations can go from very simple to complex, and there are many open source libraries that support this technique. We are going to use the Microsoft Toolkit MVVM library, which is an open source library containing the ICommand implementation as a RelayCommand.

Tip   When adding additional third-party dependencies to your project, ensure to look through various dependencies to assess the risk it might bring to your project. In some instances, it may be too much overhead to pull in a large library when you only need a few objects from it.

The Microsoft Toolkit is also known as the Windows Community Toolkit. You can find it on GitHub, which has links to the various NuGet packages:

- https://github.com/CommunityToolkit/WindowsCommunityToolkit

---

Note   The Microsoft Toolkit or Windows Community Toolkit focuses on Windows development. The Uno Platform team has forked the repository to create various Uno Platform NuGet packages that will handle the non-Windows target platforms.

The NuGet packages for the Microsoft Toolkit are split into various areas of focus and only have the required dependencies to run that code. The CommunityToolkit. Mvvm NuGet package does not depend on any Windows-specific code and can be used in any .NET cross-platform project like the Uno Platform application we are building. This package will provide us with the necessary commanding implementations and save us much needed time.

Add NuGet Packages to Target Platforms

Add the NuGet package CommunityToolkit.Mvvm to all the target platform project heads. Start with adding it to the Windows project by adding the NuGet package to UnoDrive. Windows.csproj – see Listing 10-6.

Listing 10-6. Add NuGet CommunityToolkit.Mvvm to the Windows project

```
<PackageReference
  Include=" CommunityToolkit.Mvvm"
  Version="7.1.2" />
```

Next, add the NuGet package to the WebAssembly (WASM) project just like you did for Windows. Edit the `UnoDrive.Wasm.csproj` and add the code in Listing 10-7.

Listing 10-7. Add NuGet CommunityToolkit.Mvvm to the WebAssembly (WASM) project

```
<PackageReference
  Include=" CommunityToolkit.Mvvm"
  Version="7.1.2" />
```

In the WPF project, you only need to edit the main WPF project and not the host project. Add the code snippet in Listing 10-8 to `UnoDrive.Skia.Wpf.csproj`.

Listing 10-8. Add NuGet CommunityToolkit.Mvvm to the WPF project

```
<PackageReference
  Include=" CommunityToolkit.Mvvm"
  Version="7.1.2" />
```

In the GTK project, add the NuGet package to the `UnoDrive.Skia.Gtk.csproj`. See Listing 10-9.

Listing 10-9. Add NuGet CommunityToolkit.Mvvm to the GTK project

```
<PackageReference
  Include=" CommunityToolkit.Mvvm"
  Version="7.1.2" />
```

Finally, we can take care of Android, iOS, and macOS all at once using the multi-targeted mobile project. Add the NuGet package to `UnoDrive.Mobile.csproj` and be sure to add it to the `<ItemGroup>` block that is used by all projects and not a specific target platform. See Listing 10-10 for the code snippet.

Listing 10-10. Add NuGet CommunityToolkit.Mvvm to the mobile project for Android, iOS, and macOS

```
<PackageReference
  Include="CommunityToolkit.Mvvm"
  Version="7.1.2" />
```

Add Commanding to LoginViewModel

After adding the NuGet packages to all the target platforms, we can start implementing our commanding solution in the LoginViewModel. Start by stubbing out the method and ICommand property. Add the code in Listing 10-11 to the end of your LoginViewModel class.

Listing 10-11. Add ICommand stub to LoginViewModel

```
public ICommand Login { get; }

void OnLogin()
{
  // TODO - add implementation
}
```

We now have the building blocks of our ICommand stub, and it needs to be configured in the constructor. The NuGet package CommunityToolkit.Mvvm contains the RelayCommand object, which we can connect to our OnLogin method. When the ICommand is executed, it will run the code in OnLogin. Add the code in Listing 10-12 to your constructor.

Listing 10-12. Add RelayCommand instantiation to the LoginViewModel constructor

```
Login = new RelayCommand(OnLogin);
```

Move the code from LoginPage.xaml.cs seen in Listing 10-1 to the OnLogin method of the LoginViewModel. See Listing 10-13 for the OnLogin method implementation.

Listing 10-13. OnLogin method implementation for LoginViewModel

```
void OnLogin()
{
  Window window = ((App)App.Current).Window;

  if (window.Content is Frame rootFrame)
  {
    rootFrame.Navigate(typeof(Dashboard), null);
  }
}
```

Once this code is moved, we can delete the event handler in the `LoginPage.xaml.cs` named `OnLoginClick`. This code now belongs to the `LoginViewModel`.

To complete the migration of this code to the view model, we need to add the command binding to the `LoginPage.xaml` and remove the old event handler registration. Start by removing the `Click` event handler registration seen in Listing 10-14. This code snippet should be on the `Button` control toward the bottom of the page.

Listing 10-14. Click event handler to be removed in LoginPage.xaml

```
Click="OnLoginClick"
```

The `Button` control has a built-in `Command` property. When this property is set to an `ICommand` implementation, it will execute automatically when the button is pressed. Update the `Button` control in the `LoginPage.xaml` to use the command binding and link it to the `LoginViewModel` `Login` property that is of type `ICommand`. See Listing 10-15 for the binding code snippet.

Listing 10-15. Command binding for Button in LoginPage.xaml

```
Command="{Binding Login}"
```

Test Login Flow

You have now updated the navigation for the `LoginPage` to belong to the `LoginViewModel`. You can now run the application in all the target platforms, and the application should still behave the same way. When the user clicks/presses the "Login" button, it will navigate them to the `Dashboard` page.

Create NavigationService

When building MVVM applications, you should create a navigation service that
will manage your page-to-page navigation. In the previous section, we moved our
LoginPage-to-Dashboard navigation from the code behind to the LoginViewModel. We
are now going to expand on this topic and create a NavigationService to decouple
the LoginViewModel from the navigation code. By decoupling the code, we now make
it easier to test and reduce bugs that may be introduced by keeping each class simple.
This makes it easier to test the code as you can create mock implementations of the
INavigationService.

When we are performing navigation from a view model, it shouldn't take any
dependencies on the presentation layer. We will need to implement a "Services" layer of
our application that the view model can use to perform navigation. The most common
navigation pattern in MVVM applications is creating an INavigationService, which
will manage various navigation events. Our implementation will focus on specific
navigation behaviors for the various pages we have in our application. To complete the
implementation, we will need to complete the following steps:

1. Create INavigationService and implementation for
   NavigateToDashboard() and SignOut().

2. Register INavigationService with Dependency Injection.

3. Update LoginViewModel to use INavigationService.

4. Update Dashboard code behind to use INavigationService.

5. Test code and make sure everything works as expected.

Create INavigationService and Implementation

The first thing needed will be to create a new Services folder at the root directory of the
shared project. In that folder, create two new classes, an interface and implementation
for the navigation service called INavigationService.cs and NavigationService.cs,
respectively. See Figure 10-1 for a screenshot.

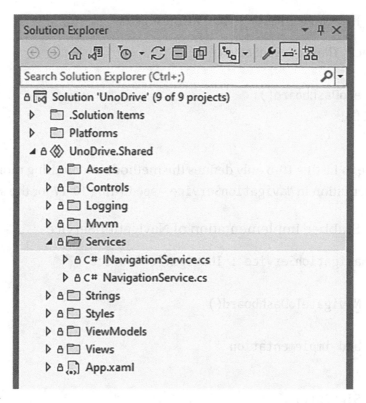

Figure 10-1. *Visual Studio Solution Explorer – Services folder*

The INavigationService is the interface or contract that will be implemented in the NavigationService.

Note   An interface is a useful tool in Dependency Injection that provides a set of APIs without implementation. It is always a good idea to have your code depend on interfaces instead of implementations. The implementation may change, but if you use a strong interface, it'll create less overhead in the consuming code.

See the code in Listing 10-16 for the INavigationService interface.

Listing 10-16. Interface code of INavigationService

```
public interface INavigationService
{
  void NavigateToDashboard();
  void SignOut();
}
```

The interface in Listing 10-6 only defines the methods and nothing more. We will add the implementation in NavigationService – see Listing 10-17 for the stubbed class.

Listing 10-17. Stubbed implementation of NavigationService

```
public class NavigationService : INavigationService
{
  public void NavigateToDashboard()
  {
    // TODO - add implementation
  }

  public void SignOut()
  {
    // TODO - add implementation
  }
}
```

We have our basic structure in place, and we can now start moving some of our code from LoginPage.xaml.cs. If we refer to Listing 10-1, we will see we need to retrieve the global root Window of the application and then perform navigation on that Frame. Since this code will be used in multiple APIs in the NavigationService, we need to create a private helper method called GetRootFrame. See Listing 10-18 for the implementation of the helper method.

Listing 10-18. NavigationService helper method GetRootFrame for retrieving the application's root frame

```
Frame GetRootFrame()
{
  Window window = ((App)App.Current).Window;
```

```
if (window.Content is Frame rootFrame)
{
    return rootFrame;
}

return null;
}
```

With our helper method implemented, we can implement both of our APIs. See Listing 10-19 for NavigateToDashboard.

Listing 10-19. NavigationService implementation of NavigateToDashboard

```
public void NavigateToDashboard()
{
  GetRootFrame()?.Navigate(typeof(Dashboard), null);
}
```

Implementing the SignOut logic will navigate the user back to the login page. Currently our application isn't configured to authentication with Azure Active Directory and the Microsoft Graph. As a placeholder, this implementation will only navigate the user back to the login page. We will be coming back to this in Chapter 11 to complete the SignOut implementation. See Listing 10-20 for the basic SignOut implementation.

Listing 10-20. NavigationService basic implementation of SignOut. This code snippet is missing authentication, which will be covered in Chapter 11

```
public void SignOut()
{
  GetRootFrame()?.GoBack();
}
```

In Listing 10-20 we use the navigation API GoBack(), which pops the current page off the navigation view stack and takes us to the previous page. In our application, the rootFrame only has two pages it is ever navigated to: the LoginPage or the Dashboard. This makes it safe to use the GoBack() API, which removes the Dashboard from the view stack and brings us back to the LoginPage.

Our new NavigationService has been implemented and can be used throughout our application.

Register INavigationService with Dependency Injection

In Chapter 9 we learned about Dependency Injection and how to register objects
with the container. We are going to put that knowledge to use and add our new
INavigationService and the implementation NavigationService to the container. This
will allow us to inject INavigationService into any view model in the application.

Register INavigationService in the App.xaml.cs by adding the code block in
Listing 10-21 to the ConfigureServices method.

Listing 10-21. Register INavigationService with the Dependency Injection
container

```
services.AddTransient<INavigationService, NavigationService>();
```

The INavigationService is considered a stateless service, which means we don't
need to maintain any data in the object injected. Each API invocation is independent
of the other because we retrieve the frame each time it is invoked. Registering the
dependency as a transient service means a new instance of NavigationService
is instantiated every time it is requested. See the current ConfigureServices
implementation with existing registrations in Listing 10-22.

Listing 10-22. Current ConfigureServices implementation in App.xaml.cs

```
protected override void ConfigureServices(
  IServiceCollection services)
{
  services.AddLoggingForUnoDrive();
  services.AddTransient<INavigationService, NavigationService>();
}
```

Add INavigationService to LoginViewModel

With the INavigationService registered with Dependency Injection, we can use it in
the LoginViewModel. This will allow us to remove the tightly coupled presentation layer
navigation code from the business rules of the view model.

To start, update the constructor to include INavigationService as a parameter
and add a local variable to store the injected property. See Listing 10-23 for updated
constructor code.

Listing 10-23. Add INavigationService to the constructor of LoginViewModel

```
INavigationService navigation;
ILogger logger;

public LoginViewModel(
  INavigationService navigation,
  ILogger<LoginViewModel> logger)
{
  this.navigation = navigation;
  this.logger = logger;
  this.logger.LogInformation("Hello logging");

  Login = new RelayCommand(OnLogin);
}
```

Tip   Always make sure you store the injected property to your local property. It is a common mistake to forget this, and you will see a `NullReferenceException` when you try to use the dependency later in your application.

Now that the `INavigationService` is injected correctly, we can update the `OnLogin` method implementation to remove all the code and use the API available on the `INavigationService`. When a user logs into the application, we want to bring them to the dashboard. Update this code to use `navigation.NavigateToDashboard()`. See Listing 10-24 for updated `OnLogin` code.

Listing 10-24. Use INavigationService in OnLogin of LoginViewModel

```
void OnLogin()
{
  navigation.NavigateToDashboard();
}
```

This code now completes our decoupling of presentation layer code from the business rules of the `LoginViewModel`. See the complete `LoginViewModel` code in Listing 10-25. This listing has the complete code so far including items added in previous chapters.

Listing 10-25. Current code for LoginViewModel

```
public class LoginViewModel
{
  INavigationService navigation;
  ILogger logger;

  public LoginViewModel(
    INavigationService navigation,
    ILogger<LoginViewModel> logger)
  {
    this.navigation = navigation;
    this.logger = logger;
    this.logger.LogInformation("Hello logging");

    Login = new RelayCommand(OnLogin);
  }

  public string Title => "Welcome to UnoDrive!";
  public string Header => "Uno Platform ♥ OneDrive = UnoDrive";
  public string ButtonText => "Login to UnoDrive";

  public ICommand Login { get; }

  void OnLogin()
  {
    navigation.NavigateToDashboard();
  }
}
```

Add INavigationService to the Dashboard

Now we need to go to the Dashboard and use the INavigationService to handle the SignOut functionality. Since this is a page and not a view model, we aren't able to use constructor injection to retrieve the INavigationService.

Caution   It may seem useful to add additional code and wrappers around the navigation APIs to support constructor injection, but proceed with caution. This may cause other problems in your application and make it more difficult to maintain. Try and use the built-in APIs for passing parameters to your page whenever possible.

Our `Dashboard` page handles navigation for the menu items. These navigation event handlers do not belong in the `NavigationService` as they are local to this page. The `SignOut` logic is different because it will pop the dashboard page off the view stack and bring the user back to the root `LoginPage`. The `SignOut` logic belongs in the `NavigationService` because of how it affects the entire window and not just the one page.

Earlier we learned about the various parameters of the navigation API and how to pass object parameters. We need to update the `NavigateToDashboard` method in the `NavigationService` to pass the current `INavigationService`. This will allow us to store and use the `INavigationService` in the dashboard, which we need to perform the `SignOut` logic.

Let's begin by updating the object parameter from `null` to `this` in the `NavigationService`. The change will take the current instance and pass it as an object parameter. See Listing 10-26 for changes to `NavigationService`.

Listing 10-26. Pass the current NavigationService when navigating to the dashboard

```
public void NavigateToDashboard()
{
  GetRootFrame().Navigate(typeof(Dashboard), this);
}
```

This change does not impact the contract of `INavigationService`, so there is no need to change the existing usages in the `LoginViewModel`.

Now that the `INavigationService` is being passed to the navigation method as an object parameter, we need to store it in the event handler. Earlier we learned about the navigation event handler `OnNavigatedTo`, which is invoked after the page is loaded and includes the parameter. Add an override for `OnNavigatedTo` in the `Dashboard.xaml.cs` – see Listing 10-27.

Listing 10-27. Add OnNavigatedTo override to Dashboard.xaml.cs

```
protected override void OnNavigatedTo(NavigationEventARgs e)
{
  base.OnNavigatedTo(e);

  if (e.Parameter is INavigationService navigation)
  {
    this.navigation = navigation;
  }
}
```

The `OnNavigatedTo` override acts as the constructor of a view model as we pass
the injected property and store it to a local variable. Now, we can use the `navigation`
variable in any method of the current `Dashboard` instance. Let's update the sign-out logic
of the event handler `MenuItemSelected`. See Listing 10-28 for a code snippet of just the
sign-out code.

Listing 10-28. Code snippet of sign-out logic in Dashboard.xaml.cs

```
void MenuItemSelected(
  NavigationView sender,
  NavigationViewItemInvokedEventArgs args)
{
  if (signOut == args.InvokedItemContainer)
  {
    navigation.SignOut();

    // return to prevent any other navigation
    return;
  }

  // omitted code
}
```

See Listing 10-29 for the complete event handler code including the navigation code
we added when we first implemented the `Dashboard`.

Listing 10-29. Complete MenuItemSelected code in Dashboard.xaml.cs

```
void MenuItemSelected(
  NavigationView sender,
  NavigationViewItemInvokedEventArgs args)
{
  if (signOut == args.InvokedItemContainer)
  {
    navigation.SignOut();

    // return to prevent any other navigation
    return;
  }

  Type pageType = default;
  if (myFiles == args.InvokedItemContainer)
    pageType = typeof(MyFilesPage);
  else if (recentFiles == args.InvokedItemContainer)
    pageType = typeof(RecentFilesPage);
  else if (sharedFiles == args.InvokedItemContainer)
    pageType = typeof(SharedFilesPage);

  else
    return;

  contentFrame.Navigate(pageType, null, new
CommonNavigationTransitionInfo());
}
```

Test the Application

We have now successfully implemented our NavigationService, and we can test the application. You can open the application in any or all target platforms and see that you can complete the following actions:

- Navigate to the dashboard.

- Sign out of the application, which will return you to the login page.

- Navigate to any of the dashboard menus.

Conclusion

In this chapter we added a `NavigationService` to our application that inherits from the `INavigationService` interface. This has been registered with the container in Dependency Injection, so we can use the contract anywhere in our application. As we move forward into authentication and various navigation elements in future chapters, we will be coming back to the `INavigationService` and `NavigationService` to make changes.

If you had trouble with any of the code in this chapter, you could find the completed code available on GitHub: `https://github.com/SkyeHoefling/UnoDrive/tree/main/Chapter%2010`.

CHAPTER 11

Authentication with Azure Active Directory

Our application is starting to take shape, and it is time to implement authentication, which will allow our users to log in and connect to their data. When adding authentication to your application, there are many tools at your disposal to choose from such as using a social authentication provider like Facebook or Twitter or using a business authentication provider like Microsoft or Google. Our application will be using the Microsoft authentication provider known as Azure Active Directory (Azure AD). The techniques covered in this chapter apply to users who want to access hosted data available in Microsoft services such as Office 365 or OneDrive. Authentication in other platforms such as Facebook and Google follows similar techniques, but the implementation will vary depending on the API.

In this chapter we will be adding Azure Active Directory authentication to our application. We will then use the access token returned by the authentication process to access OneDrive data via the Microsoft Graph APIs. These two pieces put together will give us direct access to our OneDrive data to start displaying content on the screen.

Microsoft's authentication provider is called the Microsoft Authentication Library (MSAL). This provides the necessary tools to connect to Azure Active Directory, which is the backing technology to all of Microsoft's authentication including Office 365.

How Does It Work?

Authentication providers are complex systems that allow your application to authenticate a user's identity. If you are using additional services such as requesting data from OneDrive, the authentication provider will return an access token, which can be used with the Microsoft Graph APIs to retrieve data. After the user is authenticated based

© Skye Hoefling 2022
S. Hoefling, *Getting Started with the Uno Platform and WinUI 3*,
https://doi.org/10.1007/978-1-4842-8248-9_11

on the input scopes, it will authorize the user for the data it is requesting to access. Most authentication providers implement OAuth2, which uses RESTful APIs to authenticate a user and get an access token, which can be presented when accessing the RESTful API to authorize access. The OAuth2 protocol is complicated, and our goal is to help you understand what you need to implement authentication in your application.

Note   Authentication and authorization are two different concepts that are commonly confused. Authentication is ensuring you are the user you say you are, whereas authorization is determining if you have permission and access to retrieve the data you are requesting.

When using MSAL to connect to Azure Active Directory, you will need to be familiar with a couple concepts:

- Scopes

- Access token

- Refresh token

- Redirect URIs

Scopes

The authentication scopes are a series of commands that communicate to the authentication provider what type of data the application is requesting. A scope determines the type of data that a user can retrieve in this session such as profile data, which would be reading the information about the user. A scope can be more sensitive information such as the user's OneDrive files. When the application sends the authentication request, the scopes need to be included; otherwise, the access token won't be generated correctly.

Access Token

After successfully processing the authentication request, the provider will return an access token to be used by the application. The access token is sent with every request for your session; it contains the information needed about who you are and the scopes you have requested. The access token should have a short life, typically 1–2 hours.

Important   The access token is a highly sensitive secret token and should be treated as such. Any software or person that obtains an access token while it is still valid has direct access to all the information.

Refresh Token

An access token is only valid for a certain amount of time, and then it expires. A refresh token is a special token that allows the application to request a fresh access token. The refresh token can also be used to generate individual access tokens for specific scopes. You may want to use one access token for really sensitive data and another for retrieving profile information. An access token may expire during application use, and the user may still be logged in using the application. Just like the access token, this is a sensitive token and if stored in the application will need to be encrypted.

Important   Unlike the access token, a refresh token can be revoked. Once this is done, you will not be able to generate any new access tokens.

Redirect URI

An OAuth2 implementation will use a web browser to ask the user to log into the provider with their email and password. It needs to know where to send the user after successful login. The application also needs to be listening for the authentication provider on that specific redirect URI. This is a special place in the application that will get the authorized status of the user and any access token or refresh token. Once the user is sent to the redirect URI, the application will typically finish processing their authentication request and bring them to the main application dashboard.

Azure App Registration

Prior to adding any code, we will need to add our Azure Active Directory app registration. As we go through and implement the various platforms, we will be coming back to this to tweak settings as they vary slightly between some of the platforms.

Once you log into the Azure Portal, you will need to navigate to the Azure Active Directory page. The easiest way to do this is to type in "Azure Active Directory" into the search bar at the top and then select the correct service in the menu below the search – see Figure 11-1.

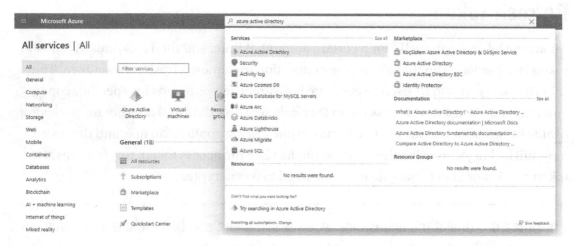

Figure 11-1. *Azure Portal search for the Azure Active Directory service*

In the Azure Active Directory service, you will select the "App registrations" option in the left menu – see Figure 11-2. This is the menu that allows us to configure our application with Azure Active Directory.

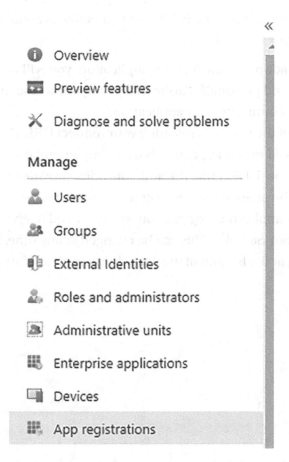

Figure 11-2. Azure Portal – Azure Active Directory left menu

You can now add a new application registration by selecting the "New registration" button at the top of this page. It will open an Azure wizard for creating the new application. The first part is where we define what type of authentication provider we want to implement. Your options are

- *Single tenant*: Only accounts in this Azure Active Directory organization

- *Multitenant*: Accounts in any Azure Active Directory organization except personal accounts

- *Multitenant and personal*: Accounts in any Azure Active Directory organization and personal accounts

- *Personal accounts only*: Only Microsoft personal accounts such as
  Skype or Xbox

To get the widest adoption rate for your application, you will want to select the third option, "multitenant and personal." This will allow anyone to use their work, school, or personal Microsoft account with your application.

The second part of the wizard is selecting your redirect URI. This is listed as optional at this point, and we will need to update this as we implement our various platforms. The redirect URI is a special URI that the authentication provider sends the user to. Your application will then be able to send the user to the correct page.

To complete your application registration, you will need to give it a name. I have chosen "UnoDrive Book Sample." This can be changed at any time. Now you can click the "Register" button at the bottom of the wizard. A completed form can be seen in Figure 11-3.

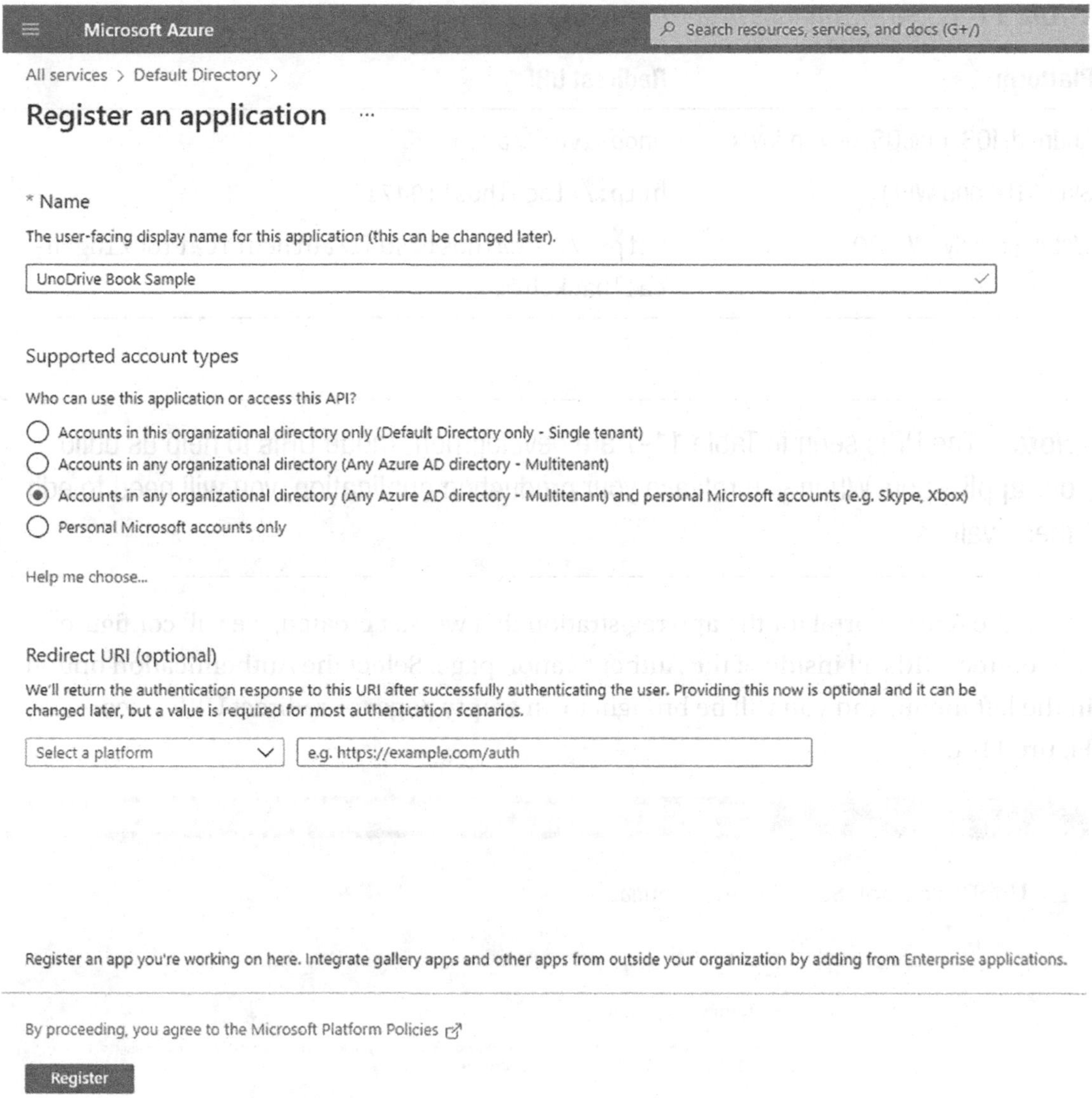

Figure 11-3. *Azure Portal – Register an application wizard*

The app registration has been created, and you will be brought to the Overview page. Next, we need to configure the various types of redirect URIs needed by the platforms we are supporting. See Table 11-1 for a mapping of redirect URIs and platforms.

Table 11-1. *Mapping of Target Platforms and Redirect URIs*

Platform	Redirect URI
Android, iOS, macOS, or Windows	`unodrive://auth`
Skia (GTK and WPF)	`http://localhost:9471`
WebAssembly (WASM)	`https://localhost:5001/authentication/login-callback.htm`

Note   The URIs seen in Table 11-1 are development mode URIs to help us build our application. When you release your production application, you will need to edit these values.

In the Azure Portal for the app registration that we just created, we will configure the redirect URIs all inside of the Authentication page. Select the Authentication option in the left menu, and you will be brought to an empty page for redirect URIs – see Figure 11-4.

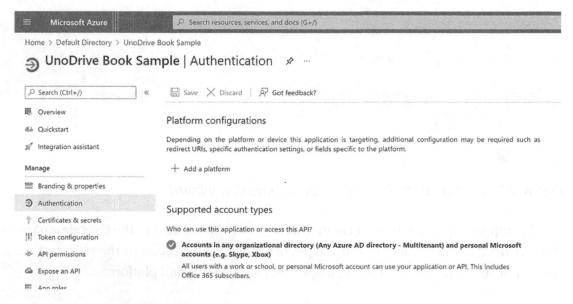

Figure 11-4. *App registration Authentication page*

To start, add the redirect URI for Windows, Android, iOS, and macOS by selecting the "Add a platform" button. A sidebar will open asking you to select the platform. You will need to select "Mobile and desktop applications" – see Figure 11-5.

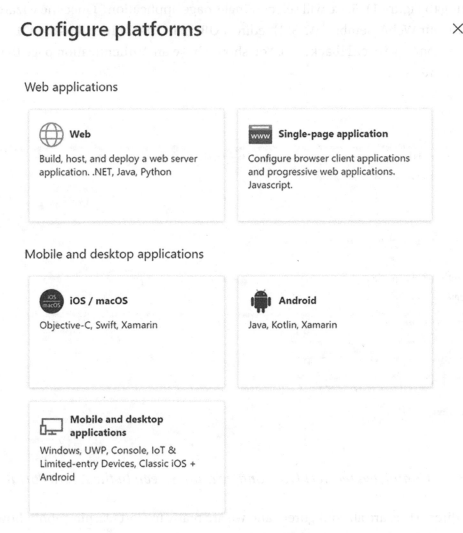

Figure 11-5. *App registration platform selection wizard for the redirect URI*

Once you select "Mobile and desktop applications," you can fill out the form with our redirect URI. Enter unodrive://auth and save the platform configuration. Now the Authentication page will update and allow you to enter another "Mobile and desktop applications" redirect URI. This time add http://localhost:9471, which will handle the GTK and WPF platforms.

Adding the redirect URI for WebAssembly (WASM) is slightly different since it uses the browser. We will need to configure it as a single-page application, also known as a SPA. Following our instructions from earlier, select the button "Add a platform," and referring to Figure 11-5, we will select "Single-page application." Once the wizard appears, use our WebAssembly (WASM) redirect URI of `https://localhost:5001/authentication/login-callback.htm`. You should have an Authentication page that looks like Figure 11-6.

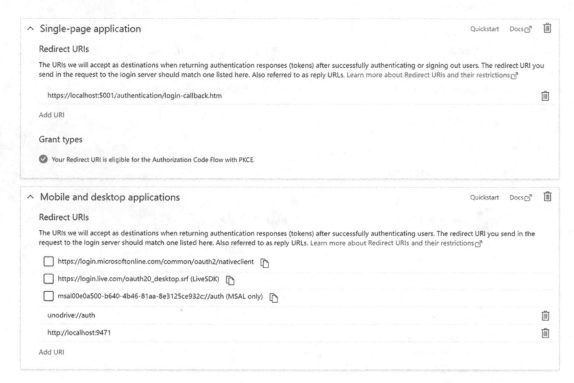

Figure 11-6. *Completed redirect URI configuration screen in the Azure Portal*

The redirect URIs are all configured, and we are ready to start learning about how to implement authentication in our application.

Implement Authentication

There are three main parts to our implementation:

- Configuration and startup logic

- Authentication service

- Application flow

When the application first opens, we need to ensure we are ready to communicate with Azure Active Directory and use the new app registration we created in the last section. Then we need to have our code flow that will perform the authentication when the user requests it.

NuGet Packages

There are three NuGet packages we will need, and they are the same across all the platforms:

- *Microsoft.Identity.Client*: MSAL from Microsoft

- *Uno.WinUI.MSAL*: Uno Platform helpers for MSAL

- *System.Text.Json*: JSON serialization and deserialization library

Add your NuGet packages to each project head – see the code in Listing 11-1. You will add this code to UnoDrive.Windows.csproj, UnoDrive.Wasm.csproj, UnoDrive. Skia.Wpf.csproj, UnoDrive.Skia.Gtk.csproj, and UnoDrive.Mobile.csproj.

Listing 11-1. Add NuGet packages for MSAL and Uno Platform helpers

```
<PackageReference
  Include="Microsoft.Identity.Client"
  Version="4.39.0" />
<PackageReference
  Include="Uno.WinUI.MSAL"
  Version="4.0.11" />
<PackageReference
  Include="System.Text.Json"
  Version="6.0.5" />
```

Configuration and Dependency Injection

With all the NuGet packages added and our app compiling, we can start configuring it to use Azure Active Directory. In this section we will configure MSAL to use the app registration that we configured in the Azure Portal.

First, you will need to create a new folder in the UnoDrive.Shared project called Authentication. Like our Logging folder, this is where we will place all our authentication code. Once you have created the new directory, add an empty class named AuthenticationConfiguration.cs. See Figure 11-7 for how the structure should look in Visual Studio.

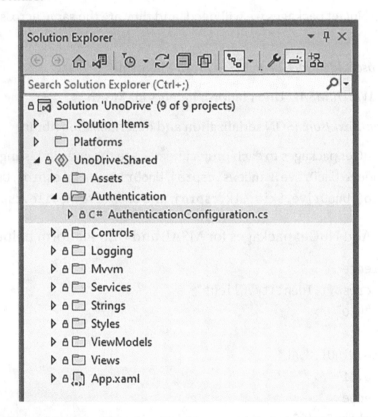

Figure 11-7. *Visual Studio Solution Explorer – AuthenticationConfiguration.cs*

Add a new method named ConfigureAuthentication(IServiceCollection services). This will be invoked from our Dependency Injection startup code. The goal of this method is to register all MSAL objects with the container so they can be used in other classes throughout our application. See code in Listing 11-2 for the stubbed-out class.

Listing 11-2. Stubbed-out AuthenticationConfiguration class

```
public class AuthenticationConfiguration
{
  public void ConfigureAuthentication(
    IServiceCollection services)
  {
    // TODO - Add implementation
  }
}
```

MSAL contains an interface named `IPublicClientApplication,` which contains all the details and APIs needed to authenticate with Azure Active Directory. To build an implementation of this interface, there is a useful builder object named `PublicClientApplicationBuilder`. When using the builder, we will add the necessary configuration values, which tell it how to connect to Azure Active Directory.

Using the Azure Portal, retrieve your application's Client ID. This can be found from the Overview page of the app registration. Open the Azure Portal, and navigate to the service Azure Active Directory. Open the app registration menu and then our application named "UnoDrive Book Sample." You will see an Overview page that looks like the image in Figure 11-8. You will be able to copy the application (Client) ID to your clipboard.

Figure 11-8. *Azure app registration Overview page*

Caution   The app registration Overview page contains many secrets available to you that may not seem like secrets. Some are more sensitive than others, but treat all the GUIDs on this page as sensitive data. Do not commit them directly to source control or share them with anyone or any software that does not need them. You should always include these as build secrets.

A bad actor that gains access to your Client ID can impersonate your application.

Our Client ID is 9f500d92-8e2e-4b91-b43a-a9ddb73e1c30. This will be used in the configuration APIs on the MSAL PublicClientApplicationBuilder.

Note   The screenshot in Figure 11-8 and Client ID we are using will not be valid anymore. You will need to use your own Client ID that you retrieve from the Azure Portal.

In Visual Studio we can now create our builder with the Client ID. Update your code in the AuthenticationConfiguration class as seen in Listing 11-3.

Listing 11-3. PublicClientApplicationBuilder with Client ID and Uno helpers

```
public class AuthenticationConfiguration
{
  public void ConfigureAuthentication(
    IServiceCollection services)
  {
    var builder = PublicClientApplicationBuilder
      .Create("9f500d92-8e2e-4b91-b43a-a9ddb73e1c30")
      .WithRedirectUri("") // TODO – Add Redirect URI
      .WithUnoHelpers();
  }
}
```

The last statement in the code block invokes the Uno Platform helpers by the extension method named WithUnoHelpers(). This is code from the NuGet package Uno. WinUI.MSAL and handles all the supported Uno Platform target platforms. It will add any special code that is required by that platform, which means your shared code does not need to add anything else to the builder.

We still need to configure the redirect URI, which we left as an empty string. Update the AuthenticationConfiguration class to be a partial class, just like the LoggingConfiguration class we implemented in Chapter 9. We will create platform-specific implementations for the various platforms to retrieve the correct redirect URI. Once the class has been updated to a partial class, you will then add a new partial method named GetRedirectUri() and invoke it as part of the builder. The new builder code for the redirect URI will be WithRedirectUri(GetRedirectUri()). See updated code for the AuthenticationConfiguration in Listing 11-4.

Listing 11-4. AuthenticationConfiguration with a partial method GetRedirectUri.

```
public partial class AuthenticationConfiguration
{
  public void ConfigureAuthentication(
    IServiceCollection services)
  {
    var builder = PublicClientApplicationBuilder
      .Create("9f500d92-8e2e-4b91-b43a-a9ddb73e1c30")
      .WithRedirectUri(GetRedirectUri())
      .WithUnoHelpers();
  }

  private partial string GetRedirectUri();
}
```

We are just about finished implementing our PublicClientApplicationBuilder. Next, we will need to add platform-specific redirect URIs and implementations. Our redirect URIs will be broken into three categories:

- Android, macOS, iOS, and Windows

- Skia

- WebAssembly (WASM)

We can group our redirect URIs this way because some projects will have an identical redirect URI. It will be fewer files for us to manage as we only need to create three platform-specific code files. In the Authentication directory of the UnoDrive.Shared project, add the following code files:

- AuthenticationConfiguration.android.ios.macos.windows.cs

- AuthenticationConfiguration.gtk.wpf.cs

- AuthenticationConfiguration.wasm.cs

See Figure 11-9 for an image of the new files in Visual Studio.

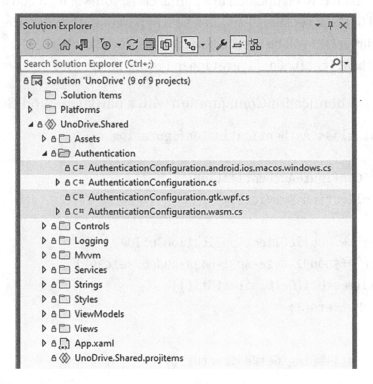

Figure 11-9. *Visual Studio Solution Explorer – partial classes for AuthenticationConfiguration*

To implement the Skia targets GTK and WPF, you will add the pre-processor directive to the top of the file #if HAS_UNO_SKIA. This will only run code on the Skia targets of GTK and WPF. Add the implementation of our partial method to return http:// localhost:9471. See Listing 11-5 for completed code.

Listing 11-5. Skia RedirectUri implementation

```
#if HAS_UNO_SKIA
namespace UnoDrive.Authentication
{
  public partial class AuthenticationConfiguration
  {
    private partial string GetRedirectUri() =>
      "http://localhost:9471";
  }
}
#endif
```

There are no project-specific implementations needed for GTK or WPF.

WebAssembly will require a few additional steps from the previous implementation. Start by adding the WebAssembly pre-processor directive of #if __WASM__ to AuthenticationConfiguration.wasm.cs. Implement the partial method and have it return https://localhost:5001/authentication/login-callback.html. See the completed WebAssembly code in Listing 11-6.

Listing 11-6. WebAssembly RedirectUri implementation

```
#if __WASM__
namespace UnoDrive.Authentication
{
  public partial class AuthenticationConfiguration
  {
    private partial string GetRedirectUri() =>
      "https://localhost:5001/authentication/login-callback.htm";
  }
}
#endif
```

The redirect URI for WebAssembly is a standard HTML file that must be added to the WebAssembly project. This file is a loading page that displays to the user while the authentication is processing. In the UnoDrive.Wasm project, add a new directory into wwwroot called Authentication. In this new folder, add a standard HTML file named login-callback.htm. See Figure 11-10 for the screenshot of the Solution Explorer.

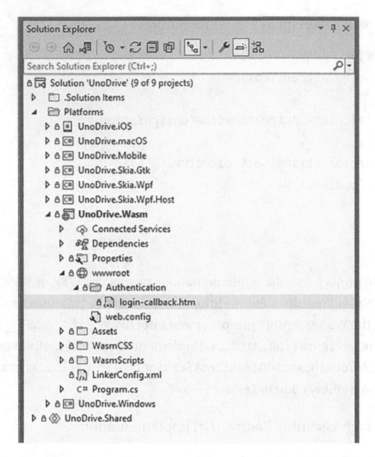

Figure 11-10. *Visual Studio Solution Explorer – login-callback.htm for the WebAssembly project*

The login-callback.htm is a static HTML page, and it can display any content that you desire. In our sample application, it is going to read a simple message of "Waiting for Authentication to process." You can see the HTML code in Listing 11-7.

Listing 11-7. login-callback.htm complete code

```
<!DOCTYPE html>
<html>
<head>
    <meta charset="utf-8" />
    <title></title>
</head>
<body>
```

```
   Waiting for Authentication to process
</body>
</html>
```

The final `AuthenticationConfiguration` redirect URI implementation is for the remaining platforms: Android, iOS, macOS, and Windows. Edit the `AuthenticationConfiguration.android.ios.macos.windows.cs` file and add pre-processor directives for each platform – see Listing 11-8.

Listing 11-8. Pre-processor directives for Android, iOS, macOS, and Windows

```
#if __ANDROID__ || __IOS__ || __MACOS || __UNO_DRIVE_WINDOWS__
```

Add the redirect URI implementation to return `unodrive://auth`. For the native application model, we can return a custom URI like this that will be handled by the application. The other platforms depend on using a website address. See Listing 11-9 for the complete code implementation.

Listing 11-9. Redirect URI implementation for Android, iOS, macOS, and Windows

```
#if __ANDROID__ || __IOS__ || __MACOS__ || __UNO_DRIVE_WINDOWS__
namespace UnoDrive.Authentication
{
  public partial class AuthenticationConfiguration
  {
    private partial string GetRedirectUri() =>
      "unodrive://auth";
  }
}
#endif
```

You will need to add the `unodrive://auth` redirect URI for Android. Windows, iOS, and macOS still require keychain configuration, which we cover in the next section. These platforms will automatically take the user to the landing page upon successful authentication.

To add the redirect URI to Android, open the UnoDrive.Mobile project and select the Android folder. You will now open the Android.Manifest.xml file and add a new activity with an intent filter to listen for the redirect. MSAL for Android includes the necessary activity and intent filters to properly listen for the redirect for the authentication. To add the new activity, you will add it into the <application> XML node that should already be in the manifest. See Listing 11-10 for new intent filter code.

Listing 11-10. Android intent filter for the unodrive://auth redirect URI

```
<activity
  android:name="microsoft.identity.client.BrowserTabActivity"
  android:configChanges="orientation|screenSize">
  <intent-filter>
    <action android:name="android.intent.action.VIEW" />
    <category android:name="android.intent.category.DEFAULT" />
    <category android:name="android.intent.category.BROWSABLE" />
    <data android:scheme="unodrive" android:host="auth" />
  </intent-filter>
</activity>
```

To complete the Android implementation, you will need to update the MainActivity. Open the MainActivity.Android.cs file and add a new override for the method OnActivityResult. In this method we will need to invoke the MSAL API for setting the continuation. See Listing 11-11 for code.

Listing 11-11. Android MainActivity OnActivityResult implementation

```
protected override void OnActivityResult(
  int requestCode, Result resultCode, Intent data)
{
  base.OnActivityResult(requestCode, resultCode, data);
  AuthenticationContinuationHelper
    .SetAuthenticationContinuationEventArgs(
      requestCode, resultCode, data);
}
```

The final step to configure the PublicClientApplicationBuilder is adding it as a singleton object for Dependency Injection. In the AuthenticationConfiguration. cs where we started, use the Build() API to create the IPublicClientApplication implementation and register it. See Listing 11-12 for registration code and Listing 11-13 for current AuthenticationConfiguration code.

Listing 11-12. PublicClientApplicationBuilder – build and register for Dependency Injection

```
services.AddSingleton(builder.Build());
```

Listing 11-13. Current AuthenticationConfiguration implementation

```
public partial class AuthenticationConfiguration
{
  public void ConfigureAuthentication(
    IServiceCollection services)
  {
    var builder = PublicClientApplicationBuilder
      .Create("9f500d92-8e2e-4b91-b43a-a9ddb73e1c30")
      .WithRedirectUri(GetRedirectUri())
      .WithUnoHelpers();

    services.AddSingleton(builder.Build());
  }

  private partial string GetRedirectUri();
}
```

We have completed our configuration code, but it isn't being used by anything yet because it hasn't been invoked as part of the Dependency Injection startup code. In the Authentication directory of the UnoDrive.Shared project, add a new class named AuthenticationExtensions.cs. This is where we can create the necessary extension method that will invoke our configuration logic. See Figure 11-11 for the screenshot of the Solution Explorer.

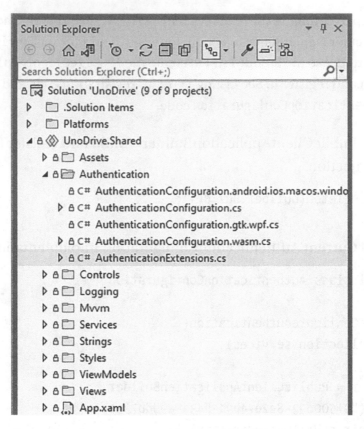

Figure 11-11. *Visual Studio Solution Explorer – AuthenticationExtensions.cs*

In the newly created AuthenticationExtensions.cs file, we will create an extension method that invokes the authentication code we have added so far. Create a new method named AddAuthentication, and then instantiate the AuthenticationConfiguration object and invoke the ConfigureAuthentication method. See Listing 11-14 for the complete extension method code.

Listing 11-14. AddAuthentication extension method code

```
public static class AuthenticationExtensions
{
  public static void AddAuthentication(
    this IServiceCollection services)
  {
    AuthenticationConfiguration configuration =
      new AuthenticationConfiguration();
```

```
    configuration.ConfigureAuthentication(services);
  }
}
```

Note We created the extension method to provide a simple API when adding authentication to Dependency Injection.

In the App.xaml.cs we can update the ConfigureServices method to use our new AddAuthentication method, which will complete our configuration code. See Listing 11-15 for the current ConfigureServices implementation.

Listing 11-15. Current ConfigureServices code in App.xaml.cs

```
protected override void ConfigureServices(
  IServiceCollection services)
{
  services.AddLoggingForUnoDrive();
  services.AddAuthentication();
  services.AddTransient<INavigationService, NavigationService>();
}
```

iOS and macOS Keychain Access

Keychain access is required for iOS and macOS because it is the secure storage mechanism in the Apple ecosystem. It allows for secure encrypted storage of data.

Configuring authentication for iOS and macOS has some additional steps:

1. Ensure the bundle identifier is unique and matches your desired name.

2. Update Info.plist.

3. Update Entitlements.plist.

4. Add keychain access to configuration.

> **Note**   The configuration for keychain access is identical between iOS and macOS. The changes will need to be duplicated in both projects.

Open the `Info.plist` file for both iOS and macOS and ensure you have your correct bundle identifier. We will be using `com.SkyeHoefling.UnoDrive` as the bundle identifier. In your code it will need to match the identifier created in your Apple developer account.

> **Note**   This book does not go into detail about creating your identifier or provisioning profile.

Add or update your `CFBundleIdentifier` **to match your bundle name. See the plist code snippet in Listing 11-16.**

Listing 11-16. iOS and macOS CFBundleIdentifier snippet for Info.plist

```
<key>CFBundleIdentifier</key>
<string>com.SkyeHoefling.UnoDrive</string>
```

MSAL uses special Apple query schemes that are needed for the library to work correctly. To enable this, add `msauthv2` and `msauthv3` to the `Info.plist`. See the plist code snippet in Listing 11-17.

Listing 11-17. iOS and macOS query schemes snippet for Info.plist

```
<key>LSApplicationQueriesSchemes</key>
<array>
  <string>msauthv2</string>
  <string>msauthv3</string>
</array>
```

Next, you will need to add the keychain access to the Entitlements.plist file. You will need to use the bundle identifier we configured in the Info.plist file. If these do not match, it will not work. Add the snippet in Listing 11-18.

Listing 11-18. iOS and macOS keychain access for Entitlements.plist

```
<key>keychain-access-groups</key>
<array>
  <string>$(AppIdentifierPrefix)com.SkyeHoefling.UnoDrive</string>
</array>
```

Everything is configured, and we can now update the AuthenticationConfiguration code to use the keychain security group. Add a new builder method in between the initial build statements and the final build invocation. This needs to only run on iOS and macOS. You will need to use the bundle identifier we defined earlier. See Listing 11-19 for the code snippet.

Listing 11-19. AuthenticationConfiguration keychain access for iOS and macOS

```
#if __IOS__ || __MACOS__
builder.WithIosKeychaingSecurityGroup(
  "com.SkyeHoefling.UnoDrive");
#endif
```

Authentication Service

With our application configuration to Azure Active Directory completed, we can start implementing the IAuthenticationService. In our MVVM application, we want our authentication code to be isolated from our standard view models. This means we will be creating a special interface and implementation to handle all the authentication code. Then in our LoginViewModel and DashboardViewModel, we can use these APIs to perform the code flow.

Start by adding two files into the UnoDrive.Shared project's Authentication folder: IAuthenticationService and AuthenticationService. These files will serve as the interface and implementation. See Figure 11-12 for a screenshot of the Solution Explorer.

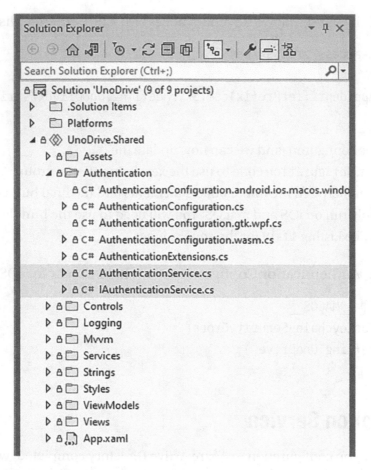

Figure 11-12. *Visual Studio Solution Explorer – AuthenticationService.cs and IAuthenticationService.cs*

Starting with the interface, let's define our contract that the view models will be using. There are two APIs that need to be added: SignOutAsync() and AcquireTokenAsync(). See interface code in Listing 11-20.

Listing 11-20. IAuthenticationService interface definition

```
public interface IAuthenticationService
{
  Task<AuthenticationResult> AcquireTokenAsync();
  Task SignOutAsync();
}
```

In the AuthenticationService.cs file, we need to update the class to inherit from IAuthenticationService and stub out the methods for implementation. See Listing 11-21 for the stubbed class.

Listing 11-21. Stubbed AuthenticationService

```
public class AuthenticationService : IAuthenticationService
{
  public async Task<AuthenticationResult> AcquireTokenAsync()
  {
    // TODO - add implementation
  }

  public async Task SignOutAsync()
  {
    // TODO - add implementation
  }
}
```

Let's review some concepts to help us understand what we are adding in the AuthenticationService. There are two types of tokens that we are concerned about: access token and refresh token. We learned at the beginning of the chapter that both are sensitive tokens but serve different purposes. The access token is used on all requests after authentication, whereas the refresh token is a way to retrieve a new access token after the current one has expired. The refresh token is also useful for silently logging into the app either in an offline mode or if the user has already logged in during a prior session.

We will break our implementation into two strategies to get toward the completed solution. To start we will focus on online mode, and after that is completed, we will handle the refresh token and offline mode.

In the AuthenticationService, add a new method stub named AcquireInteractiveTokenAsync. When you acquire an interactive token, it will ask the user for their email and password and process them through the Azure Active Directory login pages. Acquiring a silent token skips the step that prompts the user because it is using a refresh token stored in the local database. The application can then acquire the needed access token and proceed into the application. See Listing 11-22 for the method stub.

Listing 11-22. AcquireInteractiveTokenAsync method stub

```
async Task<AuthenticationResult> AcquireInteractiveTokenAsync()
{
  // TODO - add implementation
}
```

In the AcquireTokenAsync method implementation that we stubbed out earlier, we can invoke the new method AcquireInteractiveTokenAsync and return. See Listing 11-23 for updated AcquireTokenAsync code.

Listing 11-23. Updated AcquireTokenAsync to invoke the new private method AcquireInteractiveTokenAsync

```
public async Task<AuthenticationResult> AcquireTokenAsync()
{
  return await AcquireInteractiveTokenAsync()
}
```

Before we can implement our method, we need to inject our MSAL configuration that we completed in the previous section. We registered the IPublicClientApplication with Dependency Injection. Let's inject that object and store it in a local variable. See Listing 11-24 for constructor code.

Listing 11-24. IPublicClientApplication injection into the AuthenticationService

```
public class AuthenticationService : IAuthenticationService
{
  IPublicClientApplication publicClientApp;

  Public AuthenticationService(
    IPublicClientApplication publicClientApp)
  {
    this.publicClientApp = publicClientApp;
  }
  // omitted code
}
```

Next, we need to define the application scopes that determine what data we want to retrieve from Azure Active Directory. Our application is going to be interacting with the OneDrive API, so we need to be able to get files and profiles, and we want offline access. See Table 11-2 for details on each scope and what it is for.

Table 11-2. *Authentication Scopes and Their Descriptions*

Scope	Description
email	Access to the user's email address. This will be used for displaying on the dashboard.
Files. ReadWrite. All	Access to all OneDrive files including read and write. This will allow our application to perform all of the OneDrive operations.
offline_ access	Ability to store the refresh token and log in while in offline mode.
profile	Access to the user's profile information.
User.Read	Access to additional properties of the user that aren't available in the standard profile.

We will define the scopes in the constructor as it will be the same for all authentication requests. Update the constructor code to include all scopes from Table 11-2. See Listing 11-25 for updated constructor code.

Listing 11-25. Updated AuthenticationService constructor code to include scopes

```
public class AuthenticationService : IAuthenticationService
{
  string[] scopes;

  IPublicClientApplication publicClientApp;

  Public AuthenticationService(
    IPublicClientApplication publicClientApp)
  {
    this.publicClientApp = publicClientApp;

    scopes = new []
    {
      "email",
```

```
        "Files.ReadWrite.All",
        "offline_access",
        "profile",
        "User.Read"
    };
}

// omitted code
}
```

The constructor code is complete enough for us to finish the interactive authentication flow. In the method `AcquireInteractiveTokenAsync`, we will use the injected `IPublicClientApplication` to acquire the token. The first API `AcquireTokenInteractive` will take the parameters of our scopes. This is where the connection is made to Azure Active Directory, and the scopes we defined earlier will be needed. Be sure to always use the Uno Platform helpers via `WithUnoHelpers()`. This will ensure you don't need to write any platform-specific code as the application goes from shared code to native code for you. See the implementation in Listing 11-26.

Listing 11-26. Implementation for AcquireInteractiveTokenAsync

```
async Task<AuthenticationResult> AcquireInteractiveTokenAsync()
{
  return await publicClientApp
    .AcquireTokenInteractive(scopes)
    .WithUnoHelpers()
    .ExecuteAsync();
}
```

Now that we have implemented the ability to sign in, we need to implement the ability to sign out. When we acquire a token, it stores the necessary information for us through APIs provided by MSAL. It saves the concept of an account, which we will use later for silent sign-on. To sign out we simply delete the data from the local database using the MSAL APIs. Since the authentication protocol we are using requires all authenticated requests to include the access token, if we lose both our access token and refresh token, there is no way to log in. The user will need to acquire the token with an interactive session again.

Implement the SignOutAsync method by searching for the first account and removing it. See code in Listing 11-27 for basic implementation.

Listing 11-27. SignOutAsync basic implementation

```
public async Task SignOutAsync()
{
  var accounts = await publicClientApp.GetAccountsAsync();
  var firstAccount = accounts.FirstOrDefault();
  if (firstAccount == null)
  {
    return;
  }

  await publicClientApp.RemoveAsync(firstAccount);
}
```

This gets us going with the basic authentication code paths for acquiring a token for login and then removing the account and the associated details for sign-out.

Authentication code can be very tricky to debug, and it is a difficult topic among application developers. There are so many options and so many places for things to go wrong. It could be your code, your redirect URI, the token being generated incorrectly, or some configuration value. To help ease our efforts in debugging, let's add some logging statements for sign-out.

Start by injecting the ILogger into the AuthenticationService. Update the constructor to take an additional parameter of ILogger<AuthenticationService> and save the value to an instance variable. See Listing 11-28 for updated constructor code.

Listing 11-28. Add ILogger to constructor injection for AuthenticationService

```
public class AuthenticationService : IAuthenticationService
{
  string[] scopes;

  IPublicClientApplication publicClientApp;
```

```
ILogger logger;

Public AuthenticationService(
  IPublicClientApplication publicClientApp,
  ILogger logger)
{
  this.publicClientApp = publicClientApp;
  this.logger = logger;

  scopes = new []
  {
    "email",
    "Files.ReadWrite.All",
    "offline_access",
    "profile",
    "User.Read"
  };
}

// omitted code
}
```

We can now update our SignOutAsync implementation to print different messages if the user was signed out or if no account was found. See Listing 11-29 for updated SignOutAsync code.

Listing 11-29. SignOutAsync code with log statements

```
public async Task SignOutAsync()
{
  var accounts = await publicClientApp.GetAccountsAsync();
  var firstAccount = accounts.FirstOrDefault();
  if (firstAccount == null)
  {
    logger.LogInformation(
      "Unable to find any accounts to log out of.");
    return;
  }
```

```
await publicClientApp.RemoveAsync(firstAccount);
logger.LogInformation(
  $"Removed account: {firstAccount.Username}, " +
  "user successfully logged out.");
}
```

Modern applications for both mobile and desktop need to be built for offline mode. As WebAssembly becomes a more common technology, it will be useful to run these apps in an offline mode if you have all assets already downloaded on your machine or browser.

The next part to implementing authentication will be enabling offline mode. In our application we will only allow the user to sign on if they have already acquired a token successfully while connected to the Internet. At that point if the Internet connection is no longer present, they will be able to sign in again and use the data they have downloaded on the device.

In our application we want to implement the following algorithm to handle sign-in:

1. Attempt a silent sign-on by checking if the account has already been logged in.

2. If no account is present in the local database, acquire a new token interactively.

These rules will apply for both online and offline modes. The only problem with offline mode is if the user has never logged in, the account data is not cached. This is a normal operation. To use the app, you must have the Internet for the first sign-on attempt.

To get started, create a new private method stub called AcquireSilentTokenAsync. This is where our silent sign-on logic will be – see stub code in Listing 11-30.

Listing 11-30. AcquireSilentTokenAsync method stub

```
async Task<AuthenticationResult> AcquireSilentTokenAsync()
{
  // TODO - add implementation
}
```

Now we can update our main acquire token method to attempt to acquire a silent token first and then fall back to an interactive acquire. The `AuthenticationResult` will contain the access token; we can check if this value is null or empty. If it is null or empty, that means we did not perform a silent authentication, and we need to perform an interactive authentication. See updated `AcquireTokenAsync` code in Listing 11-31.

Listing 11-31. Updated AcquireTokenAsync using silent and interactive methods

```
public async Task<AuthenticationResult> AcquireTokenAsync()
{
  AuthenticationResult authentication =
    await AcquireSilentTokenAsync();

  if (string.IsNullOrEmpty(authentication?.AccessToken)
  {
    authentication = await AcquireInteractiveTokenAsync();
  }

  return authentication;
}
```

The business rules are updated for our `AcquireTokenAsync` method, and we can now implement `AcquireSilentTokenAsync`. The algorithm for acquiring a silent token is a little bit more involved than interactive because of all the things that could go wrong:

1. Check if there is an account stored in the local database. If there is one, we can continue; if not, we need to return and attempt an interactive sign-on.

2. Using the account in the local database, we will attempt a sign-on and see if we can log in:

   a. Handle various exceptions that can be thrown.

We will first implement the solution and talk about what is needed to accomplish the basics and then add exception handling and logging to help with diagnosing issues. Using similar APIs to the `SignOutAsync`, let's get our account and determine if we can attempt a silent sign-on – see code Listing 11-32.

Listing 11-32. Return if no account data in the AcquireSilentTokenAsync method

```
async Task<AuthenticationResult> AcquireSilentTokenAsync()
{
  var accounts = await publicClientApp.GetAccountsAsync();
  var firstAccount = accounts.FirstOrDefault();

  if (firstAccount == null)
  {
    return null;
  }
}
```

The base case of no prior sign-on is now implemented. We can take all the data
we have built up in other parts of the class to try and authenticate with the requested
scopes. Add the code from Listing 11-33 next.

Listing 11-33. Acquire silent token API

```
return await publicClientApp
  .AcquireTokenSilent(scopes, firstAccount)
  .WaitForRefresh(false)
  .ExecuteAsync();
```

The code put together for acquiring silent tokens can be seen in Listing 11-34.

Listing 11-34. Current code for AcquireSilentTokenAsync

```
async Task<AuthenticationResult> AcquireSilentTokenAsync()
{
  var accounts = await publicClientApp.GetAccountsAsync();
  var firstAccount = accounts.FirstOrDefault();

  if (firstAccount == null)
  {
    return null;
  }

  return await publicClientApp
    .AcquireTokenSilent(scopes, firstAccount)
```

```
    .WaitForRefresh(false)
    .ExecuteAsync();
}
```

This method is broken into two parts, checking for an existing account and then acquiring the silent token. Add new logging statements to the first part that checks for an account. This will help understand if there is no data or an account available when running the application. See the code snippet for new logging statements in Listing 11-35.

Listing 11-35. Logging statements for checking account data in the AcquireSilentTokenAsync

```
async Task<AuthenticationResult> AcquireSilentTokenAsync()
{
  var accounts = await publicClientApp.GetAccountsAsync();
  var firstAccount = accounts.FirstOrDefault();

  if (firstAccount == null)
  {
    logger.LogInformation(
      "Unable to find Account in MSAL.NET cache");
    return null;
  }

  if (accounts.Any())
  {
    logger.LogInformation(
      $"Number of Accounts: {accounts.Count()}");
  }

  // omitted code
}
```

Now we can start implementing exception handling. The goal of the exception handling for acquiring silent tokens is to allow the system to fall back to an interactive token acquisition. All exception handling that requires a user interface change should be handled in the view model and not the `AuthenticationService`.

Wrap the second part of our `AcquireSilentTokenAsync` method in a try-catch block. Then add catch statements for the following exceptions:

- `MsalUiRequiredException`: Requires the interactive token to be used to sign on. All we need to do is log the message and return.

- `HttpException`: If there is an issue sending the HTTP request such as a connection is terminated in the middle, this may be thrown.

- `Exception`: Something else has gone wrong. We will still proceed to interactive acquisition, but it will be useful to log the details.

Update the `AcquireSilentTokenAsync` method to implement the catch blocks and add logging. See Listing 11-36 for updated try-catch block implementations.

Listing 11-36. AcquireSilentTokenAsync updated try-catch implementation

```
async Task<AuthenticationResult> AcquireSilentTokenAsync()
{
  // omitted code

  AuthenticationResult result;

  try
  {
    logger.LogInformation(
      "Attempting to perform silent sign in . . .");
    logger.LogInformation(
      "Authentication Scopes: " +
      $"{JsonConvert.SerializeObject(scopes)}");
    logger.LogInformation(
      $"Account Name: {firstAccount.Username}");

    result = await publicClientApp
      .AcquireTokenSilent(scopes, firstAccount)
      .WaitForRefresh(false)
      .ExecuteAsync();
  }
  catch (MsalUiRequiredException ex)
  {
```

```
    logger.LogWarning(ex, ex.Message);
    logger.LogWarning(
      "Unable to retrieve silent sign in Access Token");
  }
  catch (HttpException ex)
  {
    logger.LogError(httpException, httpException.Message);
  }
  catch (Exception ex)
  {
    logger.LogWarning(exception, exception.Message);
    logger.LogWarning(
      "Unable to retrieve silent sign in details");
  }
}
```

The HttpException catch block is only useful if there is Internet connection. This will help diagnose network traffic. If there is no Internet connection, this exception should never be thrown. To check for Internet connectivity, we can use the WinUI API NetworkInformation. Let's create a new Dependency Injection service to check for Internet connectivity. This service will be used whenever we need to check for network connection.

In the Services directory, create a new pair of classes: INetworkConnectivityService and NetworkConnectivityService. See Figure 11-13 for a screenshot from the Solution Explorer.

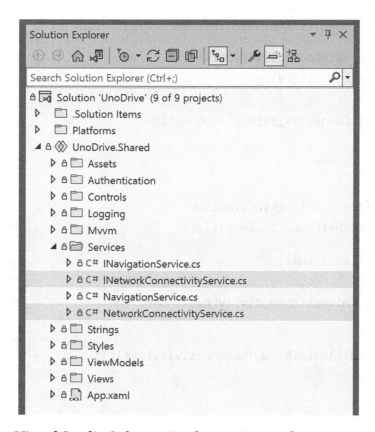

Figure 11-13. *Visual Studio Solution Explorer – NetworkConnectivityService.cs and INetworkConnectivityService.cs*

Add the interface implementation to INetworkConnectivityService, which defines our contract for checking the Internet connection. We can use the existing WinUI object of NetworkConnectivityLevel to determine what type of connection we have. See Listing 11-37 for interface code.

Listing 11-37. INetworkConnectivityService implementation

```
public interface INetworkConnectivityService
{
  NetworkConnectivityLevel Connectivity { get; }
}
```

With the interface designed, we can add the implementation in NetworkConnectivityService. Using the WinUI object NetworkInformation, we can retrieve the network status and return. See Listing 11-38 for the implementation.

Listing 11-38. NetworkConnectivityService implementation

```
public class NetworkConnectivityService :
  INetworkConnectivityService
{
  public NetworkConnectivityLevel Connection
  {
    get
    {
      var profile = NetworkInformation
        .GetInternetConnectionProfile();

      if (profile == null)
      {
        return NetworkConnectivityLevel.None;
      }

      return profile.GetNetworkConnectivityLevel();
    }
  }
}
```

With our new NetworkConnectivityService implemented, we just need to add it to the Dependency Injection registration. Add the code in Listing 11-39 to the App.xaml.cs ConfigureServices method. See Listing 11-40 for our current implementation.

Listing 11-39. INetworkConnectivityService Dependency Injection registration

```
services.AddTransient<
  INetworkConnectivityService,
  NetworkConnectivityService>();
```

Listing 11-40. Current implementation of ConfigureServices in App.xaml.cs

```
protected override void ConfigureServices(
  IServiceCollection services)
{
  services.AddLoggingForUnoDrive();
  services.AddAuthentication();
```

```
services.AddTransient<INavigationService, NavigationService>();
services.AddTransient<
  INetworkConnectivityService,
  NetworkConnectivityService>();
}
```

Heading back over to the AuthenticationService, we can now inject our new INetworkConnectivityService to the constructor. Update the existing constructor code to include the new variable, which we will use to check network status. See Listing 11-41 for the updated constructor code.

Listing 11-41. Updated AuthenticationService constructor – adds injected INetworkConnectivityService

```
public class AuthenticationService : IAuthenticationService
{
  string[] scopes;

  IPublicClientApplication publicClientApp;
  INetworkConnectivityService networkService;
  ILogger logger;

  Public AuthenticationService(
    IPublicClientApplication publicClientApp,
    INetworkConnectivityService networkService,
    ILogger logger)
  {
    this.publicClientApp = publicClientApp;
    this.networkService = networkService;
    this.logger = logger;

    scopes = new []
    {
      "email",
      "Files.ReadWrite.All",
      "offline_access",
      "profile",
      "User.Read"
```

```
    };
  }

  // omitted code
}
```

In our AcquireSilentTokenAsync method, we are handling the HttpException. This exception is only useful to us if the device has a valid network connection. If there is no connection and there is an exception, that means our refresh token has expired or we have never performed a sign-on. Update the HttpException catch block to only print the log statement if there is a valid connection – see Listing 11-42.

Listing 11-42. HttpException catch block in AcquireSilentTokenAsync of the AuthenticationService

```
catch (HttpException ex)
{
  if (networkService.Connectivity ==
    NetworkConnectivityLevel.InternetAccess)
  {
    logger.LogError(httpException, httpException.Message);
  }
}
```

The AuthenticationService is completed. There were a lot of different things we needed to properly implement the AuthenticationService. See the completed code so far in Listing 11-43.

Listing 11-43. Completed AuthenticationService

```
public class AuthenticationService : IAuthenticationService
{
  string[] scopes;

  IPublicClientApplication publicClientApp;
  INetworkConnectivityService networkService;
  ILogger logger;

  Public AuthenticationService(
```

```
  IPublicClientApplication publicClientApp,
  INetworkConnectivityService networkService,
  ILogger logger)
{
  this.publicClientApp = publicClientApp;
  this.networkService = networkService;
  this.logger = logger;

  scopes = new []
  {
    "email",
    "Files.ReadWrite.All",
    "offline_access",
    "profile",
    "User.Read"
  };
}

public async Task<AuthenticationResult> AcquireTokenAsync()
{
  AuthenticationResult authentication =
    await AcquireSilentTokenAsync();

  if (authentication == null ||
    string.IsNullOrEmpty(authentication.AccessToken)
  {
    authentication = await AcquireInteractiveTokenAsync();
  }

  return authentication;
}

public async Task SignOutAsync()
{
  var accounts = await publicClientApp.GetAccountsAsync();
  var firstAccount = accounts.FirstOrDefault();
  if (firstAccount == null)
  {
```

```
      logger.LogInformation(
        "Unable to find any accounts to log out of.");
      return;
    }

  await publicClientApp.RemoveAsync(firstAccount);
  logger.LogInformation(
    $"Removed account: {firstAccount.Username}, " +
    "user successfully logged out.");
}

async Task<AuthenticationResult> AcquireSilentTokenAsync()
{
  var accounts = await publicClientApp.GetAccountsAsync();
  var firstAccount = accounts.FirstOrDefault();

  if (firstAccount == null)
  {
    logger.LogInformation(
      "Unable to find Account in MSAL.NET cache");
    return null;
  }

  if (accounts.Any())
  {
    logger.LogInformation(
      $"Number of Accounts: {accounts.Count()}");
  }

  AuthenticationResult result;

  try
  {
    logger.LogInformation(
      "Attempting to perform silent sign in . . .");
    logger.LogInformation(
      "Authentication Scopes: " +
      $"{JsonConvert.SerializeObject(scopes)}");
```

```
      logger.LogInformation(
        $"Account Name: {firstAccount.Username}");

      result = await publicClientApp
        .AcquireTokenSilent(scopes, firstAccount)
        .WaitForRefresh(false)
        .ExecuteAsync();
    }
    catch (MsalUiRequiredException ex)
    {
      logger.LogWarning(ex, ex.Message);
      logger.LogWarning(
        "Unable to retrieve silent sign in Access Token");
    }
    catch (HttpException ex)
    {
      if (networkService.Connectivity ==
        NetworkConnectivityLevel.InternetAccess)
      {
        logger.LogError(httpException, httpException.Message);
      }
    }
    catch (Exception ex)
    {
      logger.LogWarning(exception, exception.Message);
      logger.LogWarning(
        "Unable to retrieve silent sign in details");
    }
  }
}
```

The last thing that we need to do is register the AuthenticationService with
Dependency Injection. Since all the authentication code is within the Authentication
folder, we will add this to the AuthenticationConfiguration class. At the end of the
ConfigureAuthentication method, add the code from Listing 11-44. See the completed
AuthenticationConfiguration in Listing 11-45.

Listing 11-44. Register AuthenticationService with Dependency Injection

```
services.AddTransient<
  IAuthenticationService,
  AuthenticationService>();
```

Listing 11-45. Completed AuthenticationConfiguration code

```
public partial class AuthenticationConfiguration
{
  public void ConfigureAuthentication(
    IServiceCollection services)
  {
    var builder = PublicClientApplicationBuilder
      .Create("9f500d92-8e2e-4b91-b43a-a9ddb73e1c30")
      .WithRedirectUri(GetRedirectUri())
      .WithUnoHelpers();

    services.AddSingleton(builder.Build());
    services.AddTransient<
      IAuthenticationService,
      AuthenticationService>();
  }

  private partial string GetRedirectUri();
}
```

Application Code Flow

All the authentication code is completed, and we can implement the application
flow. This section covers the code changes to the LoginViewModel for sign-
on and how the dashboard performs the sign-out via the NavigationService.
The AuthenticationService provides the ability to acquire the necessary
access token to make requests against Azure Active Directory. When designing
this class, we intentionally did not handle any exceptions from the method
AcquireInteractiveTokenAsync. This allows us to handle the errors on the user
interface and communicate clear instructions to the user if something goes wrong.

The `IAuthenticationService` API returns the MSAL object `AuthenticationResult`. Once authenticated, we will be using this object throughout the application. To make this easy to access in various parts of our application, we can add the `AuthenticationResult` to the `App.xaml.cs` class. At the beginning of the class just after the declaration, we can create an instance property to store this. See Listing 11-46 for property code.

Listing 11-46. AuthenticationResult property in App.xaml.cs

```
public AuthenticationResult AuthenticationResult { get; set; }
```

> **Note** In Listing 11-46 we add the `AuthenticationResult` property to the `App.xaml.cs` because it is an application-wide property and provides useful state. This can also be stored in the Dependency Injection container or another mechanism for lookup.

Now we can begin updating the `LoginViewModel` to use the `AuthenticationService`. Up until this point, the `LoginViewModel` would only perform the navigation action to open the dashboard. This means all the connections are in place and we just need to update our implementation of the `OnLogin` method in the `LoginViewModel`.

Start by injecting the `IAuthenticationService` and `INetworkConnectivityService` into the `LoginViewModel` and storing them as local variables. We will also update the `ICommand` instantiation of login to use the async implementation. We will be using them in our updated implementation of `OnLogin`. See Listing 11-47 for updated constructor code.

Listing 11-47. Updated LoginViewModel constructor injecting IAuthenticationService and INetworkConnectivityService

```
public class LoginViewModel : ObservableObject
{
  IAuthenticationService authentication;
  INetworkConnectivityService networkService;
  INavigationService navigationService;
  ILogger logger;
```

```
public LoginViewModel(
  IAuthenticationService authentication,
  INetworkConnectivityService networkService,
  INavigationService navigationService,
  ILogger<LoginViewModel> logger)
{
  this.authentication = authentication;
  this.networkService = networkService;
  this.navigationService = navigationService;
  this.logger = logger;

  Login = new AsyncRelayCommand(OnLoginAsync);
}
}
```

This will create a compile error, so we need to update the OnLogin method to change its signature to support async. Remove the existing OnLogin method and replace it with OnLoginAsync as seen in Listing 11-48.

Listing 11-48. OnLoginAsync updates to support async APIs

```
async Task OnLoginAsync()
{
  // TODO - add implementation
}
```

We need to create a couple bindable properties that will help us share the state of the login operation with the LoginPage. Create two properties: IsBusy to render a loading indicator and Message to display error messages to the user. Add the following properties just above the OnLoginAsync in your LoginViewModel – see Listing 11-49.

Listing 11-49. IsBusy and Message bindable properties in the LoginViewModel

```
string message;
public string Message
{
  get => message;
  set => SetProperty(ref message, value);
```

```
}

bool isBusy;
public bool IsBusy
{
  get => isBusy;
  set => SetProperty(ref isBusy, value);
}
```

When performing any long-running process, it is a good idea to set the IsBusy = true, and when the processing is done, we will set it back to IsBusy = false. Let's implement our OnLoginAsync method starting with a simple implementation focusing on the core usage of the AuthenticationService. We will then add logging and error handling. Add the code seen in Listing 11-50.

Listing 11-50. Simple implementation of authentication in LoginViewModel

```
async Task OnLoginAsync()
{
  IsBusy = true;
  Logger.LogInformation("Login tapped or clicked");

  var authenticationResult = authentication.AcquireTokenAsync();
  if (authenticationResult == null ||
    string.IsNullOrEmpty(authenticationResult.AccessToken))
  {
    // TODO - handle no result
  }
  else
  {
    ((App)App.Current).AuthenticationResult =
      authenticationResult;

    navigation.NavigateToDashboard();
  }

  IsBusy = false;
}
```

We put all the hard authentication code into the `AuthenticationService`; it makes our implementation here relatively simple. All we do is acquire the token and then navigate to the main dashboard if we get a valid token back.

Let's add some logging to this code to help us diagnose issues. We may get no `AuthenticationResult` if there is no Internet connection or the user cancels the login. If a user cancels the token acquisition, this is not an error that needs to be displayed to the user. If they don't have Internet connection, we should display a message to the user. Update the null check if block to contain logging and set the `Message` object. See code in Listing 11-51.

Listing 11-51. Handle null access token in LoginViewModel

```
logger.LogError(
  "Unable to retrieve Access Token from Azure Active Directory");

if (networkService.Connectivity !=
  NetworkConnectivityLevel.InternetAccess
{
  logger.LogInformation(
    "NO INTERNET CONNECTION: Internet required to " +
     "retrieve an Access Token for the first time");

   Message = "No Internet, try again after connecting.";
}
```

Now we can add exception handling to handle any exceptions that may be thrown by the `AcquireTokenAsync` method. Earlier we intentionally left out exception handling so we can display messages to the user interface. Let's wrap the bulk of the work in a try-catch block and handle `MsalException` and `Exception`. See exception handling code in Listing 11-52.

Listing 11-52. Exception handling in LoginViewModel

```
catch (MsalException msalException)
{
  logger.LogError(msalException, msalException.Message);
```

```
    Message = msalException.Message;
}
catch (Exception exception)
{
    logger.LogError(exception, exception.Message);
    Message = "Unable to sign-in, try again or check logs";
}
```

The last thing we will do is move the IsBusy = true to be in the finally block. This will ensure that it will always reset the screen status even if there is an issue. See the complete code for all the changes in the LoginViewModel in Listing 11-53.

Listing 11-53. Completed OnLoginAsync code

```
async Task OnLoginAsync()
{
    IsBusy = true;
    Logger.LogInformation("Login tapped or clicked");

    try
    {
        var authenticationResult = await
            authentication.AcquireTokenAsync();

        if (authenticationResult == null ||
            string.IsNullOrEmpty(authenticationResult.Accesstoken))
        {
            logger.LogError(
                "Unable to retrieve Access Token from Azure " +
                "Active Directory");

            if (networkService.Connectivity !=
                NetworkConnectivityLevel.InternetAccess
            {
                logger.LogCritical(
                    "NO INTERNET CONNECTION: Internet required to " +
                    "retrieve an Access Token for the first time");

                Message = "No Internet, try again after connecting.";
```

```
        }
      }
      else
      {
        logger.LogInformation(
          "Authentication successful, navigating to dashboard");

        ((App)App.Current).AuthenticationResult =
          authenticationResult;

        navigation.NavigateToDashboard();
      }
    }
    catch (MsalException msalException)
    {
      logger.LogError(msalException, msalException.Message);
      Message = msalException.Message;
    }
    catch (Exception exception)
    {
      logger.LogError(exception, exception.Message);
      Message = "Unable to sign-in, try again or check logs";
    }
    finally
    {
      IsBusy = false;
    }
}
```

The business rules are complete for the LoginViewModel. The last thing we need
to implement is the sign-out logic from the Dashboard. In Chapter 10 we configured
the sign-out logic to return the user to the LoginPage. This is all controlled in the
NavigationService. This means we can inject the IAuthenticationService into the
NavigationService and trigger the sign-out logic from there.

Let's start by updating the constructor to NavigationService and inject the
IAuthenticationService. See code in Listing 11-54 for the updated constructor code.

Listing 11-54. Added IAuthenticationService to the NavigationService constructor

```
public class NavigationService : INavigationService
{
  IAuthenticationService authentication;
  public NavigationService(IAuthenticationService authentication)
  {
    this.authentication = authentication;
  }

  // omitted code
}
```

Looking at our API structure between the `INavigationService` and the `IAuthenticationService,` we have navigation using synchronous APIs and authentication using asynchronous APIs. To get the service implemented correctly, we will need to update the `INavigationService` method signature for `SignOut` to be `SignOutAsync` and return a `Task` – see code in Listing 11-55 for updated interface declaration.

Listing 11-55. INavigationService.SignOutAsync declaration

```
Task SignOutAsync();
```

To update the implementation in the `NavigationService`, we will need to invoke the `IAuthenticationService.SignOutAsync()` method just before we perform the navigation. This will clear out the local data in MSAL and require the user to sign in again. See code in Listing 11-56 for updated implementation.

Listing 11-56. NavigationService.SignOutAsync implementation

```
public async Task SignOutAsync()
{
  await authentication.SignOutAsync();
  GetRootFrame().Navigate(typeof(LoginPage), this);
}
```

Note   When signing out, MSAL will remove authentication and authorization information from its local cache. If you have downloaded any data and cached it such as files from OneDrive, you may need to manually remove those.

This new API signature has created a breaking change. We will need to update the Dashboard.xaml.cs event handler of MenuItemSelected to use the new API. An event handler does not return a Task, and there is no method overload for this. You can simply add the keyword async void in place of void to use async methods. See updated event handler code in Listing 11-57.

Listing 11-57. Updated Dashboard.MenuItemSelected event handler to use new navigation API

```
async void MenuItemSelected(
  NavigationView sender,
  NavigationViewItemInvokedEventArgs args)
{
  if (signOut == args.InvokedItemContainer)
  {
    await navigation.SignOutAsync();
    return;
  }

  // omitted code
}
```

Caution   Using async void can be dangerous as it does not save the context of the Task. If you try using an inheritance tree with the event handler, you will lose the state of the current Task. It is available in the language for this exact usage in the event handler scenario. Whenever possible use async Task.

Test Authentication

We have finished implementing our authentication using Azure Active Directory for all the platforms in our project. Now we can run the application and see how it looks in the various platforms. The authentication flow is almost identical, but some platforms open the Azure Active Directory login page slightly differently.

Windows

Launch the application using the Windows target by selecting `UnoDrive.Windows` as your startup project. Once the application launches, when you click the login button, a window will pop up asking you to use your Microsoft account. See Figure 11-14.

Figure 11-14. *Windows – Microsoft login to Azure Active Directory*

Use your Microsoft account and attempt to sign on. The next page will ask the user if the application can have permission to their data. This page can be branded to your application, and all of it is controlled in the Azure Active Directory app registration portal. See the permission request page in Figure 11-15.

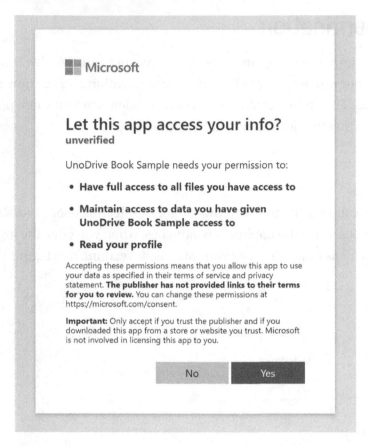

Figure 11-15. *Windows – Active Directory permission authorization page*

Once you authorize the application to access your data, you will be logged in and brought to the Dashboard page. If you go and sign out and sign back in again or from a different device, you won't need to authorize again. You only ever need to authorize permission once for any particular app.

Note   The authorization screen seen in Figure 11-15 is a one-time authorization. We will not see it in the other platforms for our testing as we have already authorized the application to access our data. To reset the authorization, you need to log in to your Microsoft account.

WebAssembly (WASM)

To test the WebAssembly (WASM) target, select UnoDrive.Wasm as your startup project. Once the application launches in the web browser, click the login button to trigger the Microsoft login page. A new browser window will open up that is requesting your login – see Figure 11-16.

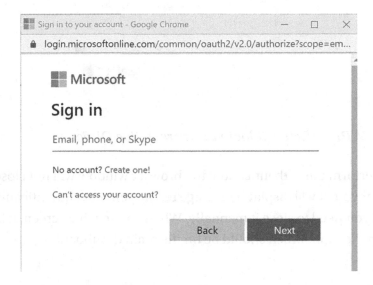

Figure 11-16. *WebAssembly (WASM) – Microsoft login to Azure Active Directory*

Upon clicking the Next button, Azure Active Directory will process your authentication attempt, and if successful it will bring you to the main dashboard page.

WPF

To test WPF you will select the `UnoDrive.Skia.Wpf` project as your startup project. Once the application launches, you can click the Next button to start the Azure Active Directory authentication. WPF will not open a popup like the other targets so far; it will open a full web browser session to launch the authentication. See the WPF Azure Active Directory authentication screen in Figure 11-17.

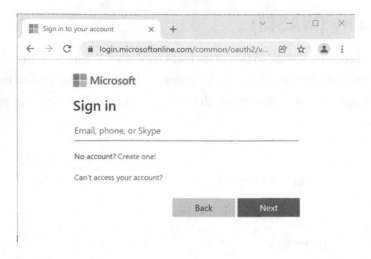

Figure 11-17. *WPF – Microsoft login to Azure Active Directory*

Once you perform the authentication, the browser window will not close automatically for you. It will display a message telling you that authentication was successful, and you need to close it manually. When you see that screen, it is safe to open up your WPF application, which should be on the main dashboard page.

GTK

To test GTK you will select `UnoDrive.Skia.Gtk` as your startup project. We have been running it within Windows Subsystem for Linux (WSL), so when you click the login button, it will open a browser in the host Windows machine and not the Linux browser. If we were running this natively on a Linux machine it, would open the native browser. To fully test this experience, in the screenshot in Figure 11-18, I have opened a browser through Linux.

Proceed with testing the GTK platform by clicking the login button. You will see the Microsoft login page for Azure Active Directory as seen in Figure 11-18. Once you successfully log in, the browser will display a success message. Just like in the WPF target, the GTK target will not automatically close the browser window. Once you close it and reopen the application, it will be loaded to the dashboard page.

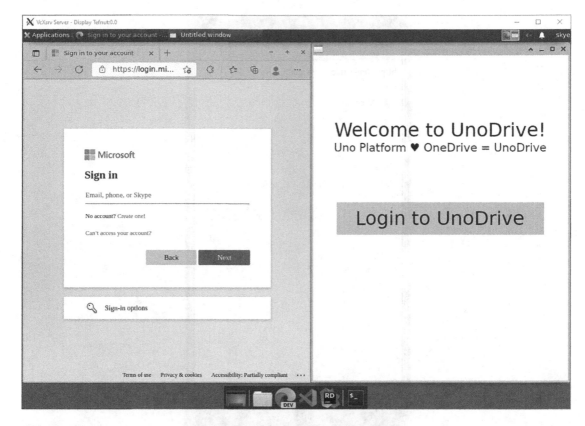

Figure 11-18. GTK – Microsoft login to Azure Active Directory

Android

Next, select UnoDrive.Mobile as your startup project and launch the application into your connected Android device. Once the application loads, click the login button to start the Azure Active Directory login flow. In Android everything happens seamlessly inside the application, which creates a very nice user experience. See Figure 11-19 for the login screen on Android.

Figure 11-19. *Android – Microsoft login to Azure Active Directory*

iOS

To test iOS ensure you are connected to your Mac agent and select UnoDrive.Moble as your startup project. Once the application loads, click the login button to start the Azure Active Directory login flow. Just like Android the iOS login flow is a seamless integration all within the application.

When the user clicks the login button, iOS will request two permission pages: application permission from the operating system and Azure Active Directory permission that is consistent with all the platforms. See Figure 11-20 for the iOS permission and Figure 11-21 for the iOS login.

Figure 11-20. *iOS – application permission for sign-in*

In Figure 11-20 you see a modal with string UnoDrive.iOS, which is the name of your app bundle. This can be configured by the name that you package your iOS application as. As for the string "microsoftonline.com," that comes directly from Azure AD.

Figure 11-21. *iOS – Microsoft login to Azure Active Directory*

After completing the permission pages and logging in using Azure Active Directory, the user will be brought to the main dashboard of the application.

macOS

To test macOS you will need to run the application from Visual Studio for Mac. Select UnoDrive.Mobile as your startup project and select the Mac as the device to run on. Once the application launches, click the login button to start the Azure Active Directory authentication flow. Like iOS and Android the integration is seamless into the application. See Figure 11-22 for macOS login.

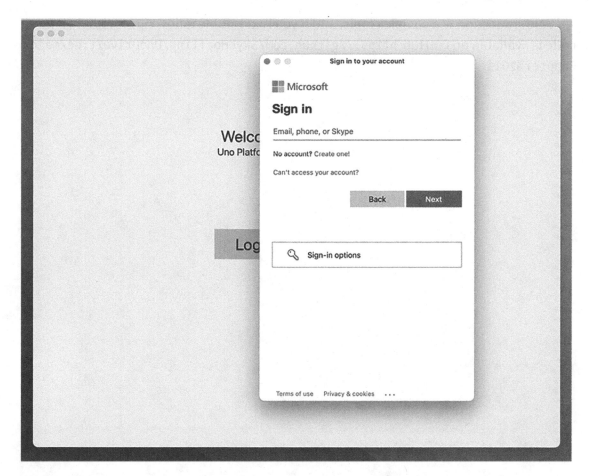

Figure 11-22. *macOS – Microsoft login to Azure Active Directory*

After completing the login process, the user will be brought to the main dashboard of the application.

Conclusion

In this chapter we did a deep dive into implementing authentication with Microsoft's Azure Active Directory as the authentication provider. At this point you should have a working application that allows you to authenticate with your Microsoft account. We will be building on these concepts in the next chapter as we learn how to use our access token for requesting data from the Microsoft Graph.

Authentication is a complex topic, and if you had trouble following along, all of the code is available on GitHub: `https://github.com/SkyeHoefling/UnoDrive/tree/main/Chapter%2011`.

CHAPTER 12

Converters

In Chapter 8 we introduced the Model-View-ViewModel application design, which includes the concept of data binding, a technique used to bind public properties from your ViewModel to various properties of a user interface control that resides in the View or page. In many cases the properties exposed by the ViewModel do not match the properties that are to be shown on the user interface control. This is when you would want to consider using a converter.

A converter is a special type of data binding that takes in the source value from the ViewModel and converts it to a target value that can be used by the user interface control. A common example of this is managing Visibility state. The ViewModel may have state controlled by a true or false bool value, where the user interface control will use the Visibility object. This will require a converter that will convert the data from bool to Visibility. When the value is bound using the converter, the control will have the correct value of Visibility set. This is because the code in the converter will provide the mapping to Visibility.

The usage of converters requires one extra step in the data binding syntax in your XAML code. Let's consider an example to illustrate how this works in practice. Consider a property on the ViewModel named MyValue. To perform the data binding in the View, you would use a simple binding syntax of {Binding MyValue}. This will work fine if the user interface control's property is the same type as MyValue. To add a converter to this, you will specify the converter syntax inside the curly braces. In Listing 12-1 we assume our binding property is MyValue and the converter is registered as a static resource named MyConverter. See Listing 12-1 for the full binding example.

Listing 12-1. Basic converter example in data binding

```
{Binding MyValue, Converter={StaticResource MyConverter}}
```

© Skye Hoefling 2022
S. Hoefling, *Getting Started with the Uno Platform and WinUI 3*,
https://doi.org/10.1007/978-1-4842-8248-9_12

> **Note**   The binding markup extension allows you to specify many optional parameters. In the case of converters, we simply add the comma and specify the keyword `Converter` to tell the binding system we want to use a converter.

How Does It Work?

To create a converter, you must have an object that implements the `IValueConverter` interface. The application won't know how to convert the object from one type to the next until you write the implementation. The interface defines all possible parameters that are available for converters. It is common to not need all the additional parameters, but they are there in case you need them. See Listing 12-2 for the interface contract.

> **Note**   In an application that needs localization, the language parameter of the `IValueConverter` from Listing 12-2 can be used to define what language to use in the `Converter`.

Listing 12-2. IValueConverter contract

```
public interface IValueConverter
{
  object Convert(
    object value,
    Type targetType,
    object parameters,
    string language);

  object ConvertBack(
    object value,
    Type targetType,
    object parameter,
    string language);
}
```

Once you have a converter that implements this interface, you will need to add it as a StaticResource to your styles. See Listing 12-3 for a simple usage.

Listing 12-3. Converter declaration example for a converter named MyCustomConverter

```
<converters:MyCustomConverter x:Key="MyCustomConverter" />
```

This could be global or for the specific page or control you would like to use it on. Once you have added the style, you can then use the syntax we saw in Listing 12-1 to add the converter to our page.

Create the Converters

We need to add two converters that we will be using in Chapter 14. The goal of this chapter is to create our building blocks that will be needed later.

Here are the converters we will be creating:

- *IsEmptyToVisibilityConverter*: Converts an empty or null string to Visibility

- *BoolToVisibilityConverter*: Converts a bool value to Visibility

These converters are both useful when determining a user interface control's Visibility state – in other words, if it can be seen by the user or not.

IsEmptyToVisibilityConverter

We want to convert a string value to Visibility by testing if the string is null or empty. Then we can determine if we want the user interface control to be Visible or Collapsed. The converter needs to be designed in a way that supports both outcomes: if the string is not empty or empty, it can be Visible or Collapsed.

In the UnoDrive.Shared project, create a new folder called "Converters." This is where we will be placing all our converter code files. Inside the new directory, create a new C# class file named IsEmptyToVisibilityConverter.cs. See Figure 12-1 for what the Visual Studio Solution Explorer should look like.

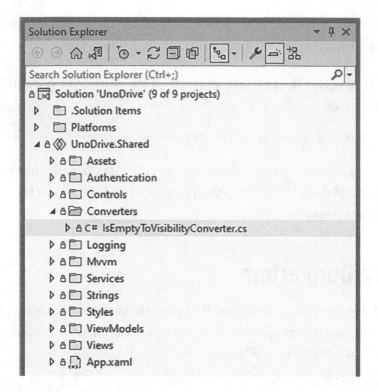

Figure 12-1. *Visual Studio Solution Explorer for IsEmptyToVisibilityConverter.cs*

In the code file, you can stub out the interface with our basic implementation that gives us the structure that we will be working with. See Listing 12-4 for the stubbed-out implementation.

Listing 12-4. Stubbed implementation of IsEmptyToVisibilityConverter

```
public class IsEmptyToVisibilityConverter : IValueConverter
{
  public object Convert(object value, Type targetType,
    object parameter, string language)
  {
    // TODO - Add implementation
  }

  public object CoverterBack(object value, Type targetType,
    object parameters, string language)
  {
```

```
    throw new NotSupportedException();
  }
}
```

In our preceding code, we are intentionally throwing a NotSupportedException in the attempt to ConvertBack. There is no way for us to take the converted value of Visibility and convert it back to a string. In this scenario it is best to throw an exception.

Tip   It is a good idea to create both implementations of Convert and ConvertBack for IValueConverter. This will allow your application to use more complex data binding techniques such as two-way binding. This goes out of scope of this chapter.

Add two properties above the Convert method to store the Visibility values for our two cases: IsEmpty and IsNotEmpty. See Listing 12-5 for property definitions.

Listing 12-5. Property definitions for IsEmpty and IsNotEmpty in IsEmptyToVisibilityConverter

```
public Visibility IsEmpty { get; set; }
public Visibility IsNotEmpty { get; set; }
```

When defining the converter in XAML, this will allow you to specify what Visibility should be returned given the input value is an empty string vs. a non-empty string. You can reference Listing 12-3 for a sample.

To implement the Convert API, you will only need to worry about the first parameter of value. First, cast it to a string, and then you can use the string.IsNullOrEmpty() API to determine which property created in Listing 12-5 to return. See Listing 12-6 for completed Convert code.

Listing 12-6. Convert implementation for IsEmptyToVisibilityConverter

```
public object Convert(object value, Type targetType,
  object parameter, string language)
{
  if (value is string message)
```

```
  {
    return string.IsNullOrEmpty(message) ? IsEmpty : IsNotEmpty;
  }
  else
  {
    return Visibility.Collapsed;;
  }
}
```

Note   In Listing 12-6 we are using a ternary operator, which is the same as an if-else block. It allows us to make our if statement be on one line of code. The property after the question mark character (?) is the true value, and the property after the colon character (:) is the false value.

Our converter implementation for IsEmptyToVisiblityConverter is complete. You can see the complete converter code in Listing 12-7.

Listing 12-7. Complete implementation for IsEmptyToVisibilityConverter

```
public class IsEmptyToVisibilityConverter : IValueConverter
{
  public Visibility IsEmpty { get; set; }
  public Visibility IsNotEmpty { get; set; }

  public object Convert(object value, Type targetType,
    object parameter, string language)
  {
    if (value is string message)
    {
      return string.IsNullOrEmpty(message) ?
        IsEmpty : IsNotEmpty;
    }
    else
    {
      return Visibility.Collapsed;;
```

```
    }
  }

  public object CoverterBack(object value, Type targetType,
    object parameters, string language)
  {
    throw new NotSupportedException();
  }
}
```

BoolToVisibilityConverter

The BoolToVisibilityConverter is very similar to the IsEmptyToVisibilityConvert except it is going to be converting a bool value instead of a string. To get started first create a new code file in the UnoDrive.Shared project under the Converters folder named BoolToVisibilityConverter.cs. See Figure 12-2 for the Visual Studio Solution Explorer with the new code file.

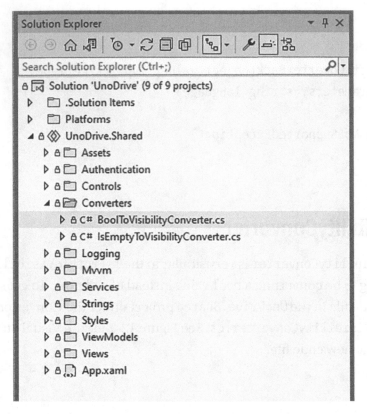

Figure 12-2. *Visual Studio Solution Explorer for BoolToVisibilityConverter.cs*

Next, you will open the code file and create a stubbed implementation of IValueConverter. See Listing 12-8 for the stubbed implementation.

Listing 12-8. Stubbed implementation of BoolToVisibilityConverter

```csharp
public class BoolToVisibilityConverter : IValueConverter
{
  public object Convert(object value, Type targetType,
    object parameter, string language)
  {
    // TODO - Add implementation
  }

  public object CoverterBack(object value, Type targetType,
    object parameters, string language)
  {
```

```
      throw new NotSupportedException();
  }
}
```

Since we need to handle both a positive and negative Visibility in this converter, just like in the other converter, create two properties to manage the TrueValue and FalseValue. See Listing 12-9 for property definitions.

Listing 12-9. Property definitions for TrueValue and FalseValue in BoolToVisibilityConverter

```
public Visibility TrueValue { get; set; }
public Visibility FalseValue { get; set; }
```

Now we can implement the Convert API. First, cast the input parameter of value to a bool, and then we can check if it is true or false and return the correct property defined in Listing 12-9. See Listing 12-10 for the implementation of the Convert API.

Listing 12-10. Convert implementation for BoolToVisibilityConverter

```
public object Convert(object value, Type targetType,
  object parameter, string language)
{
  bool boolValue = value is bool && (bool)value;
  return boolValue ? TrueValue : FalseValue;
}
```

The converter is now completed. You can see the completed BoolToVisibilityConverter implementation in Listing 12-11.

Listing 12-11. Complete implementation for BoolToVisibilityConverter

```
public class BoolToVisibilityConverter : IValueConverter
{
  public Visibility TrueValue { get; set; }
  public Visibility FalseValue { get; set; }

  public object Convert(object value, Type targetType,
    object parameter, string language)
```

```
  {
    bool boolValue = value is bool && (bool)value;
    return boolValue ? TrueValue : FalseValue;
  }

  public object CoverterBack(object value, Type targetType,
    object parameters, string language)
  {
    throw new NotSupportedException();
  }
}
```

Add Converters to Global Styles

In the previous section, we created our two converters IsEmptyToVisibilityConverter and BoolToVisibilityConverter. In this section we are going to add them to the global styles so we can start using them in any of the application pages. In Chapter 4 we created the building blocks for our application styles. We are going to build upon the concepts we learned to add the converters to our styles.

In the UnoDrive.Shared project, add a new XAML file under Styles ➤ Application named Converters.xaml. See Figure 12-3 for what the Visual Studio Solution Explorer should look like.

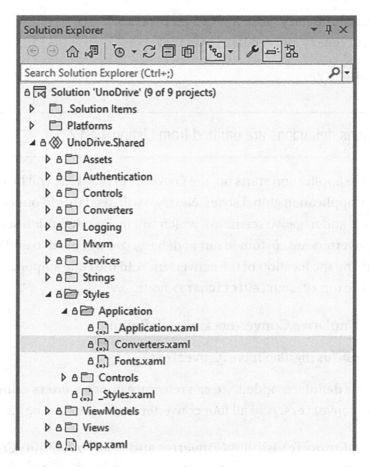

Figure 12-3. *Visual Studio Solution Explorer for Converters.xaml*

Placing the Converters.xaml file in the Application folder means it is a global application-wide style as opposed to a control-specific style. With any new application style file, we need to update the _Application.xaml to properly load it. See completed code in Listing 12-12.

Listing 12-12. Completed _Application.xaml code

```
<ResourceDictionary>

  <ResourceDictionary.MergedDictionaries>
    <XamlControlsResources
      xmlns="using:Microsoft.UI.Xaml.Controls" />
      <ResourceDictionary Source="Fonts.xaml" />
```

```
<ResourceDictionary Source="Converters.xaml" />
  </ResourceDictionary.MergedDictionaries>

</ResourceDictionary>
```

Note   The xmlns definitions are omitted from Listing 12-12.

Now, when the application starts up, the `Converters.xaml` file will be loaded correctly into the application global styles. Next, we will need to add our converters and both their positive and negative scenarios, which will be four definition statements.

Since our converters are custom to our codebase, you will need to add a new xmlns definition specifying the location of the converters. Add the code snippet from Listing 12-13 to the top `<ResourceDictionary>` node.

Listing 12-13. UnoDrive.Converters xmlns definition

```
xmlns:converters="using:UnoDrive.Converters"
```

With the xmlns definition added, we can reference our converters using the local variable name of `converters`. Add all four converters as seen in Listing 12-14.

Listing 12-14. IsEmptyToVisibilityConverter and BoolToVisibilityConverter statements

```
<converters:IsEmptyToVisibilityConverter
  x:Key="IsEmptyEqualsVisibileConverter"
  IsEmpty="Visible" IsNotEmpty="Collapsed" />

<converters:IsEmptyToVisibilityConverter
  x:Key="IsEmptyEqualsCollapsedConverter"
  IsEmpty="Collapsed" IsNotEmpty="Visible" />

<converters:BoolToVisibilityConverter
  x:Key="BoolToVisibilityConverter"
  TrueValue="Visible" FalseValue="Collapsed" />
```

```
<converters:BoolToVisibilityConverter
  x:Key="BoolNegationToVisibilityConverter"
  TrueValue="Collapsed" FalseValue="Visible" />
```

In the previous section where we defined our converters, we built them in a way so we can specify the `Visibility` for the `TrueValue` vs. `FalseValue` or the `IsEmpty` vs. `IsNotEmpty`. This allows us to create two instances of each to cover all our uses.

Usage

With the converters defined and added to our global application styles, we are ready to start using them. We will be using these converters in more real-world scenarios in Chapter 14, but the examples in this section are helpful to understand how they will be used.

Consider you have a property in the ViewModel called `IsBusy` and when it is true data is loading and when it is false data is no longer loading. In this scenario we may want to display a `ProgressRing` to denote to the user that data is loading. We can use our data binding with the converter to properly render the `ProgressRing` only when data is loading. See Listing 12-15 for a code sample.

Listing 12-15. Example of data binding BoolToVisibilityConverter on a ProgressRing

```
<ProgressRing
  Visibility="{Binding IsBusy,
    Converter={StaticResource BoolToVisibilityConverter}}" />
```

Note   When using a static resource as we are with the converters, you must always use the x:Key for the converter and not the object name. The converter is added to the style via the key in the ResourceDictionary. If you don't use the key, it will not know where to find the converter.

Conclusion

In this chapter we created some basic converters that can be used in combination with data binding to map a bound value type to another type that is needed in the user interface control. We are going to be using the converters we implemented here in Chapter 14.

Converters from third-party libraries such as NuGet packages are very easy to use. Many of the basic converters are available in projects like the Windows Community Toolkit. The converters from that project can easily be used in any Uno Platform project.

If you had any trouble following the code, you can find all the code available on GitHub at https://github.com/SkyeHoefling/UnoDrive/tree/main/Chapter%2012.

CHAPTER 13

Microsoft Graph, Web APIs, and MyFilesPage

The Microsoft Graph is the API we are going to use to communicate with Microsoft OneDrive to retrieve files and folders in our UnoDrive application. It is a RESTful API, which you can integrate with using any language, that provides read and write access to many Microsoft services, including OneDrive.

In this chapter we will be building on the authentication concepts that we learned in Chapter 11. Upon successfully logging into the application, you will have a stored access token that can be used for any Microsoft Graph API request. We will be creating the building blocks of our main user interface by implementing the Microsoft Graph integration. By the end of this chapter, we will have a full implementation that displays some items on the screen retrieved from OneDrive. This will be a basic implementation, and we will be expanding on these concepts in future chapters.

Microsoft Graph

The Microsoft Graph (the Graph) is the best way to integrate with various Microsoft services including Office 365, OneDrive, and many more. It provides a central RESTful API that applications of any language and platform can integrate with. Prior to using the Graph, you will need to obtain a valid access token, which is usually done using the Microsoft Authentication Library also, known as MSAL. When authenticating you will request scopes to gain access to various endpoints on the Graph. The authentication concepts have already been covered in Chapter 11.

© Skye Hoefling 2022
S. Hoefling, *Getting Started with the Uno Platform and WinUI 3*,
https://doi.org/10.1007/978-1-4842-8248-9_13

Our UnoDrive application is an introduction to the Microsoft Graph and what you can do with it. You can learn more about it and what you can do by going to the official Microsoft documentation: `https://docs.microsoft.com/graph/overview`. If you want to explore the Graph, you can use the Graph Explorer tool, which allows you to make API calls right from the sandbox tool: `https://developer.microsoft.com/graph/graph-explorer`.

Web APIs and Uno Platform

In Uno Platform integrating with a simple Web API is very straightforward. At the basic level, you will need to create an `HttpClient` and specify your address and any headers.

Consider a basic request that tries to read data at `https://localhost/api/`. See the standard integration in Listing 13-1.

Listing 13-1. Standard HttpClient implementation

```
string url = "https://localhost/api/";
HttpClient client = new HttpClient();
HttpResponseMessage response = await client.GetAsync(url);
```

Graph Service Implementation

As we build our Microsoft Graph and user interface in this chapter, we are going to work from the bottom up. This means we will start by implementing the necessary service code and finish with the user interface code.

Add NuGet Packages

The Microsoft Graph SDK is a NuGet package that we can include in all our project heads and is the first step in implementing any integration. Add the code from Listing 13-2 to all of your project heads: `UnoDrive.Windows`, `UnoDrive.Wasm`, `UnoDrive.Skia.Wpf`, `UnoDrive.Skia.Gtk`, and `UnoDrive.Mobile`.

Listing 13-2. Microsoft.Graph NuGet package reference

```
<PackageReference
  Include="Microsoft.Graph"
  Version="4.32.0" />
```

The WebAssembly (WASM) target needs updates to the LinkerConfig.xml; otherwise, certain APIs may be removed at compile time. Add the code from Listing 13-3 to your LinkerConfig.xml.

Listing 13-3. WebAssembly (WASM) LinkerConfig.xml updates for the Microsoft. Graph NuGet package

```
<assembly fullname="Microsoft.Graph" />
<assembly fullname="Microsoft.Graph.Core" />
```

Note   The linker is a compile-time tool that runs on various platforms to remove unused APIs, which keeps the generated assembly size small. By adding the Microsoft Graph assemblies to the LinkerConfig.xml, it prevents those APIs from being removed. This is specifically important for WASM as the first load of the application requires the assembly to be downloaded. The smaller it is, the faster the application will load.

Data Models

The data models, also known as entities, store the resulting data used in the Microsoft Graph. We will have our own data structure that we will map the results of the APIs to. These data models will be the return type on our implementation of our service integration. This helps create a clean separation between the Microsoft Graph SDK and our implementation. In our case this is valuable as we don't need all the data being returned from the SDK. Creating the data model allows us to have only properties that our application needs.

We need to capture two types of data models: an item type and item details. In the UnoDrive.Shared project, create a new root directory named Data. In that new folder, you will create two new classes named OneDriveItem.cs and OneDriveItemType.cs. See Figure 13-1 for a screenshot of the Visual Studio solution Explorer.

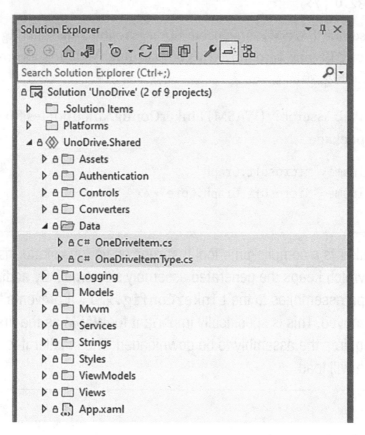

Figure 13-1. *Data models in the Visual Studio Solution Explorer*

The OneDriveItemType is a simple data model that is an enum that only stores if the item is a file or a folder. An enum is a useful structure in .NET that allows you to define a set of constants that can be strongly type-checked.

Note   .NET enums or enumerations are very useful when you have an object that needs type-checking. By encapsulating the enum values, other parts of your application can quickly check the enum values to determine various business rules and code paths.

Implement the OneDriveItemType by using the code in Listing 13-4.

Listing 13-4. OneDriveItemType implementation

```
public enum OneDriveItemType
{
  File = 0,
  Folder = 1
}
```

The OneDriveItem will store details about a specific item, which can be either a folder or a file. The OneDriveItem will encapsulate the OneDriveItemType we just defined along with other properties we will need later in the service implementation. See the full code for the OneDriveItem in Listing 13-5.

Listing 13-5. OneDriveItem implementation

```
public class OneDriveItem
{
  public string Id { get; set; }
  public string Name { get; set; }
  public string Path { get; set; }
  public string PathId { get; set; }
  public DateTime Modified { get; set; }
  public string FileSize { get; set; }
  public OneDriveItemType Type { get; set; }
  public ImageSource ThumbnailSource { get; set; }
}
```

.NET 6 Mobile Data Models

In .NET 6 there are special target frameworks for the various mobile targets such as net6.0-android, net6.0-ios, net6.0-maccatalyst, net6.0-macos, and others. The backward compatibility layer for the .NET Standard with these target frameworks is very thin. If you are using a third-party package that isn't specifically compiled for your target framework, specifically the mobile targets of .NET 6, you may get runtime errors. These errors can be hidden in very obscure error messages.

This section focuses on issues that may still happen in the Microsoft.Graph SDK or other similar libraries you are using. It is best to get a compiled binary for your specific target framework to avoid these problems. For example, if you are using net6.0-android, ensure your binary has been compiled for net6.0-android specifically.

Prior to the release of .NET 6 for mobile targets, the Microsoft.Graph SDK didn't fully support using it. When querying some of the APIs, you would see the error message in Listing 13-6.

Listing 13-6. .NET 6 mobile exception with backward compatibility issues

```
System.TypeLoadException: Could not resolve type with
  token 01000023 from typeref (expected class
  'System.Threading.Tasks.ValueTask`1' in assembly 'mscorlib,
  Version=2.0.5.0, Culture=neutral,
  PublicKeyToken=7cec85d7bea7798e')
```

This exception is unable to find a necessary object at runtime that the SDK depends on, which caused the runtime error.

The Microsoft Graph is a series of RESTful endpoints that return JSON strings of serialized data. To work around this problem, we can take the raw object and deserialize it manually instead of using the Microsoft.Graph SDK. We can write platform-specific code to handle this situation vs. using the objects directly from the SDK.

Caution   It is always best to use the third-party package the way it was intended to be used. If it doesn't natively support your target framework, this is a valid workaround.

In the `UnoDrive.Shared` project under the `Data` directory, create five new files:

- `DriveItem.android.ios.macos.cs`: Listing 13-8

- `DriveItemCollection.android.ios.macos.cs`: Listing 13-9

- `Folder.android.ios.macos.cs`: Listing 13-10

- `Thumbnail.android.ios.macos.cs`: Listing 13-11

- `ThumbnailImage.android.ios.macos.cs`: Listing 13-12

We only create data models for the mobile target frameworks because those will require manual invocations of the RESTful API. As we create the various data models that are needed, we will try and leverage the objects directly from the SDK when possible. It is not always possible to derserialize straight to the object.

Important   For each file created in this section, you will need to add the pre-processor directive for the platforms supported. Wrap the entire file in #if __ ANDROID__ || __IOS__ || __MACOS__. This needs to be done for Listings 13-8 through 13-12.

The DriveItem object is our top-level OneDrive object that contains specific details about the item, which can be a file or folder. See code in Listing 13-7.

Listing 13-7. DriveItem implementation

```
public class DriveItem
{
  [JsonPropertyName("id")]
  public string Id { get; set; }

  [JsonPropertyName("name")]
  public string Name { get; set; }

  [JsonPropertyName("parentReference")]
  public ItemReference ParentReference { get; set; }

  [JsonPropertyName("size")]
  public Int64? Size { get; set; }

  [JsonPropertyName("lastModifiedDateTime")]
  public DateTimeOffset? LastModifiedDateTime { get; set; }

  [JsonPropertyName("thumbnails")]
  public Thumbnail[] Thumbnails { get; set; }

  [JsonPropertyName("folder")]
  public Folder Folder { get; set; }
}
```

The DriveItemCollection is used when the SDK is returning a collection of DriveItem objects. Since the DriveItem defines one specific item, the DriveItemCollection is useful to see all the items in the current path. See code in Listing 13-8.

Listing 13-8. DriveItemCollection implementation

```
public class DriveItemCollection
{
    [JsonPropertyName("value")]
    public DriveItem[] Value { get; set; }
}
```

The Folder object details how many children exist in that folder. See code in Listing 13-9.

Listing 13-9. Folder implementation

```
public class Folder
{
    [JsonPropertyName("childCount")]
    public Int32? ChildCount { get; set; }
}
```

The Thumbnail object contains various ThumbnailImage objects, which are used for various sizes. This is useful when you want to display a large vs. medium vs. small thumbnail image. See code in Listing 13-10.

Listing 13-10. Thumbnail implementation

```
public class Thumbnail
{
    [JsonPropertyName("id")]
    public string Id { get; set; }

    [JsonPropertyName("large")]
    public ThumbnailImage Large { get; set; }
```

```
[JsonPropertyName("medium")]
public ThumbnailImage Medium { get; set; }

[JsonPropertyName("small")]
public ThumbnailImage Small { get; set; }
}
```

The ThumbnailImage contains the details of the image and a URL to download the file. See code in Listing 13-11.

Listing 13-11. ThumbnailImage implementation

```
public class ThumbnailImage
{
  [JsonPropertyName("height")]
  public int Height { get; set; }

  [JsonPropertyName("width")]
  public int Width { get; set; }

  [JsonPropertyName("url")]
  public string Url { get; set; }
}
```

GraphFileService Interface

The Microsoft Graph implementation will be used in our Dependency Injection system so we can inject a simple interface to be used in the view models. There are two APIs that need to be implemented:

- GetRootFilesAsync: Returns the items in the root OneDrive path

- GetFilesAsync: Returns the items by a specified unique ID

In the UnoDrive.Shared project under the Services folder, create a new file named IGraphFileService.cs. This will be the interface definition for our graph implementation. See code in Listing 13-12 for the interface definition.

Listing 13-12. IGraphFileService interface definition

```
public interface IGraphFileService
{
  Task<IEnumerable<OneDriveItem>> GetRootFilesAsync();
  Task<IEnumerable<OneDriveItem>> GetFilesAsync();
}
```

Note   The IGraphFileService interface defines a return type object of OneDriveItem. This is the data model that we defined earlier in the chapter.

GraphFileService: Stubs

All the building blocks are in place for us to implement the GraphFileService. This class will contain the code that invokes Web APIs against the Microsoft Graph, which will allow us to integrate with OneDrive as we build out our UnoDrive application.

Start by creating the basic class and stubbing out the methods from the IGraphFileService interface. In the UnoDrive.Shared project under the Services folder, create a new file named GraphFileService.cs. Open this file and add the code from Listing 13-13.

Listing 13-13. GraphFileService stubbed implementation

```
public class GraphFileService : IGraphFileService
{
  public async
    Task<IEnumerable<OneDriveItem>> GetRootFilesAsync()
  {
    // TODO - add implementation
  }
  public async
    Task<IEnumerable<OneDriveItem>> GetFilesAsync(string id)
```

```
    {
      // TODO - add implementation
    }
}
```

GraphFileService: AuthenticationProvider

The Microsoft Graph SDK requires an implementation of the IAuthenticationProvider interface. This interface provides an API that includes the HttpRequestMessage. This gives our GraphFileService implementation the necessary entry point to set the access token on any request. To implement this, we will make the GraphFileService implement IAuthenticationProvider and update the HttpRequestMessage. See the code in Listing 13-14.

Listing 13-14. GraphFileService IAuthenticationProvider implementation

```
public class GraphFileService :
  IGraphFileService, IAuthenticationProvider
{
  // omitted code

  Task IAuthenticationProvider.AuthenticateRequestAsync(
    HttpRequestMessage request)
  {
    string token = ((App)App.Current)
      .AuthenticationResult
      ?.AccessToken;

    if (string.IsNullOrEmpty(token))
    {
      throw new Exception("No Access Token");
    }

    request.Headers.Authorization =
      new AuthenticationHeaderValue("Bearer", token);
    return Task.CompletedTask;
  }
}
```

Note   In Listing 13-14 we retrieve the access token from the current session. This method will throw an exception if the user has not been authenticated. We are going to make the assumption that this class is only ever used after the user has performed authentication.

To finish the IAuthenticationProvider implementation, we need to add the constructor and a class instance of GraphServiceClient. This object will be used in the API implementations to send requests to the Micorosft Graph. We will also need to inject an instance of the ILogger interface so we can log errors as we implement the APIs. See Listing 13-15 for the constructor code.

Listing 13-15. GraphFileService constructor implementation

```
public class GraphFileService :
  IGraphFileService, IAuthenticationProvider
{
  GraphServiceClient graphClient;
  ILogger logger;

  public GraphFileService(ILogger<GraphFileService> logger)
  {
    this.logger = logger;

    var httpClient = new HttpClient();

    graphClient = new GraphServiceClient(httpClient);
    graphClient.AuthenticationProvider = this;
  }

  // omitted code
}
```

To connect our GraphFileService implementation to the Microsoft.Graph SDK, we need to set the graphClient.AuthenticationProvider to be our current instance. This will then invoke our implementation of IAuthetnicationProvider as needed by the GraphServiceClient object.

GraphFileService: GetFilesAsync

Let's work on the implementation of GetFilesAsync(string id). The goal of this API is given a unique ID value, the method will return the items at that corresponding OneDrive location. Our implementation is broken into three parts:

1. Request OneDrive data.

2. Map data to an UnoDrive object.

3. Retrieve thumbnails and write to local storage.

Using the Microsoft.Graph SDK, we can request all children given a particular unique identifier. Start building your request as seen in Listing 13-16.

Listing 13-16. GraphFileService GetFilesAsync request builder

```
public async Task<IEnumerable<OneDriveItem>>
  GetFilesAsync(string id)
{
  var request = graphClient
    .Me
    .Drive
    .Items[id]
    .Children
    .Request()
    .Expand("thumbnails");
}
```

The code in Listing 13-16 goes through several APIs to get our request object. You start by using the Me API to access the current user. Then the Drive API tells the builder that you want OneDrive data. Items[id] denotes the specific drive path to look in. Children returns all the items in that specific drive path. Then Request() generates the request object that can be invoked. Finally, the Expand("thumbnails") ensures that thumbnail data is returned as it is optional.

Next, we can invoke the request and convert the results to an array. See Listing 13-17 for the invocation added to our code.

Listing 13-17. GraphFileService GetFilesAsync request invocation

```
public async Task<IEnumerable<OneDriveItem>>
  GetFilesAsync(string id)
{
  var request = graphClient
    .Me
    .Drive
    .Items[id]
    .Children
    .Request()
    .Expand("thumbnails");

  var oneDriveItems = (await request.GetAsync()).ToArray();
}
```

We now have all the OneDrive items for the specified unique ID that was provided as a parameter to GetFilesAsync. Let's take this data and map it from the SDK model to our UnoDrive model, which will be usable by our application. See updated code in Listing 13-18.

Listing 13-18. GraphFileService GetFilesAsync data mapping to the UnoDrive object

```
public async Task<IEnumerable<OneDriveItem>>
  GetFilesAsync(string id)
{
  var request = graphClient
    .Me
    .Drive
    .Items[id]
    .Children
    .Request()
    .Expand("thumbnails");

  var oneDriveItems = (await request.GetAsync()).ToArray();

  var childrenTable = oneDriveItems
    .Select(driveItem => new OneDriveItem
```

```
    {
      Id = driveItem.Id,
      Name = driveItem.Name,
      Path = driveItem.ParentReference.Path,
      PathId = driveItem.ParentReference.Id,
      FileSize = $"{driveItem.Size}",
      Modified = driveItem.LastModifiedDateTime.HasValue ?
        driveItem.LastModifiedDateTime.Value.LocalDateTime :
        DateTime.Now,
      Type = driveItem.Folder != null ?
        OneDriveItemType.Folder :
        OneDriveItemType.File
    })
    .OrderByDescending(item => item.Type)
    .ThenBy(item => item.Name)
    .ToDictionary(item => item.Id);
}
```

The goal of the object mapping code is to simplify the data structure so we can use it in our presentation layer. We do not need all the items in the Microsoft.Graph SDK object, and it makes it easier to access when we work in a flatter structure.

With our data mapped correctly to the UnoDrive object, we can now read the thumbnail data, which is another web request. Create a new private method named `StoreThumbnailsAsync(DriveItem[] oneDriveItems, IDictionary<string, OneDriveItem> childrenTable)`. This method will contain the logic for iterating through all the items at the current path, downloading and storing the thumbnail data so it can be used in our UnoDrive object.

The Microsoft.Graph SDK stores three types of thumbnails for each item: small, medium, and large. We are only going to be using the medium thumbnail as this works well across our various form factors. Our logic for the `StoreThumbnailsAsync` method is as follows:

1. Check for thumbnails.

2. Retrieve thumbnail data.

3. Save thumbnail bytes to disk.

4.   Update ImageSource on the UnoDrive object.

See Listing 13-19 for complete StoreThumbnailsAsync() code.

Listing 13-19. GraphFileService implementation for StoreThumbnailsAsync

```
async Task StoreThumbnailsAsync(
  DriveItem[] oneDriveItems,
  IDictionary<string, OneDriveItem> childrenTable)
{
  for (int index = 0; index < oneDriveItems.Length; index++)
  {
    var currentItem = oneDriveItems[index];
    var thumbnails = currentItem.Thumbnails?.FirstOrDefault();
    if (thumbnails == null ||
        !childrenTable.ContainsKey(currentItem.Id))
    {
      continue;
    }

    var url = thumbnails.Medium.Url;

    var httpClient = new HttpClient();

    var thumbnailResponse = await httpClient.GetAsync(url);
    if (!thumbnailResponse.IsSuccessStatusCode)
    {
      continue;
    }

    var imagesFolder = Path.Combine(
      Windows.Storage.ApplicationData.Current.LocalFolder.Path,
      "thumbnails");

    var name = $"{currentItem.Id}.jpeg";
    var localFilePath = Path.Combine(imagesFolder, name);

    try
```

```
    {
      if (!System.IO.Directory.Exists(imagesFolder))
      {
        System.IO.Directory.CreateDirectory(imagesFolder);
      }

      if (System.IO.File.Exists(localFilePath))
      {
        System.IO.File.Delete(localFilePath);
      }

      var bytes = await thumbnailResponse.Content
        .ReadAsByteArrayAsync();

      await System.IO.File.WriteAllBytesAsync(
        localFilePath, bytes);

      var image = new BitmapImage(new Uri(localFilePath));
      childrenTable[currentItem.Id].ThumbnailSource = image;
    }
    catch(Exception ex)
    {
      logger.LogError(ex, ex.Message);
    }
  }
}
```

The StoreThumbnailsAsync code is completed, and we can finish up our current implementation of GetFilesAsync. Since C# is passing the objects by reference to StoreThumbnailsAsync, the childrenTable does not need to be returned.

Note   When an object is passed by reference to another method, that means you retain the same object in memory. Any updates to that object within the scope of the method are persisted to the calling member. In other words, the changes that happen in StoreThumbnailsAsync are available to that object in the GetFilesAsync method.

We can take the current object and return it as we need to. It is currently in a dictionary form, and we need to convert it to a standard IEnumerable. Update your GetFilesAsync code to invoke the new method StoreThumbnailsAsync and return the final childrenTable. See the code snippet in Listing 13-20 and complete code in Listing 13-21.

Listing 13-20. GraphFileService GetFilesAsync StoreThumbnailsAsync and return data

```
await StoreThumbnailsAsync(oneDriveItems, childrenTable);
return childrenTable.Select(x => x.Value);
```

Listing 13-21. GraphFileService GetFilesAsync current implementation

```
public async Task<IEnumerable<OneDriveItem>>
  GetFilesAsync(string id)
{
  var request = graphClient
    .Me
    .Drive
    .Items[id]
    .Children
    .Request()
    .Expand("thumbnails");

  var oneDriveItems = (await request.GetAsync()).ToArray();

  var childrenTable = oneDriveItems
    .Select(driveItem => new OneDriveItem
    {
      Id = driveItem.Id,
      Name = driveItem.Name,
      Path = driveItem.ParentReference.Path,
      PathId = driveItem.ParentReference.Id,
      FileSize = $"{driveItem.Size}",
      Modified = driveItem.LastModifiedDateTime.HasValue ?
        driveItem.LastModifiedDateTime.Value.LocalDateTime :
```

```
        DateTime.Now,
      Type = driveItem.Folder != null ?
        OneDriveItemType.Folder :
        OneDriveItemType.File
    })
    .OrderByDescending(item => item.Type)
    .ThenBy(item => item.Name)
    .ToDictionary(item => item.Id);

    await StoreThumbnailsAsync(oneDriveItems, childrenTable);
    return childrenTable.Select(x => x.Value);
}
```

.NET 6 Mobile Considerations

Earlier in this chapter, we reviewed .NET 6 considerations as some libraries do not
fully support all .NET 6 target frameworks like the mobile targets we are using in
our UnoDrive application. We will need to add platform-specific code for these and
manually deserialize the JSON string.

In the GetFilesAsync API, update the request builder and invocation code to the
snippet in Listing 13-22.

Listing 13-22. GraphFileService GetFilesAsync .NET 6 request builder snippet

```
var request = graphClient
  .Me
  .Drive
  .Items[id]
  .Children
  .Request()
  .Expand("thumbnails");

#if __ANDROID__ || __IOS__ || __MACOS__
  var response = await request.GetResponseAsync();
  var data = await response.Content.ReadAsStringAsync();

  var collection = JsonSerializer.Deserialize
    <UnoDrive.Models.DriveItemCollection>(data);
```

```
  var oneDriveItems = collection.Value;
#else
  var oneDriveItems = (await request.GetAsync()).ToArray();
#endif
```

Using the specific .NET 6 models we created creates a breaking change in the StoreThumbnailsAsync method. In the .NET 6 mobile targets, it expects UnoDrive. Models.DriveItem, and in the other platforms, it can use the Microsoft.Graph SDK. To resolve this problem, we will add a pre-processor directive to the method signature. See the updated code snippet in Listing 13-23.

Listing 13-23. GraphFileService StoreThumbnailsAsync .NET 6 method signature

```
#if __ANDROID__ || __IOS__ || __MACOS__
  async Task StoreThumbnailsAsync(
    UnoDrive.Models.DriveItem[] oneDriveItems,
    IDictionary<string, OneDriveItem> childrenTable)

#else
  async Task StoreThumbnailsAsync(
    DriveItem[] oneDriveItems,
    IDictionary<string, OneDriveItem> childrenTable)
#endif
```

WPF Considerations

In the private method StoreThumbnailsAsync, there are things to consider for the WPF platform. We are using the Windows.Storage API to determine the correct file path to place the cached thumbnail into. This path varies depending on the platform, and we will need to make sure it is being stored correctly. All the platforms do a good job at this except for WPF; it places the file in a generic temporary directory that isn't application specific. For this platform we will need to add WPF-specific code to handle the path.

Update the imageFolder declaration code in the StoreThumbnailsAsync method – see the code snippet in Listing 13-24.

Listing 13-24. GraphFileService StoreThumbnailsAsync WPF-specific imageFolder code snippet

```
#if HAS_UNO_SKIA_WPF
  var applicationFolder = Path.Combine(
    Windows.Storage.ApplicationData.Current.TemporaryFolder.Path,
    "UnoDrive");
  var imageFolder = Path.Combine(
    applicationFolder, "thumbnails");
#else
  var imageFolder = Path.Combine(
    Windows.Storage.ApplicationData.Current.LocalFolder.Path,
    "thumbnails");
#endif
```

All the other platforms support File.WriteAllBytesAsync except WPF. In this case we need to add WPF-specific code for writing the thumbnail to disk to use the synchronous API. See the code snippet in Listing 13-25.

Listing 13-25. GraphFileService StoreThumbnailsAsync WPF-specific WriteAllBytes code snippet

```
#if HAS_UNO_SKIA_WPF
  System.IO.File.WriteAllBytes(localFilePath, bytes);
#else
  await System.IO.File.WriteAllBytesAsync(localFilePath, bytes);
#endif
```

Cross-Platform ImageSource Considerations

The last step in the StoreThumbnailsAsync method is to read the bytes of the cached thumbnail file and set it to the ImageSource on our OneDriveItem. The standard way to do this is by using a BitmapImage and Uri as seen in Listing 13-26.

Listing 13-26. Instantiate BitmapImage from file

```
var image = new BitmapImage(new Uri(localFilePath));
```

This technique is only working correctly on Windows and the mobile targets. It doesn't work correctly on WebAssembly (WASM), WPF, or GTK. Update our `BitmapImage` code to handle the various platforms as seen in the code snippet in Listing 13-27.

Listing 13-27. GraphFileService StoreThumbnailsAsync cross-platform code for BitmapImage from file

```
#if __UNO_DRIVE_WINDOWS__ || __ANDROID__ || __IOS__ || __MACOS__
  var image = new BitmapImage(new Uri(localFilePath));
#else
  var image = new BitmapImage();
  image.SetSource(new MemoryStream(bytes));
#endif
```

GraphFileService: GetRootFilesAsync

The `GetRootFilesAsync` API is intended to get the files at the root path of the user's OneDrive. It does not include any parameters and depends on `GetFilesAsync`. This means we need to implement an algorithm to retrieve the unique ID for the root path. The Microsoft.Graph SDK provides a special Root API on the request builder just for this scenario.

Add basic implementation with the request builder to retrieve the correct ID. See Listing 13-28 for code.

Listing 13-28. GraphFileService GetRootFilesAsync basic implementation

```
public async Task<IEnumerable<OneDriveItem>> GetRootFilesAsync()
{
  var request = graphClient
    .Me
    .Drive
    .Root
    .Request();

  var rootNode = await request.GetAsync();
  return await GetFilesAsync(rootNode.Id);
}
```

Making web requests is always susceptible to exceptions being thrown. Let's wrap this in a try-catch block and add some error handling. See updated code in Listing 13-29.

Listing 13-29. GraphFileService GetRootFilesAsync current implementation

```
public async Task<IEnumerable<OneDriveItem>> GetRootFilesAsync()
{
  var rootPathId = string.Empty;

  try
  {
    var request = graphClient
      .Me
      .Drive
      .Root
      .Request();

    var rootNode = await request.GetAsync();
    if (rootNode == null ||
      string.IsNullOrEmpty(rootNode.Id))
    {
      throw new KeyNotFoundException(
        "Unable to find OneDrive Root Folder");
    }

    rootPathId = rootNode.Id;
  }
  catch(KeyNotFoundException ex)
  {
    logger.LogWarning("Unable to retrieve data from Graph " +
      "API, it may not exist or there could be a connection " +
      "issue";
    logger.LogWarning(ex, ex.Message);
    throw;
  }
```

```
  catch(Exception ex)
  {
    logger.LogWarning("Unable to retrieve root OneDrive folder");
    logger.LogWarning(ex, ex.Message);
  }

  return await GetFilesAsync(rootNode.Id);
}
```

.NET 6 Mobile Considerations

Earlier in this chapter, we reviewed .NET 6 considerations as some libraries do not
fully support all .NET 6 target frameworks like the mobile targets we are using in our
UnoDrive application. We will need to add platform-specific code for these platforms
and manually deserialize the JSON string.

In the GetRootFilesAsync API, update the request builder and invocation code to
the snippet in Listing 13-30.

Listing 13-30. GraphFileService GetRootFilesAsync .NET 6 request
builder snippet

```
var request = graphClient
  .Me
  .Drive
  .Root
  .Request();

#if __ANDROID__ || __IOS__ || __MACOS__
  var response = await request.GetResponseAsync();
  var data = await response.Content.ReadAsStringAsync();

  var rootNode = JsonSerializer.Deserialize<DriveItem>(data);
#else
```

```
    var rootNode = await request.GetAsync();
#endif
```

Dependency Injection Setup

The Microsoft Graph service implementation is complete, and we now have an
`IGraphFileService` interface and `GraphFileService` implementation. The next step is
to update our Dependency Injection container and register the new classes, which will
allow us to inject it into the view models.

In the `UnoDrive.Shared` project, open the file `App.xaml.cs` and add the code in
Listing 13-31 to the `ConfigureServices` method. See complete `ConfigureServices` code
in Listing 13-32.

Listing 13-31. Register IGraphFileService with the Dependency Injection
container

```
services.AddTransient<IGraphFileService, GraphFileService>();
```

Listing 13-32. App.xaml.cs complete ConfigureServices code

```
protected override void ConfigureServices(IServiceCollection services)
{
  services.AddLoggingForUnoDrive();
  services.AddAuthentication();
  services.AddTransient<INavigationService, NavigationService>();
  services.AddTransient<
    INetworkConnectivityService,
    NetworkConnectivityService>();
  services.AddTransient<IGraphFileService, GraphFileService>();
}
```

ViewModel Implementation

Moving up the stack from the OneDrive integration, we will be using the
`IGraphFileService` in the `MyFilesViewModel`. Our goal is to display all the items and the
current path and manage loading state. Right now, we are focusing just on loading the

items at the root directory, and we will be handling navigation and offline data in future chapters.

Constructor

Currently, MyFilesViewModel should be a stubbed-out empty class with nothing in it. This class needs the ILogger and IGraphFileService. Let's create local variables and inject them into the constructor. See code in Listing 13-33.

Listing 13-33. MyFilesViewModel constructor injection

```
public class MyFilesViewModel
{
  IGraphFileService graphFileService;
  ILogger logger;

  public MyFilesViewModel(
    IGraphFileService graphFileService,
    ILogger<MyFilesViewModel> logger)
  {
    this.graphFileService = graphFileService;
    this.logger = logger;
  }
}
```

The items in the current OneDrive location need to be stored in a collection that can be used in the user interface. We are going to use a basic List<T> to store our OneDriveItems. To properly notify the user interface, a view model must implement INotifyPropertyChanged, and since we are using the CommunityToolkit.Mvvm NuGet package, we have an implementation named ObservableObject that already implements the interface for us. The ObservableObject class provides a useful helper method named SetProperty(), which will update the local variable with the value. Update the MyFilesViewModel to inherit from ObservableObject. See the code snippet in Listing 13-34.

Listing 13-34. Class declaration for MyFilesViewModel inheriting from ObservableObject

```
public class MyFilesViewModel : ObservableObject
{
  // omitted code
}
```

Note   When data binding collections, you can also use an ObservableCollection, which automatically notifies the View or page when changes happen to the collection. We are not using an ObservableCollection as our entire collection changes as the page is loaded and there is no need for dynamic data loading. When designing your application, pick the data structure that makes the most sense for your business rules.

Now we can add a new property and private variable for storing the current items in the OneDrive path. Create a local variable of type List<OneDriveItem>, which will be the source of items in the current path. Then create a public property that will return that variable. The setter on this property will be used to set and notify the user interface. When we get to state management, we will need to come back to this setter and notify the user interface of other properties. See the code snippet in Listing 13-35 for the new FilesAndFolders property.

Listing 13-35. MyFilesViewModel FilesAndFolders property

```
List<OneDriveItem> filesAndFolders;
public List<OneDriveItem> FilesAndFolders
{
  get => filesAndFolders;
  set
  {
```

```
    SetProperty(ref filesAndFolders, value);
  }
}
```

Now that our `FilesAndFolders` property is created, we can instantiate it in the constructor. Add the code snippet in Listing 13-36 to the constructor.

Listing 13-36. MyFilesViewModel – instantiate FilesAndFolders list

```
FilesAndFolders = new List<OneDriveItem>();
```

The constructor code is complete. You can see the full constructor code in Listing 13-37.

Listing 13-37. MyFilesViewModel complete constructor code

```
public MyFilesViewModel(
  IGraphFileService graphFileService,
  ILogger<MyFilesViewModel> logger)
{
  this.graphFileService = graphFileService;
  this.logger = logger;

  FilesAndFolders = new List<OneDriveItem>();
}
```

Properties and Data Binding

The public properties are used as a bridge to the user interface via data binding. These are the values that are used in the various controls on the user interface. When we implemented the constructor, we added our main property `FilesAndFolders` that stores the items in the current OneDrive path. In this section we are going to add the remaining properties and make the necessary data binding updates.

We need to create four additional properties:

- `IsPageEmpty`: True if there are no items on the current page and the page is not loading data.

- `CurrentFolderPath`: A string that represents the current OneDrive path.

- NoDataMessage: A simple message that is displayed if there is no data on the current page.

- IsStatusBarLoading: If true, a ProgressRing or message is displayed telling the user that data is loading.

Let's start by stubbing out all our properties, and then we can work through them one at a time. Add the code snippet from Listing 13-38.

Listing 13-38. MyFilesViewModel property stubs

```
public bool IsPageEmpty { get; set; }
public string CurrentFolderPath { get; set; }
public string NoDataMessage { get; set; }
public bool IsStatusBarLoading { get; set; }
```

As implemented in Listing 13-38, the user interface will never be notified on changes to any of these. Some of them will not need to explicitly notify the user interface as that is managed elsewhere. IsStatusBarLoading and NoDataMessage are easy to implement as they follow the standard convention for data binding and ObservableObject. For both of them, create a private variable and use the SetProperty() method. See the updated code snippet in Listing 13-39.

Listing 13-39. MyFilesViewModel IstStatusBarLoading and NoDataMessage property implementations

```
string noDataMessage;
public string NoDataMessage
{
  get => noDataMessage;
  set => SetProperty(ref noDataMessage, value);
}

bool isStatusBarLoading;
public bool IsStatusBarLoading
{
  get => isStatusBarLoading;
  set => SetProperty(ref isStatusBarLoading, value);
}
```

> **Tip**   After implementing a property to use the data binding convention as seen in Listing 13-39, you must always interact with the property and not the local variable. If you do not follow that rule, your user interface will not be notified of changes. Example: Update the loading status via `IsStatusBarLoading` instead of `isStatusBarLoading`.

To determine if the page is empty, we need to certify that the `FilesAndFolders` list is empty and the page is not loading. There is no need for us to create a local variable as this property will be notified whenever the `FilesAndFolders` list or `IsStatusBarLoading` is updated. We will be updating the notification code for these properties in Listings 13-42 and 13-43. See the updated code snippet for `IsPageEmpty` in Listing 13-40.

Listing 13-40. MyFilesViewModel IsPageEmpty property implementation

```
public bool IsPageEmpty =>
  !IsStatusBarLoading && !FilesAndFolders.Any();
```

The last property we are going to implement is the `CurrentFolderPath` property. This is a string that represents our current path in OneDrive, and we can obtain this from any item in the `FilesAndFolders` property. We will attempt to use the first item in the list and then use the Path property. If there are no items in the list, it will return an empty string. See updated property code in Listing 13-41.

Listing 13-41. MyFilesViewModel CurrentFolderPath property implementation

```
public bool IsPageEmpty =>
  !IsStatusBarLoading && !FilesAndFolders.Any();

public string CurrentFolderPath =>
  FilesAndFolders.FirstOrDefault()?.Path;

string noDataMessage;
public string NoDataMessage
{
  get => noDataMessage;
  set => SetProperty(ref noDataMessage, value);
}
```

```
bool isStatusBarLoading;
public bool IsStatusBarLoading
{
  get => isStatusBarLoading;
  set => SetProperty(ref isStatusBarLoading, value);
}
```

The four properties have been implemented, but both IsPageEmpty and
CurrentFolderPath are not notifying the user interface on changes. As it is currently
implemented, this value will be loaded once in the user interface and never change.
Both properties are dependent on changes to the FilesAndFolders property.
We can notify the user interface by using the method OnPropertyChanged() and
providing the property. This will notify the user interface of changes. See the updated
FilesAndFolders implementation in Listing 13-42.

Listing 13-42. MyFilesViewModel updated implementation for FilesAndFolders
to notify the user interface

```
List<OneDriveItem> filesAndFolders;
public List<OneDriveItem> FilesAndFolders
{
  get => filesAndFolders;
  set
  {
    SetProperty(ref filesAndFolders, value);
    OnPropertyChanged(nameof(CurrentFolderPath));
    OnPropertyChanged(nameof(IsPageEmpty));
  }
}
```

Tip   When using OnPropertyChanged you can specify the property
name either using a string such as "CurrentFolderPath" or using
nameof(CurrentFolderPath). Using the nameof() syntax protects your code
against property name changes in the future.

The property IsPageEmpty depends on both FilesAndFolders and
IsStatusBarLoading, which means we need to manually trigger the OnPropertyChanged
from the setter of IsStatusBarLoading, just like we did in FilesAndFolders. See the
updated IsStatusBarLoading code snippet in Listing 13-43.

Listing 13-43. MyFilesViewModel IsStatusBarLoading property updates

```
bool isStatusBarLoading;
public bool IsStatusBarLoading
{
  get => isStatusBarLoading;
  set
  {
    SetProperty(ref isStatusBarLoading, value);
    OnPropertyChanged(nameof(IsPageEmpty));
  }
}
```

This completes our property and data binding code. The completed property code
can be seen in Listing 13-44.

Listing 13-44. MyFilesViewModel complete property and data binding code

```
List<OneDriveItem> filesAndFolders;
public List<OneDriveItem> FilesAndFolders
{
  get => filesAndFolders;
  set
  {
    SetProperty(ref filesAndFolders, value);
    OnPropertyChanged(nameof(CurrentFolderPath));
    OnPropertyChanged(nameof(IsPageEmpty));
  }
}

public bool IsPageEmpty =>
  !IsStatusBarLoading && !FilesAndFolders.Any();
```

```
public string CurrentFolderPath =>
  FilesAndFolders.FirstOrDefault()?.Path;

string noDataMessage;
public string NoDataMessage
{
  get => noDataMessage;
  set => SetProperty(ref noDataMessage, value);
}

bool isStatusBarLoading;
public bool IsStatusBarLoading
{
  get => isStatusBarLoading;
  set
  {
    SetProperty(ref isStatusBarLoading, value);
    OnPropertyChanged(nameof(IsPageEmpty));
  }
}
```

Data Loading

With all the properties and data binding complete, we can implement our algorithm to load the data from the `IGraphFileService` implementation. Create two method stubs, which will be used in our data loading algorithm:

- `LoadDataAsync`: Entry point for data loading

- `UpdateFiles`: Updates the `FilesAndFolders` list and handles errors if empty or null

See stubbed code in Listing 13-45.

Listing 13-45. MyFilesViewModel data loading stubbed methods

```
async Task LoadDataAsync(string pathId = null)
{
  // TODO - add implementation
```

369

```
}

void UpdateFiles(IEnumerable<OneDriveItem> files)
{
  // TODO - add implementation
}
```

Implementing the second method UpdateFiles will be an easy starting point for us. The goal of this method is to update the FilesAndFolders property or display an error message if null or empty. See the completed implementation in Listing 13-46.

Listing 13-46. MyFilesViewModel completed UpdateFiles implementation

```
void UpdateFiles(IEnumerable<OneDriveItem> files)
{
  if (files == null)
  {
    NoDataMessage = "Unable to retrieve data from API " +
      "check network connection";
    logger.LogInformation("No data retrieved from API, " +
      "ensure you have a stable internet connection");

    return;
  }
  else if (!files.Any())
  {
    NoDataMessage = "No files or folders";
  }

  FilesAndFolders = files.ToList();
}
```

Now we can start implementing the LoadDataAsync API, which will be using the IGraphFileService to get our data. We have four things we need to do for our basic algorithm:

1. Notify the user interface that data is loading.

2. Load the data.

3. Update FilesAndFolders.

4. Notify the user interface that data is done loading.

See implementation in Listing 13-47.

Listing 13-47. MyFilesViewModel LoadDataAsync basic implementation

```
async Task LoadDataAsync(string pathId = null)
{
  IsStatusBarLoading = true;

  IEnumerable<OneDriveItem> data;
  if (string.IsNullOrEmpty(pathId)
  {
    data = await graphFileService.GetRootFilesAsync();
  }
  else
  {
    data = await graphFileService.GetFilesAsync(pathId);
  }

  UpdateFiles(data);

  IsStatusBarLoading = false;
}
```

This implementation works but does not consider exceptions that may be thrown. If an exception is thrown, the IsStatusBarLoading property is never reset, so the user will see the loading indicator forever, which means the user will need to restart the application. To solve this problem, let's wrap the code in a try-catch block and handle a basic exception. See updated code in Listing 13-48.

Listing 13-48. MyFilesViewModel LoadDataAsync complete implementation

```
async Task LoadDataAsync(string pathId = null)
{
  IsStatusBarLoading = true;
  try
```

```
{
  IEnumerable<OneDriveItem> data;
  if (string.IsNullOrEmpty(pathId)
  {
    data = await graphFileService.GetRootFilesAsync();
  }
  else
  {
    data = await graphFileService.GetFilesAsync(pathId);
  }

  UpdateFiles(data);
}
catch (Exception ex)
{
  logger.LogError(ex, ex.Message);
}
finally
{
  IsStatusBarLoading = false;
}
}
```

Note   By updating the IsStatusBarLoading property in the finally block of the try-catch, it ensures that it will always be invoked even if there is an exception. This will keep the user interface responsive for the user.

ViewModel Entry Point and IInitialize

MyFilesViewModel is just about implemented. We have the constructor, properties, and data loading code all completed. When the object is instantiated, there is no entry point code that invokes LoadDataAsync(). We need to add an IInitialize interface and add it to the MyFilesViewModel. This interface will provide a simple API that we can certify is invoked at instantiation time.

In the UnoDrive.Shared project, create a new file under the Mvvm folder named
IInitialize.cs. See the screenshot in Figure 13-2.

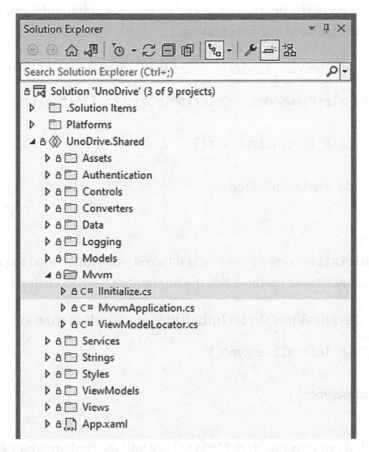

Figure 13-2. Visual Studio Solution Explorer – IInitialize.cs

Open the newly created IInitialize.cs and define our interface with an async
method named InitializeAsync(). See code in Listing 13-49 for the interface
definition.

Listing 13-49. IInitialize interface definition

```
public interface IInitialize
{
  Task InitializeAsync();
}
```

Now that we have our interface defined, we can update the MyFilesViewModel to inherit the interface and provide an implementation. The code in Listing 13-50 has all the code omitted except the new interface and an empty implementation. See code in Listing 13-50 for the stubbed implementation.

Listing 13-50. MyFilesViewModel stubbed implementation of IInitialize

```
public class MyFilesViewModel : ObservableObject, IInitialize
{
  public async Task InitializeAsync()
  {
    // TODO - add implementation
  }
}
```

When the InitializeAsync() method is invoked, we want to load the data by invoking the LoadDataAsync method. See the implementation in Listing 13-51.

Listing 13-51. MyFilesViewModel InitializeAsync implementation

```
public async Task InitializeAsync()
{
  await LoadDataAsync();
}
```

We have added our new interface IInitialize and an implementation to our MyFilesViewModel, but we have not connected this to the instantiation of the view model. To complete our implementation, we need to update the MyFilesPage.xaml.cs to invoke the interface method.

Every page has an instance of DataContext, and in our application that is the view model. We are using an automatic wireup strategy for the view model, which means we can guarantee the DataContext is set and ready to use after the constructor completes. We need to complete two tasks in the MyFilesPage.xaml.cs:

- Create a local property named ViewModel that is of type MyFilesViewModel.

- Override the OnNavigatedTo() method and invoke the InitializeAsync() method.

Add implementation for the ViewModel property as seen in Listing 13-52.

Listing 13-52. MyFilesPage ViewModel property implementation

```
public MyFilesViewModel ViewModel =>
  (MyFilesViewModel)DataContext;
```

Now that we have our property defined, we can override the OnNavigatedTo() method, which is invoked right after navigation. In this method we will check if the ViewModel property is of type IInitialize and if it is invoke the InitializeAsync() method. See the code snippet in Listing 13-53.

Listing 13-53. MyFilesPage OnNavigatedTo implementation

```
protected override async void OnNavigatedTo(
  NavigationEventArgs e)
{
  base.OnNavigatedTo(e);

  if (ViewModel is IInitialize initializeViewModel)
  {
    await initializeViewModel.InitializeAsync();
  }
}
```

Now when the page loads, the view model will be initialized, and our data loading code will be invoked.

Complete View Model Code

We implemented our MyFilesViewModel in chunks to make it easier to understand the various moving parts. You can see the completed view model code in Listing 13-54.

Listing 13-54. Complete MyFilesViewModel implementation

```
public class MyFilesViewModel : ObservableObject, IInitialize
{
  IGraphFileService graphFileService;
  ILogger logger;
```

```csharp
public MyFilesViewModel(
  IGraphFileService graphFileService,
  ILogger<MyFilesViewModel> logger)
{
  this.graphFileService = graphFileService;
  this.logger = logger;

  FilesAndFolders = new List<OneDriveItem>();
}

List<OneDriveItem> filesAndFolders;
public List<OneDriveItem> FilesAndFolders
{
  get => filesAndFolders;
  set
  {
    SetProperty(ref filesAndFolders, value);
    OnPropertyChanged(nameof(CurrentFolderPath));
    OnPropertyChanged(nameof(IsPageEmpty));
  }
}

public bool IsPageEmpty =>
  !IsStatusBarLoading && !FilesAndFolders.Any();

public string CurrentFolderPath =>
  FilesAndFolders.FirstOrDefault()?.Path;

string noDataMessage;
public string NoDataMessage
{
  get => noDataMessage;
  set => SetProperty(ref noDataMessage, value);
}

bool isStatusBarLoading;
public bool IsStatusBarLoading
{
```

```csharp
  get => isStatusBarLoading;
  set => SetProperty(ref isStatusBarLoading, value);
}

async Task LoadDataAsync(string pathId = null)
{
  IsStatusBarLoading = true;

  try
  {
    IEnumerable<OneDriveItem> data;
    if (string.IsNullOrEmpty(pathId)
    {
      data = await graphFileService.GetRootFilesAsync();
    }
    else
    {
      data = await graphFileService.GetFilesAsync(pathId);
    }

    UpdateFiles(data);
  }
  catch (Exception ex)
  {
    logger.LogError(ex, ex.Message);
  }
  finally
  {
    IsStatusBarLoading = false;
  }
}

void UpdateFiles(IEnumerable<OneDriveItem> files)
{
  if (files == null)
  {
    NoDataMessage = "Unable to retrieve data from API " +
```

```
      "check network connection";
    logger.LogInformation("No data retrieved from API, " +
      "ensure you have a stable internet connection");

    return;
  }
  else if (!files.Any())
  {
    NoDataMessage = "No files or folders";
  }

  FilesAndFolders = files.ToList();
}

public async Task InitializeAsync()
{
  await LoadDataAsync();
}
}
```

User Interface Implementation

We have now implemented the Microsoft Graph integration and the MyFilesViewModel. The last thing for us to implement in this chapter is the user interface so we can see our data on the screen.

Our plan is to add an address bar and a content area where the address bar will show the current OneDrive path and the content area will be a folders and files explorer window. We will be adding navigation to the explorer in future chapters. In this chapter we are just going to focus on the basic user interface.

Note All XAML code snippets in this section omit the xmlns and other declarations at the top of the file. Some of the snippets will explicitly mention when you need to edit them.

Create a Grid with two rows. Place a second Grid in the first row to manage the address bar and a ScrollViewer in the second row to manage the files and folders explorer. See the code snippet in Listing 13-55.

Listing 13-55. MyFilesPage basic grid structure

```
<Grid>
  <Grid.RowDefinitions>
    <RowDefinition Height="Auto" />
    <RowDefinition Height="*" />
  </Grid.RowDefinitions>

  <Grid Grid.Row="0" Margin="0, 0, 0, 20">
  </Grid>

  <ScrollViewer Grid.Row="1">
  </ScrollViewer>
</Grid>
```

Address Bar

In the first nested Grid, we are going to build our address bar. We will build upon this in future chapters. For now it will display a read-only TextBox that renders the current OneDrive path.

First, define the ColumnDefinitions to include only one column. See the code snippet in Listing 13-56.

Listing 13-56. MyFilesPage address bar grid column definition

```
<ColumnDefinitions>
  <ColumnDefinition />
</ColumnDefinitions>
```

With the grid configured, we can place our TextBox control inside. We want our TextBox to be read-only and not usable by the user. This means there are several properties that we need to swap. In the MyFilesViewModel we defined a bindable property named CurrentFolderPath. This property needs set to the Text property using the data binding markup extension. See the code snippet in Listing 13-57 for the TextBox XAML.

Listing 13-57. MyFilesPage address bar TextBox

```
<TextBox
  Grid.Column="0"
  Margin="10, 0, 0, 0"
  Padding="10, 6, 36, 5"
  IsReadOnly="True"
  IsFocusEngaged="False"
  IsEnabled="False"
  Foreground="Black"
  Background="#F2F2F2"
  Text="{Binding CurrentFolderPath}" />
```

In our design we want to have a small `ProgressRing` spinning on the right-hand side of the `TextBox` while data is loading. Since we are using a `Grid`, we can easily stack items on top of each other by placing the `ProgressRing` in the same column. When stacking controls using this technique, the last item is always on top as items are added to the view stack from top to bottom. Add your `ProgressRing` and right-align it as seen in Listing 13-58.

Listing 13-58. MyFilesPage address bar ProgressRing

```
<ProgressRing
  Grid.Column="0"
  Width="20"
  Height="20"
  HorizontalAlignment="Right"
  Margin="0, 0, 10, 0" />
```

In Chapter 12 we implemented converters to help us display controls on the screen by data binding `bool` values. To manage the `Visibility` of the `ProgressRing,` we are going to put those converters to use. See updated `ProgressRing` code in Listing 13-59.

Listing 13-59. MyFilesPage address bar ProgressRing with Visibility

```
<ProgressRing
  Grid.Column="0"
  Width="20"
```

```
Height="20"
HorizontalAlignment="Right"
Margin="0, 0, 10, 0"
IsActive="{Binding IsStatusBarLoading}"
Visibility="{Binding IsStatusBarLoading,
  Converter={StaticResource BoolToVisibilityConverter}}" />
```

With the additions of IsActive and Visibility, the ProgressRing will only render and spin when IsStatusBarLoading is set to true in the MyFilesViewModel.

We now need to consider cross-platform scenarios as not every platform will render the ProgressRing correctly or at all. We will need to adjust the sizing for Android slightly. All platforms that use Skia will also need updates as the ProgressRing does not currently work with WinUI Uno Platform.

Add a custom style for the ProgressRing so we can simplify the XAML slightly. In the UnoDrive.Shared project under Styles ➤ Controls, create a new file named ProgressRing.xaml. See the screenshot in Figure 13-3.

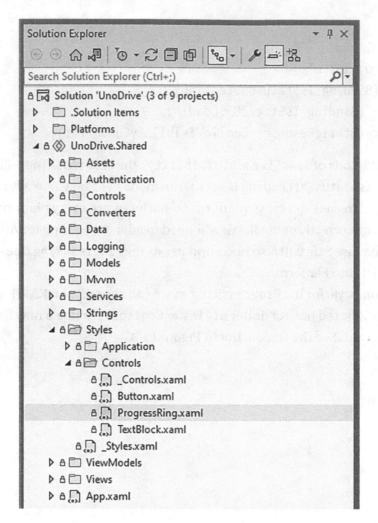

Figure 13-3. *Visual Studio Solution Explorer for ProgressRing.xaml*

To include our new `ProgressRing.xaml` file into our global styles, we need to ensure that the `ResourceDictionary` is added in the `_Controls.xaml`. See the code snippet in Listing 13-60 for updated styles in `_Controls.xaml`.

Listing 13-60. Updated _Controls.xaml to include ProgressRing.xaml

```
<ResourceDictionary>
  <ResourceDictionary Source="Button.xaml" />
  <ResourceDictionary Source="TextBlock.xaml" />
  <ResourceDictionary Source="ProgressRing.xaml" />
</ResourceDictionary>
```

Now we can add our styles to the `ProgressRing.xaml` file. At the top of the file, we need to ensure we add our xmlns for Android so we can add platform-specific XAML. Then we need to add the Android xmlns to the ignorable. See xmlns definitions in Listing 13-61.

Listing 13-61. ProgressRing.xaml Android-specific xmlns

```
xmlns:android="http://uno.ui/android"
mc:Ignorable="android"
```

Once you have updated the root `ResourceDictionary` node with the correct xmlns, we can start adding our address bar–specific `ProgressRing` style. All platforms will use a `Width` and `Height` of `20,` and Android will use a value of `15`. See the code snippet in Listing 13-62.

Listing 13-62. ProgressRing.xaml AddressBarProgressRing style

```
<Style x:Name="AddressBarProgressRing" TargetType="ProgressRing">
  <Setter Property="Width" Value="20" />
  <Setter Property="Height" Value="20" />
  <android:Setter Property="Width" Value="15" />
  <android:Setter Property="Height" Value="15" />
</Style>
```

To use this new style, we need to explicitly reference it by name `AddressBarProgressRing`. Back in the `MyFilesPage.xaml,` update the `ProgressRing` we defined in our address bar to use this style, and then remove the Height and Width properties. See the updated code snippet in Listing 13-63.

Listing 13-63. MyFilesPage address bar completed ProgressRing

```
<ProgressRing
  Grid.Column="0"
  Style="{StaticResource AddressBarProgressRing}"
  HorizontalAlignment="Right"
  Margin="0, 0, 10, 0"
  IsActive="{Binding IsStatusBarLoading}"
  Visibility="{Binding IsStatusBarLoading,
    Converter={StaticResource BoolToVisibilityConverter}}" />
```

Next, we need to handle Skia platforms as none of them on WinUI are rendering the ProgressRing correctly. Instead, we will render a TextBlock that displays the message Loading . . . to communicate to the user that data is loading. At the top of the MyFilesPage.xaml, you will need to add the skia xmlns and not_skia xmlns and add only the skia xmlns to the ignorable. See xmlns definitions in Listing 13-64.

Listing 13-64. MyFilesPage skia and not_skia xmlns definitions

```
xmlns:not_skia="http://schemas.microsoft.com/winfx/2006/xaml/presentation"
xmlns:skia="http://uno.ui/skia"
mc:Ignorable="d skia"
```

Note If you add not_skia to the ignorable from Listing 13-64, then it will not include the not_skia items correctly on Windows targets. It is important to only include skia to the ignorable in this case.

To start we can update our existing ProgressRing to use the not_skia platform – see updated code in Listing 13-65.

Listing 13-65. MyFilesPage address bar – added not_skia target to ProgressRing

```
<not_skia:ProgressRing
  Grid.Column="0"
  Style="{StaticResource AddressBarProgressRing}"
  HorizontalAlignment="Right"
  Margin="0, 0, 10, 0"
  IsActive="{Binding IsStatusBarLoading}"
  Visibility="{Binding IsStatusBarLoading,
    Converter={StaticResource BoolToVisibilityConverter}}" />
```

Now, we can add our Skia-specific TextBlock. It will follow similar rendering rules to the ProgressRing as it will be aligned on the right side of the TextBox. See the code snippet in Listing 13-66.

Listing 13-66. MyFilesPage address bar Skia-specific loading TextBlock

```
<skia:TextBlock
  Grid.Column="0"
  Text="Loading . . ."
  FontSize="12"
  Margin="0, 0, 10, 0"
  Foreground="Black"
  HorizontalAlignment="Right"
  VerticalAlignment="Center"
  Visibility="{Binding IsStatusBarLoading,
    Converter={StaticResource BoolToVisibilityConverter}}" />
```

Files and Folders Explorer

The ScrollViewer is the second control we added earlier, and that will contain our files and folders explorer. Our ScrollViewer will use a StackPanel to contain the various user interface controls that make up our explorer. See the code snippet in Listing 13-67.

Listing 13-67. MyFilesPage explorer StackPanel definition

```
<ScrollViewer Grid.Row="1">
  <StackPanel>
  </StackPanel>
</ScrollViewer>
```

We are going to use a GridView to display our various items as it provides a nice way to display a collection of data in a grid instead of a list. Before we add it to the MyFilesPage.xaml, we need to add a global style. In the UnoDrive.Shared project under Styles ➤ Controls, create a new file named GridView.xaml. See Figure 13-4 for a screenshot of the Visual Studio Solution Explorer.

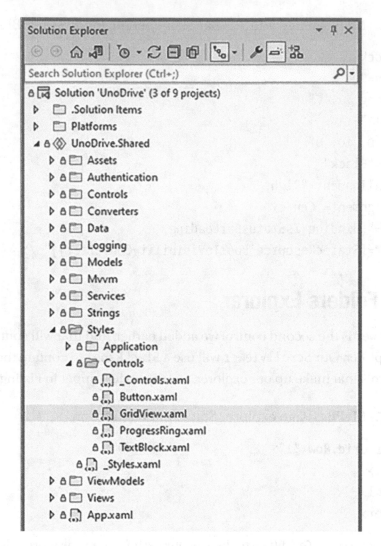

Figure 13-4. *Visual Studio Solution Explorer GridView.xaml*

Just like the ProgressRing.xaml file, we will need to ensure it is included in our
ResourceDictionary. Update the _Controls.xaml file to include our new GridView.
xaml – see code in Listing 13-68.

Listing 13-68. Add GridView.xaml to _Controls.xaml

```
<ResourceDictionary>
  <ResourceDictionary Source="Button.xaml" />
  <ResourceDictionary Source="TextBlock.xaml" />
```

```
<ResourceDictionary Source="GridView.xaml" />
<ResourceDictionary Source="ProgressRing.xaml" />
</ResourceDictionary>
```

In the GridView.xaml we can add our default style for the GridView control. This style is going to be a global style, which means it will be used on any GridView used in the entire application. There will be no need to add an explicit Style property in the MyFilesPage.xaml file. See the style XAML code in Listing 13-69.

Listing 13-69. GridView.xaml global style implementation

```
<Style TargetType="GridView">
  <Setter Property="CanDragItems" Value="False" />
  <Setter Property="AllowDrop" Value="False" />
  <Setter Property="CanReorderItems" Value="False" />
  <Setter Property="SelectionMode" Value="Single" />
  <Setter Property="FlowDirection" Value="LeftToRight" />
  <Setter Property="HorizontalContentAlignment" Value="Center" />
  <Setter Property="IsItemClickEnabled" Value="True" />
</Style>
```

Now that the global style is implemented, we can add our GridView to the MyFilesPage in our ScrollViewer. In the MyFilesViewModel we defined a public property named FilesAndFolders that is a list; this will be data bound to the ItemsSource property. The ItemsSource property on the GridView represents all the items to display. If there are no items in FilesAndFolders, we should hide the GridView so we can display other controls. You will need to bind IsPageEmpty to Visibility. See the code snippet in Listing 13-70.

Listing 13-70. MyFilesPage explorer GridView

```
<GridView
  ItemsSource="{Binding FilesAndFolders}"
  Visibility="{Binding IsPageEmpty, Converter=
    {StaticResource BoolNegationToVisibilityConverter}}" />
```

If the page is empty, we need to communicate to the user that there is no data by rendering a message No data found in a TextBlock. See the code snippet in Listing 13-71.

Listing 13-71. MyFilesPage explorer TextBlock for no data found

```
<TextBlock
  Text="No data found"
  Visibility="{Binding IsPageEmpty,
    Converter={StaticResource BoolToVisibilityConverter}}" />
```

The last step for our files and folders explorer is to render the ProgressRing in the center of the content area if data is loading. Just like the address bar earlier, we will need to use our not_skia vs. skia xmlns to display a ProgressRing or TextBlock. First, add the ProgressRing using the not_skia xmlns as seen in Listing 13-72.

Listing 13-72. MyFilesPage explorer ProgressRing for not_skia

```
<not_skia:ProgressRing
  Width="300"
  Height="300"
  IsActive="{Binding IsStatusBarLoading}"
  Visibility="{Binding IsStatusBarLoading,
    Converter={StaticResource BoolToVisibilityConverter}}" />
```

Now, we need to add the skia-specific XAML to display the TextBlock. See the code in Listing 13-73.

Listing 13-73. MyFilesPage explorer TextBlock for skia

```
<skia:TextBlock
  Text="Loading . . ."
  FontSize="40"
  Foreground="Black"
  HorizontalAlignment="Center"
  VerticalAlignment="Center"
  Visibility="{Binding IsStatusBarLoading,
    Converter={StaticResource BoolToVisibilityConverter}}" />
```

Note   In the address bar styles for the `ProgressRing,` we added a style to handle the `Width` and `Height` for Android vs. the other platforms. We are not doing that here as the center of the page has more screen space than the small TextBox from earlier.

MyFilesPage.xaml Complete Code

This completes our implementation of `MyFilesPage.xaml` for this chapter. We will be adding to it in future chapters. See the completed code in Listing 13-74.

Listing 13-74.   MyFilesPage.xaml completed code

```
<Grid>
  <Grid.RowDefinitions>
    <RowDefinition Height="Auto" />
    <RowDefinition Height="*" />
  </Grid.RowDefinitions>

  <Grid Grid.Row="0" Margin="0, 0, 0, 20">
    <Grid.ColumnDefinitions>
      <ColumnDefinition />
    </Grid.ColumnDefinitions>

    <TextBox
      Grid.Column="0"
      Margin="10, 0, 0, 0"
      Padding="10, 6, 36, 5"
      IsReadOnly="True"
      IsFocusEngaged="False"
      IsEnabled="False"
      Foreground="Black"
      Background="#F2F2F2"
      Text="{Binding CurrentFolderPath}" />
```

```xml
    <not_skia:ProgressRing
      Grid.Column="0"
      Style="{StaticResource AddressBarProgressRing}"
      HorizontalAlignment="Right"
      Margin="0, 0, 10, 0"
      IsActive="{Binding IsStatusBarLoading}"
      Visibility="{Binding IsStatusBarLoading, Converter=
        {StaticResource BoolToVisibilityConverter}}" />

    <skia:TextBlock
      Grid.Column="0"
      Text="Loading . . ."
      FontSize="12"
      Margin="0, 0, 10, 0"
      Foreground="Black"
      HorizontalAlignment="Right"
      VerticalAlignment="Center"
      Visibility="{Binding IsStatusBarLoading, Converter=
        {StaticResource BoolToVisibilityConverter}}" />
  </Grid>

  <ScrollViewer Grid.Row="1">
    <StackPanel>
      <GridView
        ItemsSource="{Binding FilesAndFolders}"
        Visibility="{Binding IsPageEmtpy, Converter=
          {StaticResource BoolNegationToVisibilityConverter}}" />

      <TextBlock
        Text="No data found"
        Visibility="{Binding IsPageEmpty, Converter=
          {StaticResource BoolToVisibilityConverter}}" />

      <not_skia:ProgressRing
        Width="300"
        Height="300"
        IsActive="{Binding IsStatusBarLoading}"
```

```
    Visibility="{Binding IsStatusBarLoading, Converter=
      {StaticResource BoolToVisibilityConverter}}" />

  <skia:TextBlock
    Text="Loading . . ."
    FontSize="40"
    Foreground="Black"
    HorizontalAlignment="Center"
    VerticalAlignment="Center"
    Visibility="{Binding IsStatusBarLoading, Converter=
      {StaticResource BoolToVisibilityConverter}}" />

    </StackPanel>
  </ScrollViewer>
</Grid>
```

Testing the Code

We now have a full-stack implementation of using the Microsoft Graph to pull data from OneDrive and render something on the screen. The address bar will work as we expect, but the files and folders explorer is just going to display object names on the screen and not the files and folders. That is intentional as we will implement images in Chapter 14. Now go and run the app on your various platforms. See screenshots of the running application in Figure 13-5 and Figure 13-6 for Windows, Figure 13-7 and Figure 13-8 for WASM, Figure 13-9 and Figure 13-10 for WPF, Figure 13-11 and Figure 13-12 for Linux, Figure 13-13 for Android, Figure 13-14 for iOS, and Figure 13-15 and Figure 13-16 for macOS.

Windows

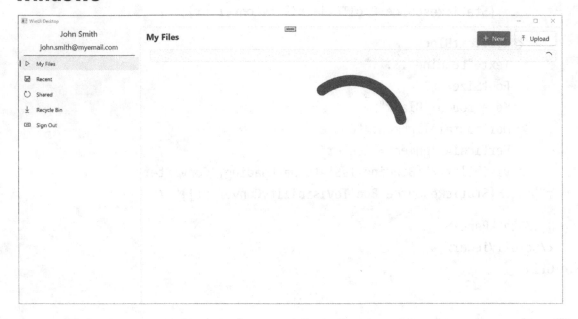

Figure 13-5. *Windows application with ProgressRing spinning*

Figure 13-6. *Windows application with root OneDrive path loaded*

WebAssembly (WASM)

Figure 13-7. *WebAssembly (WASM) application with ProgressRing spinning*

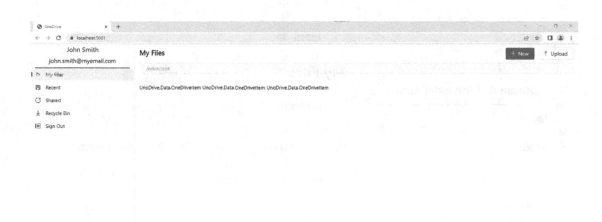

Figure 13-8. *WebAssembly (WASM) application with root OneDrive path loaded*

WPF

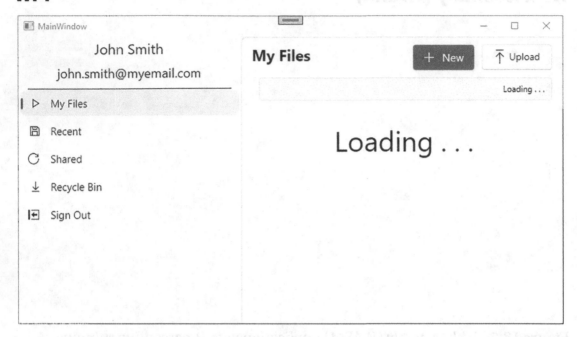

Figure 13-9. *WPF application with Loading... TextBlock*

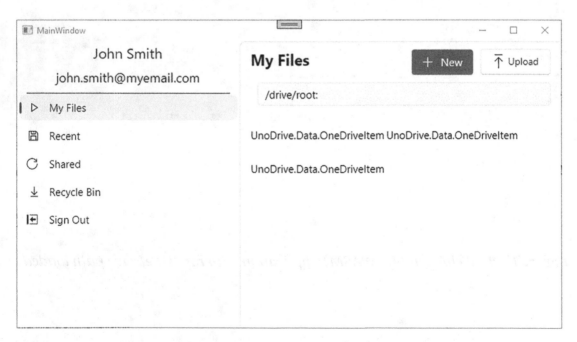

Figure 13-10. *WPF application with root OneDrive path loaded*

GTK

Figure 13-11. *GTK application with Loading... TextBlock*

Figure 13-12. *GTK application with root OneDrive path loaded*

Android

Figure 13-13. *Android application with ProgressRing spinning on the left and root OneDrive path loaded on the right*

iOS

Figure 13-14. *iOS application with ProgressRing spinning on the left and root OneDrive path loaded on the right*

macOS

Figure 13-15. *macOS application with ProgressRing spinning*

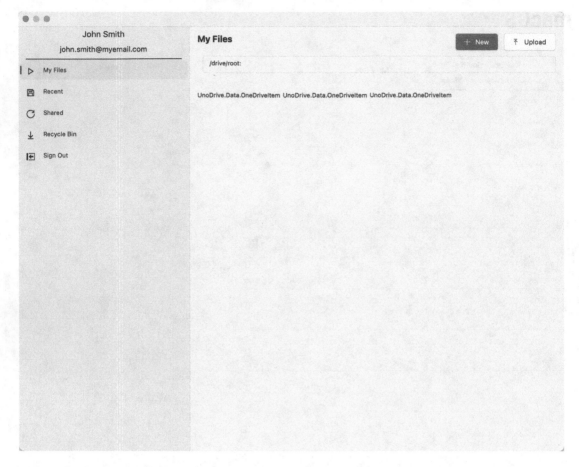

Figure 13-16. *macOS application with root OneDrive path loaded*

Conclusion

In this chapter we covered a lot of material with retrieving data from OneDrive and displaying it on the main landing page of the application. We are going to be building on the code in future chapters. If you had any trouble following along or your application isn't working right, go and download the sample code before moving on to the next chapter: `https://github.com/SkyeHoefling/UnoDrive/tree/main/Chapter%2013`.

CHAPTER 14

Microsoft Graph and Dashboard Menu

In the previous chapter, we implemented the full-stack solution for retrieving data from OneDrive and displaying it on the MyFilesPage. We are going to take some of those concepts and update the Dashboard menu to include personalized information for the user's email and name in the left corner.

Retrieving the personalized information is much simpler than loading the OneDrive files, so we will not be creating any service layer or additional Dependency Injection objects. In this chapter we will be calling into the graph right from the view model.

Tip This chapter demonstrates that you do not always need to add API calls to a service layer. If you have a set of simple APIs, it is valid and sometimes easier to invoke them from the view model. Always evaluate your situation and make the best decision for your project. **It is okay to mix and match these concepts.**

In this chapter we will be updating the DashboardPage and the DashboardViewModel. We will start from the bottom of the stack and work our way up to the presentation layer.

DashboardViewModel

Earlier in this book, we created the DashboardViewModel and do not have much of any implementation. The DashboardPage has the user's name and email address hard-coded. We will be updating this to pull the actual user display name and email from the Microsoft Graph. In the last chapter, we already added the necessary NuGet packages to integrate with the Microsoft Graph, so we can jump right into the implementation.

© Skye Hoefling 2022
S. Hoefling, *Getting Started with the Uno Platform and WinUI 3*,
https://doi.org/10.1007/978-1-4842-8248-9_14

We need to complete the following steps to finish our implementation:

- Injecting ILogger to the constructor
- Public properties for data binding
- Microsoft Graph invocations
- Implementing IInitialize

Implement the Constructor

We will need an instance of the ILogger to handle logging throughout this class. Update the constructor to inject an instance of it and save it to a local variable. See constructor code in Listing 14-1.

Listing 14-1. DashboardViewModel constructor implementation

```
public class DashboardViewModel
{
  ILogger logger;
  public DashboardViewModel(ILogger<DashboardViewModel> logger)
  {
    this.logger = logger;
  }
}
```

Note   In Listing 14-1 we resolve the ILogger by using
ILogger<DashboardViewModel>. This is the standard way to resolve any
ILogger implementation using the Microsoft Logging library.

Public Properties

In our MVVM application, the public properties are used for data binding to the view or page. Before we can add our properties, we need to update the class definition to inherit from ObservableObject. This will give us access to the SetProperty() method, which we will use to notify the view of changes. See the updated class definition in Listing 14-2.

Listing 14-2. DashboardViewModel updated class definition to include ObservableObject

```
public DashboardViewModel : ObservableObject
{
  // omitted code
}
```

We can now add our public properties Name and Email. Following the public property data binding convention, the setter will use the SetProperty() method to notify the view that there is a change. See the property code snippet in Listing 14-3.

Listing 14-3. DashboardViewModel public property implementations

```
string name;
public string Name
{
  get => name;
  set => SetProperty(ref name, value);
}

string email;
public string Email
{
  get => email;
  set => SetProperty(ref email, value);
}
```

Note When using the SetProperty() method to notify the user interface, you must pass the primitive variable as a parameter using the ref keyword. This ensures that the primitive is passed by reference instead of passed by value.

Microsoft Graph Integration

To load data from the Microsoft Graph, we will create a simple method that retrieves the Name and Email to be set to the properties we created in the last section. Create a method stub named LoadDataAsync() – see the code snippet in Listing 14-4.

Listing 14-4. DashboardViewModel LoadDataAsync method stub

```
public async Task LoadDataAsync()
{
  // TODO - add implementation
}
```

Before we can add our implementation of LoadDataAsync, we need to implement the IAuthenticationProvider interface, which is included in the Microsoft Graph SDK. This interface contains the AuthenticateRequestAsync method, which allows us to attach our access token to the outgoing HttpRequestMessage generated by the Microsoft Graph SDK. In the previous chapter, we implemented this interface in the GraphFileService. Our implementation in the DashboardViewModel will be very similar.

Update the class definition to inherit from IAuthenticationProvider – see the code snippet in Listing 14-5.

Listing 14-5. DashboardViewModel adds IAuthenticationProvider to the class definition

```
public class DashboardViewModel :
  ObservableObject, IAuthenticationProvider
{
  // omitted code
}
```

Next, we can add our implementation for the AuthenticateRequestAsync method. See the implementation in Listing 14-6.

Listing 14-6. DashboardViewModel AuthenticateRequestAsync method
implementation

```
public Task AuthenticateRequestAsync(HttpRequestMessage message)
{
  var token = ((App)App.Current)
    .AuthenticationResult
    ?.AccessToken;

  if (string.IsNullOrEmpty(token))
  {
    throw new Exception("No Access Token");
  }

  request.Headers.Authorization =
    new AuthenticationHeaderValue("Bearer", token);
  return Task.CompletedTask;
}
```

Let's work on our implementation of LoadDataAsync. We need to create an
instance of the GraphServiceClient and then retrieve our data. Our Name property
will be mapped from the DisplayName property, and the Email property will come
from the UserPrincipalName. In the last chapter, we learned that we always need
to create a special HttpHandler for WebAssembly (WASM) prior to creating the
GraphServiceClient. See the implementation of LoadDataAsync in Listing 14-7.

Listing 14-7. DashboardViewModel basic implementation of the
LoadDataAsync method

```
public async Task LoadDataAsync()
{
  try
  {
    var httpClient = new HttpClient();

    var graphClient = new GraphServiceClient(httpClient);
    graphClient.AuthenticationProvider = this;

    var me = await graphClient
```

```
        .Me
        .Request()
        .Select(user => new
        {
          Id = user.Id,
          DisplayName = user.DisplayName,
          UserPrincipalName = user.UserPrincipalName
        })
        .GetAsync();

    if (me != null)
    {
      Name = me.DisplayName;
      Email = me.UserPrincipalName;
    }
  }
  catch (Exception ex)
  {
    logger.LogError(ex, ex.Message);
  }
}
```

.NET 6 Mobile Considerations

In the last chapter while implementing the GraphFileService, we learned that if
a library is not compiled against a .NET 6 mobile target such as net6.0-android or
net6.0-ios, some objects may not work correctly. This is because the backward
compatibility layer is very thin. To resolve this, we will be manually retrieving the JSON
and deserializing it.

Update the code in LoadDataAsync where we create our request builder and generate
the local variable me. See updated code in Listing 14-8.

Listing 14-8. DashboardViewModel LoadDataAsync request builder snippet for
.NET 6 mobile targets

```
var request = await graphClient
  .Me
```

```
.Request()
.Select(user => new
{
  Id = user.Id,
  DisplayName = user.DisplayName,
  UserPrincipalName = user.UserPrincipalName
});

#if __ANDROID__ || __IOS__ || __MACOS__
  var response = await request.GetResponseAsync();
  var data = await response.Content.ReadAsStringAsync();
  var me = JsonSerializer.Deserialize<User>(data);
#else
  var me = await request.GetAsync();
#endif
```

IInitialize Implementation

The LoadDataAsync method will not be invoked unless there is something in place to tell it to load data when the page loads. In the previous chapter, we learned about our IInitialize interface and how to implement it on the view model and invoke it from the page. We need to add this code to both the DashboardViewModel and the code behind of the Dashboard in the Dashboard.xaml.cs file.

First, add the IInitialize to the class definition of the DashboardViewModel. See the code snippet in Listing 14-9.

Listing 14-9. DashboardViewModel class definition snippet adds IInitialize

```
public class DashboardViewModel :
  ObservableObject, IAuthenticationProvider, IInitialize
{
  // omitted code
}
```

The IInitialize interface defines the method InitializeAsync, which is where we will invoke our LoadDataAsync method from. We can guarantee this method is invoked just after the page is loaded. See InitializeAsync implementation in Listing 14-10.

Listing 14-10. DashboardViewModel InitializeAsync method implementation

```
public async Task InitializeAsync()
{
  await LoadDataAsync();
}
```

We need to make sure the IInitialize interface is properly invoked from the Dashboard.xaml.cs file, also known as the code behind. The implementation will be very similar to what we did in the previous chapter for the MyFilesPage.xaml.cs. In the code behind, we will create a ViewModel property that casts the DataContext to the type of DashboardViewModel. Then we will override the OnNavigatedTo method, which will invoke the InitializeAsync method on the IInitialize interface. See the code snippet in Listing 14-11.

Listing 14-11. Dashboard.xaml.cs – invoke the IInitialize interface

```
public DashboardViewModel ViewModel =>
  (DashboardViewModel)DataContext;

protected override async void OnNavigatedTo(
  NavigationEventArgs e)
{
  base.OnNavigatedTo(e);

  // Existing code
  if (e.Parameter is INavigationService navigation)
  {
    this.navigation = navigation;
  }

  // New code
  if (ViewModel is IInitialize initializeViewModel)
  {
    await initializeViewModel.InitializeAsync();
  }
}
```

Complete DashboardViewModel Implementation

We have completed our DashboardViewModel implementation – see the complete view model code in Listing 14-12.

Listing 14-12. DashboardViewModel complete implementation

```
public class DashboardViewModel :
  ObservableObject, IAuthenticationProvider, IInitialize
{
  ILogger logger;
  public DashboardViewModel(ILogger<DashboardViewModel> logger)
  {
    this.logger = logger;
  }

  string name;
  public string Name
  {
    get => name;
    set => SetProperty(ref name, value);
  }

  string email;
  public string Email
  {
    get => email;
    set => SetProperty(ref email, value);
  }

  public async Task LoadDataAsync()
  {
    try
    {

      var httpClient = new HttpClient();

      var graphClient = new GraphServiceClient(httpClient);
      graphClient.AuthenticationProvider = this;
```

```csharp
      var request = await graphClient
        .Me
        .Request()
        .Select(user => new
        {
          Id = user.Id,
          DisplayName = user.DisplayName,
          UserPrincipalName = user.UserPrincipalName
        });

#if __ANDROID__ || __IOS__ || __MACOS__
      var response = await request.GetResponseAsync();
      var data = await response.Content.ReadAsStringAsync();

      var me = JsonSerializer.Deserialize<User>(data);
#else
      var me = await request.GetAsync();
#endif

      if (me != null)
      {
        Name = me.DisplayName;
        Email = me.UserPrincipalName;
      }
    }
    catch (Exception ex)
    {
      logger.LogError(ex, ex.Message);
    }
  }

  public Task AuthenticateRequestAsync(
    HttpRequestMessage message)
  {
    var token = ((App)App.Current)
      .AuthenticationResult
      ?.AccessToken;
```

```
  if (string.IsNullOrEmpty(token))
  {
    throw new Exception("No Access Token");
  }

  request.Headers.Authorization =
    new AuthenticationHeaderValue("Bearer", token);
  return Task.CompletedTask;
  }

  public async Task InitializeAsync()
  {
    await LoadDataAsync();
  }
}
```

Dashboard Changes

We already have the Dashboard XAML code implemented and only need to update the name and email TextBlock controls to bind to the DashboardViewModel. Find the TextBlock that has the display name in it and update the Text property to bind to the Name property on the DashboardViewModel. See the code snippet in Listing 14-13.

Listing 14-13. Dashboard display name data binding snippet

```
<TextBlock
  Text="{Binding Name}"
  FontSize="20"
  skia:HorizontalAlignment="Center"
  HorizontalAlignment="Center" />
```

Next, add data binding to the email TextBlock, which should be the next control in the XAML code. Update the Text property to bind to the Email property on the DashboardViewModel. See the code snippet in Listing 14-14.

Listing 14-14. Dashboard email data binding snippet

```
<TextBlock
  Text="{Binding Email}"
  FontSize="18"
  skia:HorizontalAlignment="Center"
  HorizontalAlignment="Center" />
```

User Interface Testing

All the code is completed, and it is time to test the various platforms. Screenshots will have the email address omitted. See screenshots of running application in Figure 14-1 for Windows, Figure 14-2 for WASM, Figure 14-3 for WPF, Figure 14-4 for Linux, Figure 14-5 for Android, Figure 14-6 for iOS, and Figure 14-7 for macOS.

Windows

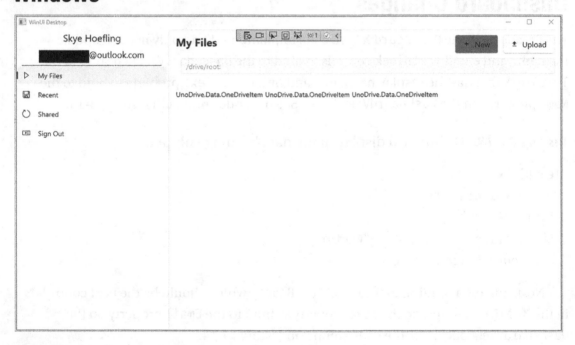

Figure 14-1. *Windows application with display name and email in the dashboard*

WebAssembly (WASM)

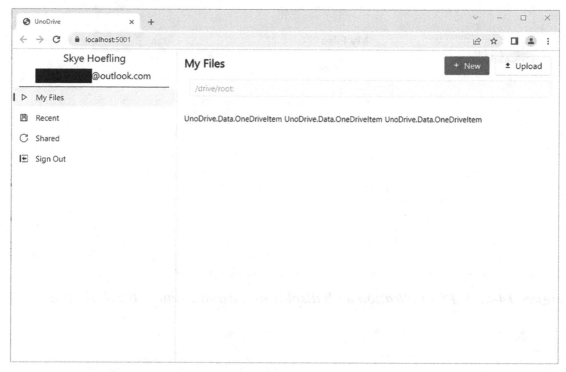

Figure 14-2. *WebAssembly (WASM) application with display name and email in the dashboard*

WPF

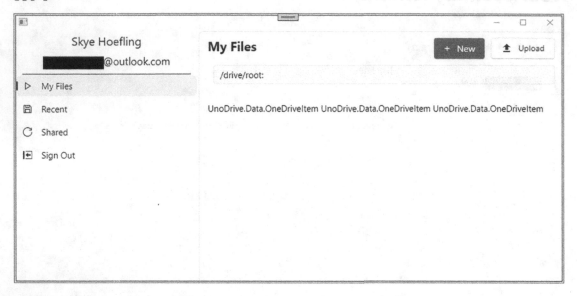

Figure 14-3. *WPF application with display name and email in the dashboard*

GTK

Figure 14-4. *GTK application with display name and email in the dashboard*

Android

Figure 14-5. *Android application with display name and email in the dashboard*

iOS

Figure 14-6. iOS application with display name and email in the dashboard

macOS

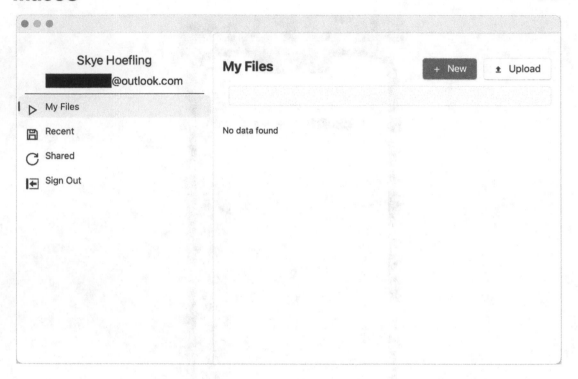

Figure 14-7. *macOS application with display name and email in the dashboard*

Conclusion

In this chapter we built on the Microsoft Graph concepts we learned in Chapter 13 while we added more personalization to the dashboard menu. If you had any trouble implementing the code, go and download the sample code before moving on to the next chapter: https://github.com/SkyeHoefling/UnoDrive/tree/main/Chapter%2014.

CHAPTER 15

Images and GridView

Adding images to an application is important to give your product a final customized look and feel. This is true for all applications from a general consumer product to a line-of-business product that is more focused on filling out forms. The images are vital in helping the user navigate through the application and perform their tasks. In this chapter we are going to review the basics of adding images and how to render them on the screen.

Adding images to your Uno Platform application is very simple compared with other cross-platform tools you may have used. It is still important to understand conceptually some of the things that are happening when working with images. In Uno Platform there is no need to manage assets in each individual target platform. You can add them all to the shared code, and the core Uno Platform toolkit will properly add them to bundles, resources, and other native locations so they are available across the platforms.

In this chapter we will be updating the `GridView` control that displays our OneDrive items to render image representations of those items. Folders that can be navigated to will use a folder icon, and individual files will attempt to render the thumbnail URL generated by the Microsoft Graph API that we cached earlier.

Uno Platform Image Layer

Adding images to an Uno Platform application is a simple process. In the shared code, you will add images into the Assets folder that is included in the project template. There you will find a `SharedAssets.md` file that explains how to add assets of various sizes. The various platforms require scaled assets depending on the screen size, and these vary depending on the platform. For example, iOS uses the terminology `@1x`, `@2x`, and `@3x`, whereas Android uses `mdpi`, `hdpi`, `xhdpi`, `xxhdpi`, and `xxxhdpi`. Typically, in a native application, you would manually add images of various sizes following that platform-specific convention. This is not required in Uno Platform as the core platform code automatically handles this at compile time. Your image assets are required to be in the shared code.

419

© Skye Hoefling 2022
S. Hoefling, *Getting Started with the Uno Platform and WinUI 3*,
https://doi.org/10.1007/978-1-4842-8248-9_15

When adding images to your project, you will need to follow the Uno Platform asset convention as documented in the SharedAssets.md. The scaling algorithm uses the syntax scale-100, scale-125, scale-150, scale-200, scale-300, and scale-400, where scale-100 is the started image and each number represents a multiplier in size from that original image. See the scaling chart in Table 15-1.

Table 15-1. *Asset Scaling Table That Shows How Scaling Will Be Applied on Various Platforms. Not All Scales Are Supported on All Platforms*

Scale	Windows	iOS	Android
100	scale-100	@1x	mdpi
125	scale-125	N/A	N/A
150	scale-150	N/A	hdpi
200	scale-200	@2x	xhdpi
300	scale-300	@3x	xxhdpi
400	scale-400	N/A	xxxhdpi

To add the image to your project, you can use one of two techniques:

1. Place all the scaled files in a scaled folder as seen in Listing 15-1.

2. Use a naming convention for each file as seen in Listing 15-2.

Listing 15-1. Image assets using the folder convention

```
\Assets\Images\scale-100\logo.png
\Assets\Images\scale-200\logo.png
\Assets\Images\scale-400\logo.png
```

Listing 15-2. Image assets using the file name convention

```
\Assets\Images\logo.scale-100.png
\Assets\Images\logo.scale-200.png
\Assets\Images\logo.scale-400.png
```

Note   These approaches are both valid and have their own advantages and disadvantages. This is purely a style and code organization preference.

Once you have added an image to the shared code's Assets folder, you can then reference it in any page using the standard `ms-appx` URI. See the URI example for accessing the `logo.png` file in Listing 15-3.

Note   `ms-appx:///` is the standard prefix for reference files packaged as `Content`. This can be files located in the shared project's `Assets` directory or anything in a target platform project that is compiled as `Content`.

Listing 15-3. ms-appx URI example

```
ms-appx:///Assets/Images/logo.png
```

When using the `ms-appx` syntax, there is no need to specify the scaling convention by file name or folder. The core platform code will automatically determine the device size and render the correct asset.

If we want to use this in a standard `Image` control on a user interface page, you will set the `ms-appx` to the `Source` property. See an example of using an Image control in Listing 15-4.

Listing 15-4. Image control using the ms-appx URI example

```
<Image Source="ms-appx:///Assets/Images/logo.png" />
```

In the next sections, we will be taking the concepts we have reviewed and putting them to practice – adding image assets to our shared project and rendering them in the user interface.

Adding Images

In this section we will be adding images to the shared project that we will be rendering in the user interface. The images we are using are available in the GitHub source for this chapter: `https://github.com/ahoefling/UnoDrive/tree/main/Chapter%2015`.

In the UnoDrive.Shared project under the Assets folder, create a new folder named Images. We will use the file name convention referenced in Listing 15-2, which means we will be adding the images in the same folder using ".scale-100.png" as the suffix for each image.

Add the following images:

```
folder.scale-100.png
folder.scale-125.png
folder.scale-150.png
folder.scale-200.png
folder.scale-300.png
folder.scale-400.png
```

See a screenshot of the Visual Studio Solution Explorer with added images in Figure 15-1.

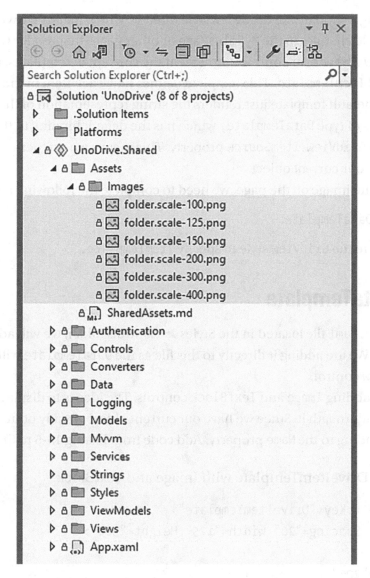

Figure 15-1. *Visual Studio Solution Explorer folder images added to the project*

Displaying Images

Currently when the user logs into the application, it renders the MyFilesPage, and the results will be displayed as a string representation of the object. Let's update our GridView to render either the folder image that we just added or the cached OneDrive thumbnail for the image.

We are going to update the `GridView` style directly, which means we will not need to make any code changes to the `MyFilesPage` or other pages that render OneDrive items. `GridView` and similar controls implement the concept of templates, and in our case, it is called `ItemTemplate`. This template defines how each item in the `GridView` is rendered. The default template just renders the string representation of the object. An `ItemTemplate` is of type `DataTemplate,` which has the default binding to the current object from the `GridView ItemSource` property. This means we can perform data binding right to our current object.

To display the image on the page, we need to complete the following tasks:

- Add `DataTemplate`.

- Update the `GridView` style to specify `ItemTemplate`.

Create DataTemplate

In the `GridView.xaml` file located in the Styles ➤ Controls folder, we will add the `DataTemplate`. We are adding it directly to this file as the `DataTemplate` will only be used by our `GridView` control.

Start off by adding `Image` and `TextBlock` controls. The idea is to display the icon and then a name underneath it. Since we have our current object already bounded, we can perform the binding to the `Name` property. Add code from Listing 15-5 to `GridView.xaml`.

Listing 15-5. DriveItemTemplate with Image and TextBlock

```
<DataTemplate x:Key="DriveItemTemplate">
  <StackPanel Spacing="20" Width="175" Height="300">
    <Image
      Height="200"
      Source="ms-appx://Assets/Images/folder.png" />
    <TextBlock
      Text="{Binding Name}"
      HorizontalAlignment="Center"
      HorizontalTextAlignment="Center"
      TextWrapping="WrapWholeWords" />
  </StackPanel>
</DataTemplate>
```

> **Note**   In Listing 15-5 we set the StackPanel to a specific Height and Width. Then we set the Image to a specific Height, which is less. This is to prevent the Image from pushing the TextBlock out of the StackPanel, which could hide it from the user.

This DataTemplate assumes everything should use the folder.png icon, which includes files and folders, which is not the behavior we want. We know that the OneDriveItem contains an ImageSource property that we can bind directly to the image. We can update the code to display the thumbnail if a thumbnail exists by using the NullEqualsVisibleConverter and NullEqualsCollapsedConverter. See the updated code snippet in Listing 15-6.

Listing 15-6. DriveItemTemplate add ThumbnailSource and Visibility converters

```
<DataTemplate x:Key="DriveItemTemplate">
  <StackPanel Spacing="20" Width="175" Height="300">
    <Image
      Height="200"
      Source="ms-appx://Assets/Images/folder.png"
      Visibility="{Binding ThumbnailSource, Converter=
        {StaticResource NullEqualsVisibleConverter}}" />
    <Image
      Source="{Binding ThumbnailSource}"
      Visibility="{Binding ThumbnailSource, Converter=
        {StaticResource NullEqualsCollapsedConverter}}" />
    <TextBlock
      Text="{Binding Name}"
      HorizontalAlignment="Center"
      HorizontalTextAlignment="Center"
      TextWrapping="WrapWholeWords" />
  </StackPanel>
</DataTemplate>
```

macOS Considerations

Some platforms do not implement the automatic asset scaling, but those assets are still added to the bundle correctly. This means you may need to add platform-specific code to get the image to render correctly. On macOS the assets are added, but not scaled, which means the ms-appx syntax needs to be adjusted to the URI in Listing 15-7.

Listing 15-7. macOS-specific image URI workaround

```
ms-appx:///Assets/Images/folder.scale-300.png
```

In the workaround, notice that it uses the exact file name instead of the convention we have been using.

Note   The Uno Platform bug and workaround cited in Listing 15-7 is a known issue for macOS. You can track the current status on GitHub at `https://github.com/unoplatform/uno/issues/8385`.

To fix this in our GridView.xaml styles, we will add platform-specific code for the concepts of macos and not_macos. Start by ensuring that the root ResourceDictionary contains platform-specific declarations so we can use them in the style. See code in Listing 15-8.

Listing 15-8. GridView.xaml ResourceDictionary declarations for platform-specific XAML

```
xmlns:mc="http://schemas.openxmlformats.org/markup-compatibility/2006"
xmlns:not_macos="http://schemas.microsoft.com/winfx/2006/xaml/presentation"
xmlns:macos="http://uno.ui/macos"
mc:Ignorable="macos"
```

We only want the macos xmlns added to ignorable in this case; otherwise, the Windows project will not compile correctly.

Now you can update the DataTemplate to include platform-specific XAML for the image folder. See updated code in Listing 15-9.

Listing 15-9. DriveItemTemplate add macOS-specific XAML for loading folder. png images

```
<DataTemplate x:Key="DriveItemTemplate">
  <StackPanel Spacing="20" Width="175" Height="300">
    <Image
      Height="200"
      not_macos:Source="ms-appx://Assets/Images/folder.png"
      macos:Source="ms-appx://Assets/Images/folder.scale-300.png"
      Visibility="{Binding ThumbnailSource, Converter=
        {StaticResource NullEqualsVisibleConverter}}" />
    <Image
      Source="{Binding ThumbnailSource}"
      Visibility="{Binding ThumbnailSource, Converter=
        {StaticResource NullEqualsCollapsedConverter}}" />
    <TextBlock
      Text="{Binding Name}"
      HorizontalAlignment="Center"
      HorizontalTextAlignment="Center"
      TextWrapping="WrapWholeWords" />
  </StackPanel>
</DataTemplate>
```

Test the User Interface

Let's launch the application on our various platforms. See the running application in Figure 15-2 for Windows, Figure 15-3 for WASM, Figure 15-4 for WPF, Figure 15-5 for Linux, Figure 15-6 for Android, Figure 15-7 for iOS, and Figure 15-8 for macOS.

Windows

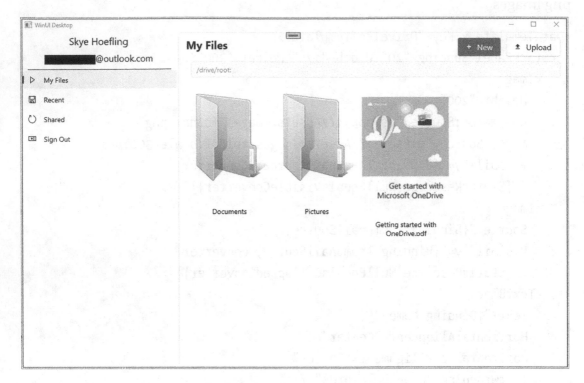

Figure 15-2. *Windows application with images rendering on the page*

WebAssembly (WASM)

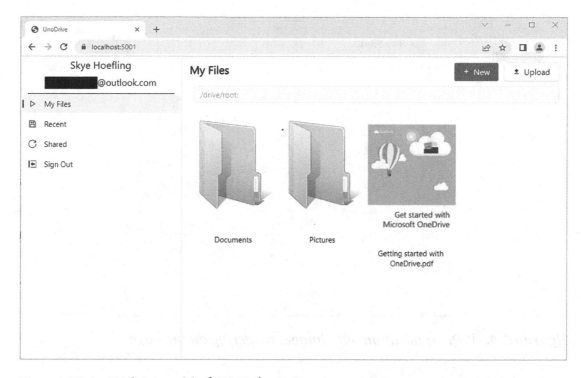

Figure 15-3. *WebAssembly (WASM) application with images rendering on the page*

WFP

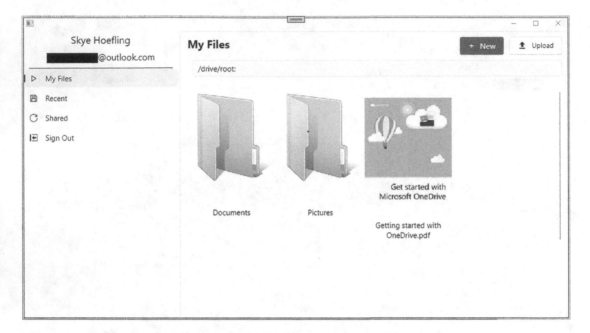

Figure 15-4. WPF application with images rendering on the page

GTK

Figure 15-5. *GTK application with images rendering on the page*

Android

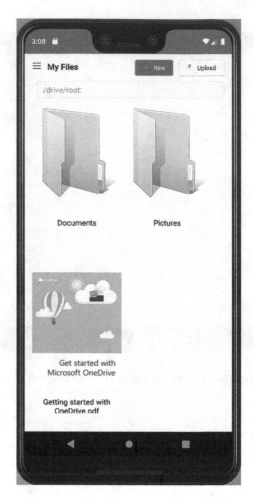

Figure 15-6. *Android application with images rendering on the page*

iOS

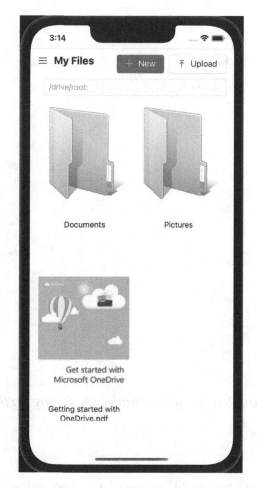

Figure 15-7. *iOS application with images rendering on the page*

macOS

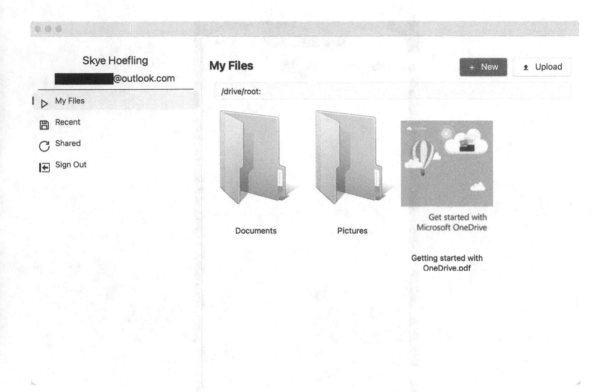

Figure 15-8. *macOS application with images rendering on the page*

Conclusion

In this chapter we learned how to add images to the page and updated our `GridView` to display a folder icon or the OneDrive thumbnail image to render the various items on the page. We will be building on these concepts as we move into the next chapter. If you had any trouble implementing the techniques, you can download the latest code from GitHub: `https://github.com/SkyeHoefling/UnoDrive/tree/main/Chapter%2015`.

CHAPTER 16

Selectors

In Chapter 12 we learned about converters. In this chapter, we will be learning about selectors, which are conceptually very similar but solve a different problem. A selector is used when you are binding a collection to a list control or similar. When displaying multiple items in a list and you need to render the row differently based on the type of data in that row, you will use a selector to determine the correct `DataTemplate` to render. A selector will run a code block for each item in the collection, which allows us to determine how to render the row.

In our UnoDrive application, we will want a selector for displaying the default folder or file icon. In Chapter 15 we added images and are using thumbnails for the files. This works as expected in our testing, but not every file is guaranteed to have a thumbnail, so we need to use a selector to render the file icon vs. the folder icon.

How Do Selectors Work?

To create a selector, you will need to define a new class that inherits from `DataTemplateSelector`, a class provided in the Uno Platform core code. You need to override the `SelectTemplateCore` method and return the `DataTemplate` you would like to render.

Consider a common selector example where you want to display one of two `DataTemplates`. In this example you need to create two properties that represent each type of `DataTemplate` you want to render. Then in the `SelectTemplateCore` method, you will determine when to render one or the other. Let's assume our collection is a list of `bool` values and return one if `true` and the other if `false`. See example code in Listing 16-1.

© Skye Hoefling 2022
S. Hoefling, *Getting Started with the Uno Platform and WinUI 3*,
https://doi.org/10.1007/978-1-4842-8248-9_16

Listing 16-1. Selector example implementation

```
public class SampleSelector : DataTemplateSelector
{
  public DataTemplate TrueTemplate { get; set; }
  public DataTemplate FalseTemplate { get; set; }

  protected override DataTemplate SelectTemplateCore(object item)
  {
    return (bool)item ? TrueTemplate : FalseTemplate;
  }
}
```

The selector is defined, and we can move on to the XAML code that creates a `StaticResource`. Just like we did with converters, a selector needs to be defined as a `StaticResource` to be used in a control or style. You will need to define two `DataTemplate` styles and then the selector itself.

In our sample here, we will render a hard-coded message for each data template. See Listing 16-2 for the `DataTemplate` and selector definition in the XAML code.

Listing 16-2. DataTemplate and selector definition in XAML

```
<DataTemplate x:Key="TrueMessageTemplate">
  <TextBlock Text="The current row is true!" />
</DataTemplate>

<DataTemplate x:Key="TrueMessageTemplate">
  <TextBlock Text="The current row is false!" />
</DataTemplate>

<selectors:SampleSelector
  x:Key="SampleSelector"
  TrueTemplate="{StaticResource TrueMessageTemplate}"
  FalseTemplate="{StaticResource FalseMessageTemplate}" />
```

Everything for our selector is defined and ready to use, and it can be added to a collection-based user interface control such as a `GridView`. The `GridView` control has a special property named `ItemTemplateSelector`, which needs to be used instead of `ItemTemplate`. This will run the code in `SampleSelector` and return the correct `DataTemplate`. See code in Listing 16-3 for the `GridView` implementation.

Listing 16-3. SampleSelector GridView implementation

```
<GridView
  ItemsSource="{Binding Items}"
  ItemTemplateSelector="{StaticResource SampleSelector}" />
```

Note   In Listing 16-2 the DataTemplate and SampleSelector both use the x:Key statement to define a unique name for the resource. This is required so it can be referenced as a StaticResource in the markup extension.

Implement the Selector

In our UnoDrive application, we need a selector that will pick the correct DataTemplate depending on if the row is for a file or a folder. The MyFilesViewModel defines a property named FilesAndFolders of type List<OneDriveItem>. In our selector code, we can determine the type of the OneDriveItem and return the correct DataTemplate.

Add the Selector

In the UnoDrive.Shared project, create a new folder named Selectors, and inside that folder create a new empty class named OneDriveItemTemplateSelector.cs. See Figure 16-1 for the screenshot.

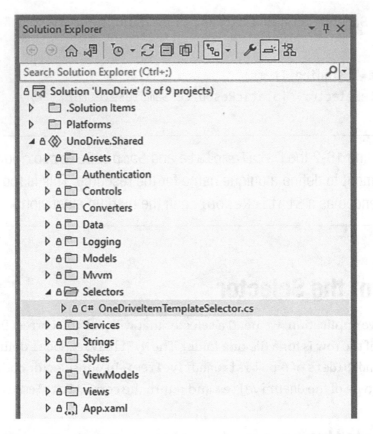

Figure 16-1. Visual Studio Solution Explorer OneDriveItemTemplateSelector.cs

Now we can implement our class by inheriting from the DataTemplateSelector
and defining our DataTemplate properties. When overriding SelectTemplateCore we
can cast our parameter to OneDriveItem and then determine if it is a folder or file. If
we are unable to determine the type, we can assume it is a folder. See the complete
implementation in Listing 16-4.

Listing 16-4. OneDriveItemTemplateSelector implementation

```
public class OneDriveItemTemplateSelector : DataTemplateSelector
{
  public DataTemplate FolderTemplate { get; set; }
  public DataTemplate ItemTemplate { get; set; }

  protected override DataTemplate SelectTemplateCore(object item)
  {
```

```
    if (item is not OneDriveItem oneDriveItem)
    {
      return FolderTemplate;
    }

    return oneDriveItem.Type == OneDriveItemType.Folder ?
      FolderTemplate : ItemTemplate;
  }
}
```

Update GridView Styles

The selector implementation is complete, and we can start updating the GridView global styles to use it. In the Styles ➤ Controls folder, open the GridView.xaml file, which is where we will be adding our new OneDriveItemTemplateSelector.

The root ResourceDictionary node at the top of the file needs to include a new namespace for the selector we just created. Add the xmlns as seen in Listing 16-5.

Listing 16-5. GridView.xaml xmlns for selectors

```
xmlns:selectors="using:UnoDrive.Selectors"
```

Currently there is only one DataTemplate in the GridView.xaml file. We need to define a DataTemplate for both files and folders. Update the name of the current DataTemplate from DriveItemTemplate to DriveFolderTemplate. None of the XAML should change, but you can see complete DriveFolderTemplate XAML in Listing 16-6.

Listing 16-6. GridView.xaml DriveFolderTemplate DataTemplate

```
<DataTemplate x:Key="DriveFolderTemplate">
  <StackPanel Spacing="20" Width="175" Height="300">
    <Image
      not_macos:Source="ms-appx:///Assets/Images/folder.png"
      macos:Source=
        "ms-appx:///Assets/Images/folder.scale-300.png"
      Visibility="{Binding ThumbnailSource, Converter=
        {StaticResource NullEqualsVisibileConverter}}" />
    <Image
```

```
      Source="{Binding ThumbnailSource}"
      Visibility="{Binding ThumbnailSource, Converter=
        {StaticResource NullEqualsCollapsedConverter}}" />
    <TextBlock
      Text="{Binding Name}"
      HorizontalAlignment="Center"
      HorizontalTextAlignment="Center"
      TextWrapping="WrapWholeWords" />
  </StackPanel>
</DataTemplate>
```

Next, we will need to create a DriveItemTemplate. This template will use a new image asset name file.png. You can download the assets from the code source on GitHub for this chapter:

- file.scale-100.png

- file.scale-125.png

- file.scale-150.png

- file.scale-200.png

- file.scale-300.png

Upload the image assets in the UnoDrive.Shared project under the folder Assets ➤ Images and ensure they are added to the project.

With the new image assets added, we can implement the DriveItemTemplate. This DataTemplate is almost identical to the DriveFolderTemplate, but we will be using file.png and file.scale-300.png for the ImageSource property. See DriveItemTemplate code in Listing 16-7.

Listing 16-7. GridView.xaml DriveItemTemplate DataTemplate

```
<DataTemplate x:Key="DriveItemTemplate">
  <StackPanel Spacing="20" Width="175" Height="300">
    <Image
      not_macos:Source="ms-appx:///Assets/Images/item.png"
      macos:Source=
        "ms-appx:///Assets/Images/item.scale-300.png"
```

```
      Visibility="{Binding ThumbnailSource, Converter=
        {StaticResource NullEqualsVisibileConverter}}" />
    <Image
      Source="{Binding ThumbnailSource}"
      Visibility="{Binding ThumbnailSource, Converter=
        {StaticResource NullEqualsCollapsedConverter}}" />
    <TextBlock
      Text="{Binding Name}"
      HorizontalAlignment="Center"
      HorizontalTextAlignment="Center"
      TextWrapping="WrapWholeWords" />
  </StackPanel>
</DataTemplate>
```

Our two DataTemplates have been created, and we can now define our selector. Add a new entry into the GridView.xaml file that defines the OneDriveItemTemplateSelector and specifies the FolderTemplate and ItemTemplate. See code in Listing 16-8.

Listing 16-8. GridView.xaml OneDriveItemTemplateSelector definition

```
<selectors:OneDriveItemTemplateSelector
  x:Key="OneDriveItemTemplateSelector"
  FolderTemplate="{StaticResource DriveFolderTemplate}"
  ItemTemplate="{StaticResource DriveItemTemplate}" />
```

The final step of our implementation is to update the default GridView style. You will remove the Setter for ItemTemplate and add a new Setter for ItemTemplateSelector. See code in Listing 16-9 for the complete GridView style.

Listing 16-9. Updated GridView default style

```
<Style TargetType="GridView">
  <Setter
    Property="ItemTemplateSelector"
    Value="{StaticResource OneDriveItemTemplateSelector}" />
  <Setter Property="IsItemClickEnabled" Value="False" />
  <Setter Property="CanDragItems" Value="False" />
  <Setter Property="AllowDrop" Value="False" />
```

```
  <Setter Property="CanReorderItems" Value="False" />
  <Setter Property="SelectionMode" Value="Single" />
  <Setter Property="FlowDirection" Value="LeftToRight" />
  <Setter Property="HorizontalContentAlignment" Value="Center" />
  <Setter Property="IsItemClickEnabled" Value="True" />
</Style>
```

That completes our implementation of the OneDriveItemTemplateSelector. When you run your application, nothing will look different with the default OneDrive files. This is useful if there are issues downloading the thumbnail or one is not included for the OneDrive item.

Conclusion

In this chapter we learned how to implement a custom selector. We added a new selector called OneDriveItemTemplateSelector, which is used to render the DataTemplate for files vs. folders. In our UnoDrive application, this selector is useful as a backup strategy in case the thumbnail data is not available from OneDrive. If you had any trouble following along with the code in this chapter, you can download it from GitHub: https://github.com/SkyeHoefling/UnoDrive/tree/main/Chapter%2016.

CHAPTER 17

OneDrive Navigation

In Chapters 13–16, we have been implementing the MyFilesPage that accesses OneDrive files from the user's account and loads them onto the screen. Currently, the application only allows you to access files in the root OneDrive directory. In this chapter we will learn how to add navigation through the various pages by applying the concepts we have learned so far on MVVM applications.

In this chapter we will be implementing the following features:

- Item click navigation

- *Forward navigation*: History

- *Backward navigatio*n: History

Update Models

Earlier we created a model named Location, which only stores an Id for the OneDrive current path of the given location. We need this to store more data to help us navigate through the different locations on OneDrive. To help us navigate through the locations, we will update the Location model to implement a doubly linked list data structure.

In this data structure, you can have any object point to the next item in the list and the previous one. This means we will easily be able to determine if we can go back or forward. If there is a null object for either, that means the operation cannot happen. If there is a valid value for it, we can start navigating in that direction.

Start off by adding two properties to the Location class to store a reference to the Back or Forward position in the doubly linked list. See Listing 17-1 for the code snippet.

© Skye Hoefling 2022
S. Hoefling, *Getting Started with the Uno Platform and WinUI 3*,
https://doi.org/10.1007/978-1-4842-8248-9_17

Listing 17-1. Location model – add Back and Forward properties

```
public class Location
{
  public string Id { get; set; }
  public Location Back { get; set; }
  public Location Forward { get; set; }
}
```

To help us determine if we can move forward or backward, we will add two properties that check if we can move in each direction. Update the Location model to include two new properties CanMoveBack and CanMoveForward. See Listing 17-2 for complete Location model code.

Listing 17-2. Location model complete code

```
public class Location
{
  public string Id { get; set; }

  public Location Back { get; set; }
  public Location Forward { get; set; }

  public bool CanMoveBack => Back != null;
  public Bool CanMoveForward => Forward != null;
}
```

The Location model is now updated, and these changes will be used as we implement navigation in the next two sections.

Item Click Navigation

Our files and folders are rendered in the MyFilesPage using a standard GridView control. This control provides an easy item click event handler named ItemClick. To implement the folder-style navigation, you will create a new method in the MyFilesViewModel and then add the data binding to the MyFilesPage.

Start by opening the MyFilesViewModel and creating a method stub that the event handler will use. Create a new method named OnItemClick as seen in Listing 17-3.

Listing 17-3. MyFilesViewModel OnItemClick method stub

```
public async void OnItemClick(
  object sender, ItemClickEventArgs args)
{
  // TODO - add implementation
}
```

Note   OnItemClick uses async void as the method signature as we will be loading data by invoking LoadDataAsync. As an event handler, it is okay to use async void in this scenario.

Now that we have the method created in the view model, we can update the MyFilesPage to use that method. Since we want to use the event handler arguments directly, we are not using an ICommand or the simple data binding using the {Binding} syntax. We will use the {x:Bind} syntax, which will give us direct access to the .NET objects and can directly invoke the method.

Earlier, we created a special property in the MyFilesPage code behind called ViewModel. This property is a casted instance of the DataContext, which is of type MyFilesViewModel. We can use {x:Bind} with that property to directly access the OnItemClick method of the MyFilesViewModel. See the updated GridView declaration in Listing 17-4.

Listing 17-4. MyFilesPage GridView update for the ItemClick event

```
<GridView
  ItemSource="{Binding FilesAndFolders}"
  ItemClick="{x:Bind ViewModel.OnItemClick}"
  Visibility="{Binding IsPageEmpty, Converter=
    {StaticResource BoolNegationToVisibilityConverter}}" />
```

Everything is connected, and we can add our OnItemClick implementation in the MyFilesViewModel. Our implementation strategy is determining if the clicked item is of type OneDriveItem and a folder. Then we can load the data and set the properties on the Location model.

Start off by adding a location variable to track the `Location` at the top of the MyFilesViewModel. See the code snippet in Listing 17-5.

Listing 17-5. MyFilesViewModel – add a location variable at the top of the file

```
public class MyFilesViewModel : ObservableObject, IInitialize
{
  Location location = new Location();

  // omitted code
}
```

In the `OnItemClick` method, we can add our implementation to load data and update our position. See code in Listing 17-6.

Listing 17-6. MyFilesViewModel OnItemClick implementation

```
public async void OnItemClick(
  object sender, ItemClickEventArgs args)
{
  if (args.ClickedItem is not OneDriveItem oneDriveItem)
  {
    return;
  }

  if (oneDriveItem.Type == OneDriveItemType.Folder)
  {
    try
    {
      location.Forward = new Location
      {
        Id = oneDriveItem.Id,
        Back = location
      };
      location = location.Forward;

      await LoadDataAsync(oneDriveItem.Id);
    }
    catch (Exception ex)
```

```
  {
    logger.LogError(ex, ex.Message);
  }
 }
}
```

Forward and Back Navigation

After the user clicks a folder, they begin navigating through the folder structure of OneDrive. Our application tracks the location as we implemented in the last section. If the user wants to go back or forward depending on their history, we need to navigate the doubly linked list we built earlier. In this section we will add the necessary controls to the MyFilesPage and add the implementation for navigation in MyFilesViewModel.

Start by creating two new properties just after the constructor. These properties will be of type IRelayCommand named Forward and Back. This time we are using the IRelayCommand, which allows us to use the CanExecute() method and NotifyCanExecuteChange(). These APIs will allow us to turn the buttons on and off depending on the page state. They will be configured with the buttons added to the MyFilesPage to perform forward and back history navigation. See the code snippet in Listing 17-7.

Note   We are using both x:Bind and ICommand on the same page and ViewModel to document the various ways to communicate with the ViewModel. For the ItemClick event, it is easier to pass the parameters using x:Bind than it is with ICommand, which is why we are using it for that.

Listing 17-7. MyFilesViewModel property definitions for Forward and Back ICommand

```
public IRelayCommand Forward { get; }
public IRelayCommand Back { get; }
```

Next, add method stubs for these commands named OnForwardAsync and
OnBackAsync. These methods will have a return type Task as they will need to invoke
LoadDataAsync if an action is successful. See Listing 17-8 for method stubs.

Listing 17-8. MyFilesViewModel OnForwardAsync and OnBackAsync
method stubs

```
Task OnForwardAsync()
{
  // TODO - add implementation
}

Task OnBackAsync()
{
  // TODO - add implementation
}
```

The constructor needs to be updated to instantiate the Forward and Back properties.
They should only be set once in the constructor, and every time the ICommand is invoked,
it will invoke the methods correctly. Since we are using the MVVM toolkit, we get a
special commanding implementation that includes AsyncRelayCommand. This has an
async/await-friendly command implementation to use since our OnBackAsync and
OnForwardAsync both return a Task. Update the constructor code to match the snippet in
Listing 17-9.

Listing 17-9. MyFilesViewModel updated constructor to instantiate Forward and
Back properties

```
public MyFilesViewModel(
  IGraphFileService graphFileService,
  ILogger<MyFilesViewModel> logger)
{
  this.graphFileService = graphFileService;
  this.logger = logger;

  Forward = new AsyncRelayCommand(OnForwardAsync,
    () => location.CanMoveForward);
  Back = new AsyncRelayCommand(OnBackAsync,
```

```
    () => location.CanMoveBack);

  FilesAndFolders = new List<OneDriveItem>();
}
```

Now that the Forward and Back properties are instantiated, we can add our implementations. The strategy is to leverage the doubly linked list and move to the next item if it exists and load the data. See the complete implementation for OnForwardAsync and OnBackAsync in Listing 17-10.

Listing 17-10. MyFilesViewModel OnForwardAsync and OnBackAsync implementation

```
Task OnForwardAsync()
{
  var forwardId = location.Forward.Id;
  location = location.Forward;
  return LoadDataAsync(forwardId);
}

Task OnBackAsync()
{
  var backId = location.Back.Id;
  location = location.Back;
  return LoadDataAsync(backId);
}
```

Since we are using the CanExecute feature of the AsyncRelayCommand, we need to update the private method LoadDataAsync() to check both Forward and Back if they are able to perform navigation. This method has a try-catch-finally block, and we will place this in the finally block so it always runs when this method completes. That will ensure we always have a good test if the Forward or Back button can perform a navigation action. See updated code in Listing 17-11 – changes are highlighted in bold.

Listing 17-11. MyFilesViewModel LoadDataAsync method notifies Forward and Back commands to check if they CanExecute

```
async Task LoadDataAsync(string pathId = null)
{
```

```
IsStatusBarLoading = true;

try
{
  IEnumerable<OneDriveItem> data;
  if (string.IsNullOrEmpty(pathId)
  {
    data = await graphFileService.GetRootFilesAsync();
  }
  else
  {
    data = await graphFileService.GetFilesAsync(pathId);
  }

  UpdateFiles(data);
}
catch (Exception ex)
{
  logger.LogError(ex, ex.Message);
}
finally
{
  Forward.NotifyCanExecuteChanged();
  Back.NotifyCanExecuteChanged();

  IsStatusBarLoading = false;
}
}
```

Our changes to the MyFilesViewModel are complete, and we can now update the MyFilesPage to include new user interface controls and add data binding to the ICommand properties.

In the MyFilesPage, we created two nested Grid objects. The top one is where we placed our TextBox that displays the OneDrive current path; this is the one we will be editing in this section. You will need to add a new ColumnDefinition so we can add our forward and back buttons to the left of the address bar. Update your Grid. ColumnDefinitions to match the code in Listing 17-12.

Listing 17-12. MyFilesPage address bar ColumnDefinitions

```
<Grid.ColumnDefinitions>
  <ColumnDefinition Width="Auto" />
  <ColumnDefinition />
</Grid.ColumnDefinitions>
```

Next, we can add a new `StackPanel` to contain two buttons that will include bindings to the `MyFilesViewModel`. Add the code in Listing 17-13 just after the `Grid.ColumnDefinitions` and before the `TextBox`.

Listing 17-13. MyFilesPage forward and back button complete implementation

```
<StackPanel
  Grid.Column="0"
  Orientation="Horizontal"
  Spacing="10">

  <Button Content="Back" Command="{Binding Back}" />
  <Button Content="Forward" Command="{Binding Forward}" />

</StackPanel>
```

To wrap up our changes in the `MyFilesPage`, you will need to update the rest of the controls in this `Grid` to use `Grid.Column="1"` instead of `Grid.Column="0"`. That will be the `TextBox`, `ProgressRing`, and `TextBlock` that follow our newly added `StackPanel`.

Testing the User Interface

The OneDrive navigation is complete, and you can run your application on the various platforms. When you click the folder icons, it will navigate to the next page. This will update the OneDrive address bar with your new path. After performing any navigation, the history is updated, and you can navigate back or forward depending on your application state.

Conclusion

In this chapter we added navigation for the MyFilesPage that allows the user to navigate through different folders as well as navigate through history with back and forward buttons. We used existing skills we learned earlier in the book with MVVM techniques to accomplish this. If you had any trouble following along, you can download the completed code from GitHub: `https://github.com/SkyeHoefling/UnoDrive/tree/main/Chapter%2017`.

CHAPTER 18

Offline Data Access

When building a mobile application, there is no guarantee that you will always have a stable Internet connection. It is best to build your application with the expectation that the connection will be severed, and it should seamlessly transition between offline mode and online mode. Since more and more devices are becoming more portable such as hybrid laptops that act as tablets, our applications need to handle this on other platforms than just mobile.

The mark of a good application is one where the user does not know when it is in online mode or offline mode. The data they are interested in viewing is available to them.

To handle offline data, you will need to add a local data store such as a database stored on device that can cache any data that you retrieve while in online mode. This means records, files, etc. need to be saved on device so they can be accessed when the network status changes.

In this chapter we will be updating our UnoDrive application to add support for offline mode. We will be adding a local data store to cache our data and present it to the user regardless of network connection.

Offline Data Access Strategies

When building an offline-first application, the data access techniques vary from an application that is guaranteed to always have a stable connection or no formal offline mode. In a typical application that guarantees a connection, you will be querying the API directly and storing that data in memory as it is presented to the user. Many requests in modern applications have a very fast response time, so this technique is valid when we have a guaranteed connection.

Our current application implementation follows the standard data retrieval pattern that renders it directly to the page. This is common of web, desktop, and some mobile applications because offline data is not required:

© Skye Hoefling 2022
S. Hoefling, *Getting Started with the Uno Platform and WinUI 3*,
https://doi.org/10.1007/978-1-4842-8248-9_18

1. Retrieve data from the API.

2. Display on page.

Consider a page that retrieves a user's name and wants to display it on the screen like our dashboard. An application that guarantees a stable connection will have code like Listing 18-1. In this code snippet, we call our remote API to retrieve our data and store it into a local property, which will render it to the screen.

Listing 18-1. Sample code for retrieving the user's name with stable connection

```
Void LoadData()
{
  var myData = GetDataFromApi();
  Name = myData.Name;
}
```

In contrast, an offline-first application adds a few extra steps when retrieving the same data. The data should be stored in a local data store, and the presentation code will always be retrieving data from that data store, never the in-memory data directly from the API. This means you should read from the local data store first and then try and refresh the data from the API. The order of operations will look like this:

1. Read data from the local data store.

2. Display on page.

3. Retrieve data from the API.

4. Write data to the local data store.

5. Update the display on page.

Updating our preceding small sample code to handle offline data can be seen in Listing 18-2.

Listing 18-2. Sample code for retrieving the user's name with the offline data store

```
void LoadData()
{
  var localData = GetLocalData();
  if (localData != null)
```

```
{
  Name = localData.Name;
}

var myData = GetDataFromApi();
WriteLocalData(myData);
Name = myData.Name;
}
```

When working with offline data, you have the potential to update the user interface two times with our current strategy. The final solution means you will have a user interface that renders very quickly.

Tip When implementing an offline data access strategy, once you render the cached data, there should still be an indicator such as a spinner to communicate to the user that data is still loading. It will create a jarring user experience if the page flashes after loading the live data.

Caching Strategies

There are two main caching strategies that are used when building offline-capable applications:

- Cache everything at startup.
- Cache at time of read.

Both strategies have their own advantages and disadvantages, and it is best to choose the right one for your application.

Caching everything at startup is typically used on mission-critical enterprise line-of-business applications. These applications need everything to be available when the application loads. This means during the application startup sequence, there needs to be a stable connection to download all the data on device and synchronize any data that has not been sent to the central API. A downside of this technique is it can take a long time for all the data to be synchronized in both download and upload tasks. In the context of a line-of-business application, this is typically an acceptable compromise. The user will know they need to wait before they can use the application in an offline mode.

Caching at time of read means the application will have a fast startup time and the user will not have any delays to getting into their application and performing their tasks. As the user performs tasks in the application, that data will be cached, and when the user needs to load it again, the data will be available in both offline mode and online mode. The major downside to caching at time of read is if the user needs to access data while in offline mode, they must view it at least once during an online session. This technique is more suitable for applications that are not running business-critical software and is okay for stale data. It is also useful for applications that do more writing than reading, such as an application that requires the user to insert new records into a database.

In our UnoDrive application, we will be implementing a caching strategy that caches at the time of read. This strategy makes the most sense as downloading all the possible OneDrive data for a user can be a very long task and the user may not need it all.

Local Data Store and LiteDB

A local data store is a database or file that is stored in the application that is used to cache data to be retrieved at runtime. When choosing the correct local data store, there are many options available in the .NET community, and it is important to pick the one that makes the most sense for you and your team. You can use a SQL or NoSQL database or even a flat file that stores the data in JSON, XML, or your favorite markup language.

There are many data store and caching tools available in the .NET ecosystem. In our application we are using LiteDB. You should decide what is best for you and your team. Akavache is a popular alternative to LiteDB as it offers a powerful caching data store that is popular with the reactiveui community:

- https://github.com/reactiveui/Akavache

- https://github.com/reactiveui/refit

Our UnoDrive application is going to use LiteDB as it is a lightweight NoSQL database that is fast and works across all the platforms in Uno Platform. You can learn more about LiteDB from their website or GitHub page:

- www.litedb.org/

- https://github.com/mbdavid/litedb

> **Tip**   The most important thing to look for when selecting your local data store is the platform support. You may find something that is great in some of your platforms, but not all of them. Ensure it works across all the platforms that your application will be targeting.

LiteDB makes the most sense for UnoDrive as it is more than capable of storing our OneDrive records and returning them quickly. All images and assets we will want to download will be stored as a file and not in the database.

Add the LiteDB NuGet Package

Add the LiteDB NuGet package to all of the target platform head projects:

- `UnoDrive.Mobile`
- `UnoDrive.Skia.Gtk`
- `UnoDrive.Skia.Wpf`
- `UnoDrive.Wasm`
- `UnoDrive.Windows`

Add the `PackageReference` code to each `csproj` file as seen in Listing 18-3.

Listing 18-3. Add PackageReference for LiteDB in all target platform head projects

```
<PackageReference Include="LiteDB" Version="5.0.11" />
```

Create the DataStore

The local data store LiteDB is unlike a centralized database that guarantees to be created and available. We will need to ensure our LiteDB is created and saved on device prior to using it. This means we need to define where on the device the file is saved and reference that file when instantiating an instance of the `LiteDatabase` object.

In our UnoDrive.Shared project, create two new files in the Data folder named IDataStore and DataStore. See Figure 18-1 for a screenshot of the Visual Studio Solution Explorer.

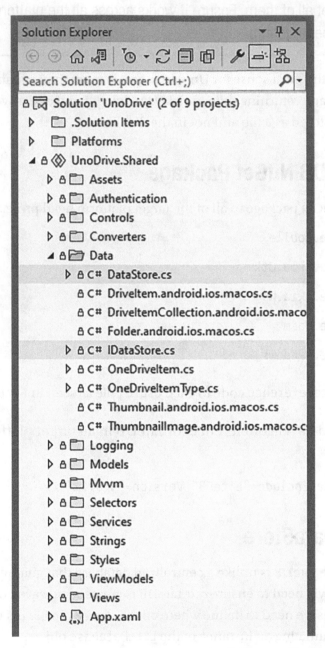

Figure 18-1. *Visual Studio Solution Explorer – DataStore and IDataStore added to the project*

Right now, we are not going to define any methods in the IDataStore as we are just configuring our database file. The DataStore will be our implementation of writing and reading data to and from the LiteDB database file. We are going to define our database file location and handle the differences between WPF and the rest of the platforms. We learned earlier in this book that WPF has a different application local folder, so we will add platform-specific code to handle the location. See code in Listing 18-4 with an initial DataStore implementation of the constructor and the database file location.

Listing 18-4. DataStore – define databaseFile and the constructor

```
public class DataStore : IDataStore
{
  readonly string databaseFile;

  public DataStore()
  {
#if HAS_UNO_SKIA_WPF
    var applicationFolder = Path.Combine(
      ApplicationData.Current.TemporaryFolder.Path,
      "UnoDrive");
    databaseFile = Path.Combine(
      applicationFolder, "UnoDriveData.db");
#else
    databaseFile = Path.Combine(
      ApplicationData.Current.LocalFolder.Path,
      "UnoDriveData.db");
#endif
  }
}
```

Note   LiteDB will automatically create the database file if it does not exist. If the database file does exist, it will use the file.

Next, we will need to register our `DataStore` with the Dependency Injection container so it can be used in various classes throughout our application. In the `App.xaml.cs` file, update the `ConfigureServices` method to register our `DataStore` as a transient service. See Listing 18-5 for new registration code and Listing 18-6 for complete `ConfigureServices` code.

Listing 18-5. Register IDataStore with the Dependency Injection container

```
services.AddTransient<IDataStore, DataStore>();
```

Listing 18-6. Complete App.xaml.cs ConfigureServices method

```
protected override void ConfigureServices(
  IServiceCollection services)
{
  services.AddLoggingForUnoDrive();
  services.AddAuthentication();
  services.AddTransient<INavigationService, NavigationService>();
  services.AddTransient<
    INetworkConnectivityService, NetworkConnectivityService>();
  services.AddTransient<IGraphFileService, GraphFileService>();
  services.AddTransient<IDataStore, DataStore>();
}
```

Authentication and Token Caching

The UnoDrive authentication is using the Microsoft Authentication Library (MSAL) to connect to Azure Active Directory. The .NET library MSAL.NET provides the concept of token caching, which means when you log in, it can cache your token and automatically log in when you launch the application. This also allows you to log in using the MSAL. NET APIs when in offline mode.

iOS and Android have built-in token caching, and this works out of the box with no additional code. As for the rest of the platforms, we will need to implement our own token caching mechanism to fully support offline mode.

MSAL.NET provides an ITokenCache interface, which has extension points to configure custom serialization and deserialization of the token cache. The extension points allow you to configure a callback, which will be called for writes and reads.

We are going to implement our own custom token caching strategy that uses an encrypted LiteDB as the data store. LiteDB provides a simple way to encrypt the database by supplying any password in the connection string. To start, create a new file in the UnoDrive.Shared project under the Authentication folder named TokenCacheStorage.cs. See Figure 18-2 for a screenshot of the Visual Studio Solution Explorer.

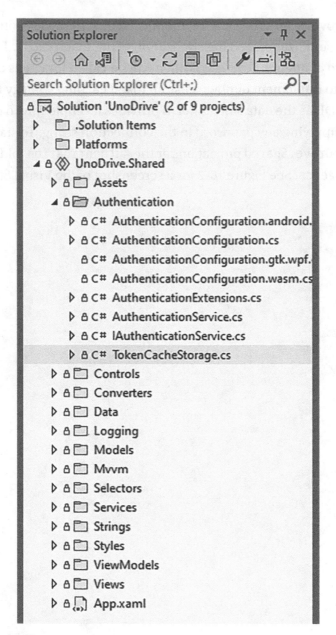

Figure 18-2. *Visual Studio Solution Explorer – TokenCacheStorage.cs*

The TokenCacheStorage class is going to be a static class, so there are not going to be any instance variables to store in the connection string. Create a private static method that returns the connection string. We will follow a similar pattern as we did in the `DataStore` class except we will specify a file name and password. To encrypt a LiteDB file, you only need to specify a password, and it happens automatically. See code in Listing 18-7 for the initial creation of `TokenCacheStorage` and method to retrieve the connection string.

Listing 18-7. TokenCacheStorage – GetConnectionString method implementation

```
static class TokenCacheStorage
{
  static string GetConnectionString()
  {
#if HAS_UNO_SKIA_WPF
    var applicationFolder = Path.Combine(
      ApplicationData.Current.TemporaryFolder.Path,
      "UnoDrive");
    var databaseFile = Path.Combine(
      applicationFolder,
      "UnoDrive_MSAL_TokenCache.db");
#else
    var databaseFile = Path.Combine(
      ApplicationData.Current.LocalFolder.Path,
      "UnoDrive_MSAL_TokenCache.db");
#endif

    return $"Filename={databaseFile};Password=UnoIsGreat!";
  }
}
```

Note   We supplied a hard-coded password, which accomplishes the goal of encryption. In an application that requires more security, this password should be install dependent by using a key unique to the device or installation.

Create the entry point for the TokenCacheStorage with a static method named EnableSerialization. This method will take a parameter of ITokenCache, which we get from the built MSAL.NET object. The ITokenCache has two methods SetBeforeAccess and SetAfterAccess, which allow us to hook into the token data and store it. Create a method stub for both SetBeforeAccess and SetAfterAccess. See the code snippet in Listing 18-8.

Listing 18-8. TokenCacheStorage – EnableSerialization and method stubs

```
static class TokenCacheStorage
{
  // omitted GetConnectionString() method

  public static void EnableSerialization(ITokenCache tokenCache)
  {
    tokenCache.SetBeforeAccess(BeforeAccessNotification);
    tokenCache.SetAfterAccess(AfterAccessNotification);
  }

  static void BeforeAccessNotification(
    TokenCacheNotificationArgs args)
  {
    // TODO - add implementation
  }

  static void AfterAccessNotification(
    TokenCacheNotification args)
  {
    // TODO - add implementation
  }
}
```

At this point when the token is acquired, the BeforeAccessNotification and AfterAccessNotification methods will be invoked, but they do not have any implementation yet.

The BeforeAccessNotifcation method is used just prior to the authentication action. We will add code that uses the LiteDB and checks for an existing cached token. If a token is found, it will allow the authentication to perform a silent login.

The `AfterAccessNotification` method is used just after a successful authentication action. A token is provided in the method arguments, and then we will use the LiteDB to store the token for a future login attempt.

We need to define a data model to store our cached token data. We are going to dump the entire string into a single column on the data model. Create a private nested class named `TokenRecord`, which will make it only accessible from inside the scope of `TokenCacheStorage`. See the code snippet in Listing 18-9.

Listing 18-9. TokenCacheStorage – add the TokenRecord data model

```
static class TokenCacheStorage
{
  // omitted code

  class TokenRecord
  {
    public string Data { get; set; }
  }
}
```

Next, we can implement both the `BeforeAccessNotification` and `AfterAccessNotification` methods. The `BeforeAccessNotification` method will be retrieving any data in the LiteDB file, and the `AfterAccessNotification` method will be writing the data to the LiteDB file. To ensure we don't have additional rows in our `TokenRecord`, be sure to delete all records prior to writing. See the code snippet in Listings 18-10 and 18-11.

Listing 18-10. TokenCacheStorage – BeforeAccessNotification method implementation

```
static void BeforeAccessNotification(
  TokenCacheNotificationArgs args)
{
  using (var db = new LiteDatabase(GetConnectionString()))
  {
    var tokens = db.GetCollection<TokenRecord>();
    var tokenRecord = tokens.Query().FirstOrDefault();
    var serializedCache = tokenRecord != null ?
```

465

```
      Convert.FromBase64String(tokenRecord.Data) : null;

   args.TokenCache.DeserializeMsalV3(serializedCache);
  }
}
```

Listing 18-11. TokenCacheStorage – AfterAccessNotification method implementation

```
static void AfterAccessNotification(
  TokenCacheNotificationArgs args)
{
  var data = args.TokenCache.SerializeMsalV3();
  var serializedCache = Convert.ToBase64String(data);

  using (var db = new LiteDatabase(GetConnectionString()))
  {
    var tokens = db.GetCollection<TokenRecord>();
    tokens.DeleteAll();
    tokens.Insert(new TokenRecord
      { Data = serializedCache });
  }
}
```

That completes the TokenCacheStorage implementation – see Listing 18-12 for the complete code.

Listing 18-12. TokenCacheStorage – complete implementation

```
Static class TokenCacheStorage
{
  static string GetConnectionString()
  {
#if HAS_UNO_SKIA_WPF
    var applicationFolder = Path.Combine(
      ApplicationData.Current.TemporaryFolder.Path,
      "UnoDrive");
    var databaseFile = Path.Combine(
```

```
      applicationFolder,
      "UnoDrive_MSAL_TokenCache.db");
#else
    var databaseFile = Path.Combine(
      ApplicationData.Current.LocalFolder.Path,
      "UnoDrive_MSAL_TokenCache.db");
#endif

    return $"Filename={databaseFile};Password=UnoIsGreat!";
  }

  public static void EnableSerialization(ITokenCache tokenCache)
  {
    tokenCache.SetBeforeAccess(BeforeAccessNotification);
    tokenCache.SetAfterAccess(AfterAccessNotification);
  }

  static void BeforeAccessNotification(
    TokenCacheNotificationArgs args)
  {
    using (var db = new LiteDatabase(GetConnectionString()))
    {
      var tokens = db.GetCollection<TokenRecord>();
      var tokenRecord = tokens.Query().FirstOrDefault();
      var serializedCache = tokenRecord != null ?
        Convert.FromBase64String(tokenRecord.Data) : null;

      args.TokenCache.DeserializeMsalV3(serializedCache);
    }
  }

  static void AfterAccessNotification(
    TokenCacheNotificationArgs args)
  {
    var data = args.TokenCache.SerializeMsalV3();
    var serializedCache = Convert.ToBase64String(data);

    using (var db = new LiteDatabase(GetConnectionString()))
```

```
    {
      var tokens = db.GetCollection<TokenRecord>();
      tokens.DeleteAll();
      tokens.Insert(new TokenRecord
        { Data = serializedCache });
    }
  }

  class TokenRecord
  {
    public string Data { get; set; }
  }
}
```

To finish our changes to the authentication system, we need to invoke the
EnableSerialization method right after building the IPublicClientApplication.
In the UnoDrive.Shared project under the Authentication folder, open the
AuthenticationConfiguration.cs file. Update the ConfigureAuthentication
method to match the code in Listing 18-13. The changes we are making are
storing the IPublicClientApplication in a local variable and then calling the
EnableSerialization method with the UserTokenCache.

Listing 18-13. AuthenticationConfiguration updates for UserTokenCache

```
public void ConfigureAuthentication(IServiceCollection services)
{
  var builder = PublicClientApplicationBuilder
    .Create("9f500d92-8e2e-4b91-b43a-a9ddb73e1c30")
    .WithRedirectUri(GetRedirectUri())
    .WithUnoHelpers();

  var app = builder.Build();

#if !__ANDROID__ && !__IOS__
  TokenCacheStorage.EnableSerialization(app.UserTokenCache);
#endif

  services.AddSingleton(app);
  services.AddTransient<
```

```
    IAuthenticationService,
    AuthenticationService>();
}
```

This completes the authentication changes, and we now have our token caching strategy implemented across all the platforms. Now when you run the application and log in, it will cache the user. Following attempts to log in will use the cached data.

Simple Caching in the Dashboard

The Dashboard in UnoDrive is our application shell or container that provides all the menus and content for the user. In our left-pane menu, we pull information from the Microsoft Graph to display the user's display name and email address. If the application is in offline mode, this data will not load. In this section we are going to apply the basics of data caching that we reviewed earlier in this chapter. As a quick refresher, our algorithm will be as follows:

1. Load cached data if it exists.

2. Pull data from the Microsoft Graph if network is available.

3. Write latest data to the data store.

4. Present the user interface.

To implement this algorithm, we will need to make changes to both the DataStore, which we started introducing in this chapter, and the Dashboard.

Add APIs to the DataStore

Before we can start adding methods to the DataStore, we need to create a new database model that represents the user information we would like to save. In the UnoDrive. Shared project under the Data folder, create a new file named UserInfo.cs. This class will contain the properties for the user's display name and email address. See Figure 18-3 for a screenshot of the Visual Studio Solution Explorer.

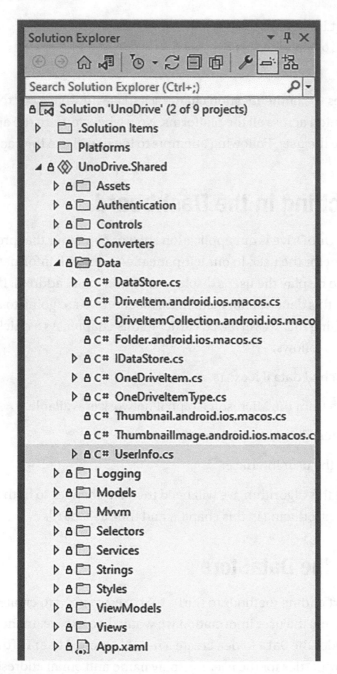

Figure 18-3. *Visual Studio Solution Explorer – UserInfo.cs*

The UserInfo class will be used by LiteDB to write information to the local database. We will need to create three simple properties, an Id, Name, and Email. See the full code for this model in Listing 18-14.

Listing 18-14. UserInfo model definition for storing the user's information

```
public class UserInfo
{
  public string Id { get; set; }
  public string Name { get; set; }
  public string Email { get; set; }
}
```

We can now start implementing the DataStore that uses the new UserInfo model. Open the IDataStore interface and define two new methods for storing and retrieving the user's information. See Listing 18-15 for the interface definition.

Listing 18-15. IDataStore interface definition for SaveUserInfo and GetUserInfoById methods

```
public interface IDataStore
{
  void SaveUserInfo(UserInfo userInfo);
  UserInfo GetUserInfoById(string id);
}
```

Next, we will implement the GetUserInfoById method as it is the easier of the two APIs. We already defined a local variable named databaseFile in the DataStore class. This will be used to instantiate an instance of the LiteDatabase so we can retrieve our records. To implement this, you will create the LiteDatabase, get our collection of UserInfo, and then try and read a record matching the input parameter. See the GetUserInfoById implementation in Listing 18-16.

Tip   When working with the LiteDatabase object, always ensure you are instantiating it with a using block or statement. This will dispose of the object at the end of the block and free up any file or memory locks on the data store. If you do not add the using block, you will need to manually invoke the Dispose() method. If you use the newer using statement syntax, that does not have any curly braces. It will automatically Dispose() at the end of the method.

Listing 18-16. DataStore GetUserInfoById method implementation

```
public UserInfo GetUserInfoById(string userId)
{
  using (var db = new LiteDatabase(databaseFile))
  {
    var users = db.GetCollection<UserInfo>();
    return users.FindById(userId);
  }
}
```

Next, we will implement the SaveUserInfo method, which has a few additional steps. Again, you will instantiate the LiteDatabase object using the local variable databaseFile. Then you will try and find an existing record that matches the ID from the supplied UserInfo parameter. If it exists, go and update the values, but if it does not exist, you will create a new record in the database. See the SaveUserInfo implementation in Listing 18-17.

Listing 18-17. DataStore SaveUserInfo method implementation

```
public void SaveUserInfo(UserInfo userInfo)
{
  using (var db = new LiteDatabase(databaseFile))
  {
    var users = db.GetCollection<UserInfo>();
    var findUserInfo = users.FindById(userInfo.Id);

    if (findUserInfo != null)
    {
      findUserInfo.Name = userInfo.Name;
      findUserInfo.Email = userInfo.Email;

      users.Update(findUserInfo);
    }
    else
    {
```

```
      users.Insert(userInfo);
    }
  }
}
```

That completes our changes to the `DataStore` for now, and we can start using it in the dashboard.

Add Offline Code to the Dashboard

To add data caching to the dashboard, we will be updating code in the `DashboardViewModel`. We have not started any work in this file yet for offline access, so we will need to inject the `IDataStore` and `INetworkConnectivityService` to give us access to the caching APIs as well as network status. Add new local variables to store references and inject them into the constructor. See updated constructor code for the `DashboardViewModel` in Listing 18-18.

Listing 18-18. DashboardViewModel updated constructor with IDataStore injection. Changes highlighted in bold

```
public class DashboardViewModel :
  ObservableObject, IAuthenticationProvider, IInitialize
{
  IDataStore datastore;
  INetworkConnectivityService networkService;
  ILogger logger;

  public DashboardViewModel(
    IDataStore datastore,
    INetworkConnectivityService networkService,
    ILogger<DashboardViewModel> logger)
  {
    this.dataStore = datastore;
    this.networkService = networkService;
    this.logger = logger;
  }
}
```

Next, we can update the `LoadDataAsync` method to perform caching. Following our algorithm from earlier, we need to try and read from the cache first and then load data and write it to the database. Now that we have access to both the `INetworkConnectivityService` and `IDataStore`, we can complete these tasks. See the updated implementation in Listing 18-19 with changes highlighted in bold.

Listing 18-19. DashboardViewModel LoadDataAsync implementation updates for caching. Changes are in bold

```
public async Task LoadDataAsync()
{
  try
  {
    var objectId = ((App)App.Current)
      .AuthenticationResult.Account.HomeAccountId.ObjectId
    var userInfo = datastore.GetUserInfoById(objectId);
    if (userInfo != null)
    {
      Name = userInfo.Name;
      Email = userInfo.Email;
    }

    if (networkService.Connectivity !=
      NetworkConnectivityLevel.InternetAccess)
    {
      return;
    }
#if __WASM__
    var httpClient = new HttpClient(
      new Uno.UI.Wasm.WasmHttpHandler());
#else
    var httpClient = new HttpClient();
#endif

    var graphClient = new GraphServiceClient(httpClient);
    graphClient.AuthenticationProvider = this;
```

```
    var request = graphClient.Me
      .Request()
      .Select(user => new
      {
        Id = user.Id,
        DisplayName = user.DisplayName,
        UserPrincipalName = user.PrincipalName
      });
#if __ANDROID__ || __IOS__ || __MACOS__
    var response = await request.GetResponseAsync();
    var data = await response.Content.ReadAsStringAsync();
    var me = JsonConvert.DeserializeObject<User>(data);
#else
    var me = await request.GetAsync();
#endif

    if (me != null)
    {
      Name = me.DisplayName;
      Email = me.UserPrincipalName;

      userInfo = new UserInfo
      {
        Id = objectId,
        Name = Name,
        Email = Email
      };
      datastore.SaveUserInfo(userInfo);
    }
  }
  catch (Exception ex)
  {
    logger.LogError(ex, ex.Message);
  }
}
```

That completes the data caching algorithm for the `DashboardViewModel`. There are no user interface changes needed as the change is just on how we store the data.

GraphFileService and MyFilesPage Caching

Adding data caching for the `MyFilesPage` is a little bit more involved than it was for the dashboard as we have more classes and interactions to handle. Conceptually, the implementation is the same. Since the `MyFilesPage` has loading indicators, we want to update the state of those as well as how we cache the data.

When the user starts loading the `MyFilesPage`, there are two spinning indicators that render: that in the status bar and that in the main content area. When we have cached data, we want to render the data as quickly as possible, so the main content indicator can go away. Since we will still be loading data, it is important to notify the user that it is processing, so we will keep the loading indicator in the status bar. Once we get our live data in online mode, all the indicators will disappear as it is implemented already.

To add data caching for the `MyFilesPage`, we have a few areas that need updating:

- New APIs in the `DataStore`

- Updates to the `GraphFileService`

- Loading indicator changes in `MyFilesPage` and `MyFilesViewModel`

Add APIs to DataStore

The `GraphFileService` has two main APIs that we need to cache data from: `GetRootFilesAsync` and `GetFilesAsync`. These APIs convert into our data store as saving and reading the root files and saving and reading the files. Start by opening the `IDataStore` interface and adding new APIs to support this:

- `SaveRootId`

- `GetRootId`

- `GetCachedFiles`

- `SaveCachedFiles`

- `UpdateCachedFileById`

See updated code for the IDataStore in Listing 18-20, which contains the interface definitions. New APIs are highlighted in bold.

Listing 18-20. IDataStore GraphFileService data caching APIs. New APIs highlighted in bold

```
public interface IDataStore
{
  void SaveUserInfo(UserInfo userInfo);
  UserInfo GetUserInfoById(string id);
  void SaveRootId(string rootId);
  string GetRootId();
  IEnumerable<OneDriveItem> GetCachedFiles(string pathId);
  void SaveCachedFiles(
    IEnumerable<OneDriveItem> children, string pathId);
  void UpdateCachedFileById(string itemId, string localFilePath);
}
```

Now we can add the implementations in the DataStore class one at time in order with SaveRootId first. This will be like SaveUserInfo. Before we can add the implementation, we will need to add a new database model to store the rootId. In the UnoDrive.Shared project under the Data folder, create a new file named Setting. See Figure 18-4 for a screenshot of the Visual Studio Solution Explorer.

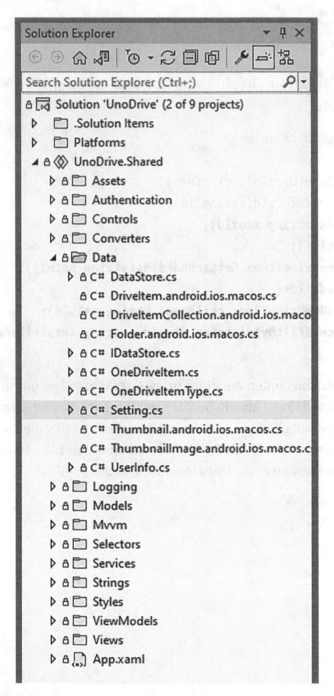

Figure 18-4. *Visual Studio Solution Explorer – Setting*

The Setting data model is a simple key/value pair model. This means the ID or key is the unique identifier and it stores some data with it. In our case we will use it to store the root ID. See Listing 18-21.

Listing 18-21. Setting data model definition

```
public class Setting
{
  public string Id { get; set; }
  public string Value { get; set; }
}
```

Now we can start implementing our DataStore APIs. The SaveRootId method is going to retrieve the Setting data model and try and find the hard-coded value "RootId" if it exists, and we will update it. Otherwise, we insert a new record. See Listing 18-22 for the method implementation.

Listing 18-22. DataStore SaveRootId method implementation

```
public void SaveRootId(string rootId)
{
  using (var db = new LiteDatabase(databaseFile))
  {
    var settings = db.GetCollection<Setting>();
    var findRootIdSetting = settings.FindById("RootId");

    if (findRootIdSetting != null)
    {
      findRootIdSetting.Value = rootId;
      settings.Update(findRootIdSetting);
    }
    else
    {
      var newSetting = new Setting
      {
        Id = "RootId",
        Value = rootId
      };
```

```
      settings.Insert(newSetting);
  }
 }
}
```

The GetRootId method will just be returning the stored Setting value. It will retrieve the hard-coded ID of "RootId". See Listing 18-23 for the GetRootId method implementation.

Listing 18-23. DataStore GetRootId method implementation

```
public string GetRootId()
{
  using (var db = new LiteDatabase(databaseFile))
  {
    var settings = db.GetCollection<Setting>();
    var rootId = settings.FindById("RootId");
    return rootId != null ? rootId.Value : string.Empty;
  }
}
```

Before implementing the APIs that manage the OneDriveItem, we need to update the data model. This data model uses an ImageSource property named ThumbnailSource, and it is not a compatible database type. To solve this problem, we can ignore the property by adding the [BsonIgnore] attribute over the property. See Listing 18-24 for the updated OneDriveItem implementation with the change highlighted in bold.

Listing 18-24. OneDriveItem – ignore ThumbnailSource. Change highlighted in bold

```
public class OneDriveItem
{
  public string Id { get; set; }
  public string Name { get; set; }
  public string Path { get; set; }
  public string PathId { get; set; }
  public DateTime Modified { get; set; }
  public string FileSize { get; set; }
```

```
public OneDriveItemType Type { get; set; }
public string ThumbnailPath { get; set; }
```

[BsonIgnore]
```
public ImageSource ThumbnailSource { get; set; }
}
```

Next, we are going to implement the GetCachedFiles method. This will return all the OneDriveItem files that are stored in the database. These can both be files and folders and are the core items displayed in the MyFilesPage. Our strategy for this method is to handle input errors such as a null or empty pathId parameter. Then we retrieve all items that match the input pathId parameter. The LiteDB engine provides LINQ queries that makes it easy to add filters to your request. See the GetCachedFiles method implementation in Listing 18-25.

Listing 18-25. DataStore GetCachedFiles method implementation

```
public IEnumerable<OneDriveItem> GetCachedFIles(string pathId)
{
  if (string.IsNullOrEmpty(pathId))
  {
    return new OneDriveItem[0];
  }

  using (var db = new LiteDatabase(databaseFile))
  {
    var items = db.GetCollection<OneDriveItem>();
    return items
      .Query()
      .Where(item => item.PathId == pathId)
      .ToArray();
  }
}
```

To implement SaveCachedFiles, we have a few additional steps from our other save methods. We will need to delete the stale items from the database in the current directory. In other words, all items at the current path are considered stale and need to be removed. Once that is done, we will delete each `ThumbnailPath` from local storage in the stale devices and then proceed to save new items. See the `SaveCachedFiles` method implementation in Listing 18-26.

Note   Our application assumes that the thumbnails will be written to the local storage after this method is called. That means it is safe for us to delete the thumbnail file as part of updating the cache.

Listing 18-26. DataStore SaveCachedFiles method implementation

```
public void SaveCachedFiles(
  IEnumerable<OneDriveItem> children, string pathId)
{
  using (var db = new LiteDatabase(databaseFile))
  {
    var items = db.GetCollection<OneDriveItem>();
    var staleItems = items
      .Query()
      .Where(i => i.PathId == pathId)
      .ToArray();

    if (staleItems != null && staleItems.Any())
    {
      items.DeleteMany(x => staleItems.Contains(x));
      foreach (var item in staleItems.Where(i =>
        !string.IsNullOrEmpty(i.ThumbnailPath)))
      {
        if (File.Exists(item.ThumbnailPath))
        {
          File.Delete(item.ThumbnailPath);
        }
      }
    }

    foreach (var item in children)
```

```
    {
      var findItem = items.FindById(item.Id);
      if (findItem != null)
      {
        items.Update()item);
      }
      else
      {
        items.Insert(item);
      }
    }
  }
}
```

The last method we are going to implement in the DataStore is
UpdateCachedFileById. The purpose of this method is when the GraphFileService is
downloading a new thumbnail file and saving it to local storage, it will invoke this API
and update the ThumbnailPath property on the OneDriveItem stored in the database.
The implementation strategy is to get the matching OneDriveItem by the ID and then
update the value and update the record. See Listing 18-27 for the UpdateCachedFileById
method implementation.

Listing 18-27. DataStore UpdateCachedFileById method implementation

```
public void UpdateCachedFileById(
  string itemId, string localFilePath)
{
  using (var db = new LiteDatabase(databaseFile))
  {
    var items = db.GetCollection<OneDriveItem>();
    var findItems = items.FindById(itemId);

    if (findItem != null)
    {
      findItem.ThumbnailPath = localFilePath;
```

```
      items.Update(findItem);
    }
  }
}
```

That completes all our changes to the IDataStore interface and DataStore. We will be using these APIs in the next section as we update the GraphFileService to support offline data caching.

Add Offline Code to GraphFileService

Now that we have completed our changes to the IDataStore interface and DataStore implementation, we can start integrating these changes into the GraphFileService. In this section we will be making code changes to update our APIs to support offline data access with our caching library. The APIs are a bit more complicated than what we did earlier in the DashboardViewModel, but the algorithm is still the same:

1. Load cached data.

2. Attempt to pull live data from the Microsoft Graph.

3. Store data in the database.

4. Return results.

Note   Our algorithm is still the same, but we do not mention presenting the user interface as the GraphFileService returns data and is not part of the presentation layer of the application.

Before we start updating the GraphFileService, we need to update the IGraphFileService contract. When a user opens a page and it loads cached data, they can click a folder on that page to start opening the next page. This means we will be handling race conditions as well as offline data. To help us solve this problem, we need to include a CancellationToken to every API in the IGraphFileService interface. This will allow the presentation layer to cancel the request from user interaction and start a new request.

Consider the user is loading the main page and there is a lot of data to pull and they already have cached folders rendering on the screen. If they click one of the folders and the data payload is smaller, it could render the second page first. Then when the first page load Task completes, it would overwrite the current state. With the CancellationToken we can stop the first request where it is and move on, which will effectively stop our race conditions.

In addition to the CancellationToken, the APIs will need to include a callback that can be triggered in the presentation layer. The callback can be thought of as a function pointer that allows your service code to invoke a method or segment of code in the presentation layer. It will be used to update the user interface at various steps along the way in the GraphFileService.

Open the IGraphFileService interface and update all the methods to include a callback function and CancellationToken parameter. See the updated interface in Listing 18-28.

Listing 18-28. IGraphFileService interface methods updated to accept CancellationToken. Changes are highlighted in bold

```
public interface IGraphFileService
{
  Task<IEnumerable<OneDriveItem>> GetRootFilesAsync(
    Action<IEnumerable<OneDriveItem>, bool> cacheCallback = null,
    CancellationToken cancellationToken = default);

  Task<IEnumerable<OneDriveItem>> GetFilesAsync(
    string id,
    Action<IEnumerable<OneDriveItem>, bool> cacheCallback = null,
    CancellationToken cancellationToken = default);
}
```

Next, you will need to update the method signatures in your GraphFileService implementation. You can see the final method signatures as we go through the implementation details of each.

Let's update the constructor code with our injectable services. We need to add INetworkConnectivityService for determining network status and IDataStore for access to the caching APIs. See Listing 18-29 for the updated constructor definition; the new code is highlighted in bold.

Listing 18-29. GraphFileService constructor updates for INetworkConnectivityService and IDataStore. Changes highlighted in bold

```
public class GraphFileService :
  IGraphFileService, IAuthenticationProvider
{

  GraphServiceClient graphClient;
  IDataStore dataStore;
  INetworkConnectivityService networkConnectivity;
  ILogger logger;

  public GraphFileService(
    IDataStore dataStore,
    INetworkConnectivityService networkConnectivity,
    ILogget<GraphFileService> logger)
  {
    this.dataStore = dataStore;
    this.networkConnectivity = networkConnectivity;
    this.logger = logger;

#if __WASM__
    var httpClient = new HttpClient(
      new Uno.UI.Wasm.WasmHttpHandler());
#else
    var httpClient = new HttpClient();
#endif

    graphClient = new GraphServiceClient(httpClient);
    graphClient.AuthenticationProvider = this;
  }

  // omitted code
}
```

We are going to update our implementation of GetFilesAsync first as that is the primary method in the GraphFileService. The GetRootFilesAsync depends on it, so it makes sense to complete GetFilesAsync first.

To update the GetFilesAsync implementation, we have a few things that need completing:

- Update the method signature to match the interface.

- Invoke the caching callback method if we can retrieve cached data.

- Skip network requests to the Microsoft Graph if there is no network availability.

- Store data to the local data store prior to returning.

You can see the complete updated implementation of GetFilesAsync in Listing 18-30; the changes will be highlighted in bold.

Listing 18-30. GraphFileService GetFilesAsync updates for data caching and task cancellation. Changes highlighted in bold

```
public async Task<IEnumerable<OneDriveItem>> GetFilesAsync(
  string id,
  Action<IEnumerable<OneDriveItem>, bool> cachedCallback = null,
  CancellationToken cancellationToken = default)
{
  if (cachedCallback != null)
  {
    var cachedChildren = dataStore
      .GetCachedFiles(id)
      .OrderByDescending(item => item.Type)
      .ThenBy(item => item.Name);

    cachedCallback(cachedChildren, true);
  }

  logger.LogInformation(
    $"Network Connectivity: {networkConnectivity.Connectivity}");
  if (networkConnectivity.Connectivity !=
    NetworkConnectivityLevel.InternetAccess)
  {
    return default;
  }
```

```
  cancellationToken.ThrowIfCancellationRequested();

  var request = graphClient.Me.Drive.Items[id].Children
    .Request()
    .Expand("thumbnails");

#if __ANDROID__ || __IOS__ || __MACOS__
  var response =
    await request.GetResponseAsync(cancellationToken);
  var data = await response.Content.ReadAsStringAsync();
  var collection = JsonConvert.DeserializeObject<
    UnoDrive.Models.DriveItemCollection>(data);
  var oneDriveItems = collection.Value;
#else
  var oneDriveItems = (await request.GetAsync(cancellationToken))
    .ToArray();
#endif

  var childrenTable = oneDriveItems
    .Select(driveItem => new OneDriveItem
    {
      Id = driveItem.Id,
      Name = driveItem.Name,
      Path = driveItem.ParentReference.Path,
      PathId = driveItem.ParentReference.Id,
      FileSize = $"{driveItem.Size}",
      Modified = driveItem.LastModifiedDateTime.HasValue ?
        driveItem.LastModifiedDateTime.Value.LocalDateTime :
        DateTime.Now,
      Type = driveItem.Folder != null ?
        OneDriveItemType.Folder :
        OneDriveItemType.File
    })
    .OrderByDescending(item => item.Type)
    .ThenBy(item => item.Name)
    .ToDictionary(item => item.Id);
```

```
cancellationToken.ThrowIfCancellationRequested();

var children = childrenTable
  .Select(item => item.Value)
  .ToArray();
if (cachedCallback != null)
{
  cachedCallback(children, false);
}

dataStore.SaveCachedFiles(children, id);
await StoreThumbnailsAsync(oneDriveItems, childrenTable
  cachedCallback, cancellationToken);
return childrenTable.Select(x => x.Value);
}
```

In the GetFilesAsync API, we passed the cachedCallback and cancellationToken to the private method StoreThumbnailsAsync. This is done because there are network requests to the Microsoft Graph that we may want to cancel. This method will be used only for writing to the data cache and invoking the callback if we detect changes. There is no need for an early load like in GetFilesAsync. See updated StoreThumbnailsAsync code in Listing 18-31; the changes are highlighted in bold.

Listing 18-31. GraphFileService StoreThumbnailsAsync updates for data caching and task cancellation. Changes highlighted in bold

```
#if __ANDROID__ || __IOS__ || __MACOS__
async Task StoreThumbnailsAsync(
  UnoDrive.Models[] oneDriveItems,
  IDictionary<string, OneDriveItem> childrenTable,
  Action<IEnumerable<OneDriveItem>, bool> cachedCallback = null,
  CancellationToken cancellationToken = default)
#else
  DriveItem[] oneDriveItems,
  IDictionary<string, OneDriveItem> childrenTable,
  Action<IEnumerable<OneDriveItem>, bool> cachedCallback = null,
  CancellationToken cancellationToken = default)
#endif
```

```
{
  for (int index = 0; index < oneDriveItems.Length; index++)
  {
    var currentItem = oneDriveItem[index];
    var thumbnails = currentItem.Thumbnails?.FirstOrDefault();
    if (thumbnails == null ||
      !childrenTable.ContainsKey(currentItem.Id))
    {
      Continue;
    }
#if __WASM__
    var httpClient = new HttpClient(
      new Uno.UI.Wasm.WasmHttpHandler());
#else
    var httpClient = new HttpClient();
#endif
    var thumbnailResponse = await httpClient.GetAsync(
      url, cancellationToken);
    if (!thumbnailResponse.IsSuccessStatusCode)
    {
      Continue;
    }
#if HAS_UNO_SKIA_WPF
    var applicationFolder = Path.Combine(
      ApplicationData.Current.TemporaryFolder.Path,
      "UnoDrive");
    var imagesFolder = Path.Combine(
      applicationFolder, "thumbnails");
#else
    var imagesFolder = Path.Combine(
      ApplicationData.Current.LocalFolder.Path,
      "thumbnails");
#endif
```

```
      var name = $"{currentItem.Id}.jpeg";
      var localFilePath = Path.Combine(imagesFolder, name);

      try
      {
        if (!System.IO.Directory.Exists(imagesFolder))
        {
          System.IO.Directory.CreateDirectory(imagesFolder);
        }

        if (System.IO.File.Exists(localFilePath))
        {
          System.IO.File.Delete(localFilePath);
        }

        var bytes = await thumbnailResponse.Content
          .ReadAsByteArrayAsync();

#if HAS_UNO_SKIA_WPF
      System.IO.File.WriteAllBytes(localFilePath, bytes);
#else
      await System.IO.File.WriteAllBytesAsync(
        localFilePath, bytes, cancellationToken);
#endif

#if __UNO_DRIVE_WINDOWS__ || __ANDROID__ || __IOS__
      var image = new BitmapImage(new Uri(localFilePath));
#else
      var image = new BitmapImage();
      image.SetSource(new MemoryStream(bytes));
#endif

      childrenTable[currentItem.Id].ThumbnailSource = image;

      if (cachedCallback != null)
      {
        var children = childrenTable
          .Select(item => item.Value)
          .ToArray();
```

```
      cachedCallback(children, value);
    }

    dataStore.UpdateCachedFileById(
      currentItem.Id, localFilePath);
    cancellationToken.ThrowIfCancellationRequested();
  }
  catch (TaskCanceledException ex)
  {
    logger.LogWarning(ex, ex.Message);
    throw;
  }
  catch (Exception ex)
  {
    logger.LogError(ex, ex.Message);
  }
  }
}
```

That completes most of the work for updating the GraphFileService, getting the presentation layer to update and storing the cached data in our LiteDB data store. The last method we need to update is GetRootFilesAsync. We need to complete the following tasks in this method:

- Update the method signature to include callback and CancellationToken.

- Read the root ID from the data store.

- Check network connectivity.

- Write the root ID to the data store.

See updated code for GetRootFilesAsync in Listing 18-32; the updated code will be highlighted in bold.

Listing 18-32. GraphFileService GetRootFilesAsync updates for data caching and task cancellation. Changes highlighted in bold

```
public async TaskIEnumerable<OneDriveItem> GetRootFilesAsync(
  Action<IEnumerable<OneDriveItem>, bool> cachedCallback = null,
  CancellationToken cancellationToken = default)
{
  var rootPathId = dataStore.GetRootId();
  if (networkConnectivity.Connectivity ==
    NetworkConnectivityLevel.InternetAccess)
  {
    try
    {
#if __ANDROID__ || __IOS__ || __MACOS__
      var response = await request
        .GetResponseAsync(cancellationToken);
      var data = await response.Content.ReadAsStringAsync();
      var rootNode = JsonConvert
        .DeserializeObject<DriveItem>(data);
#else
      var rootNode = await request.GetAsync(cancellationToken);
#endif

      if (rootNode == null || string.IsNullOrEmpty(rootNode.Id))
      {
        throw new KeyNotFoundException("Unable to find " +
          "OneDrive Root Folder");
      }

      rootPathId = rootNode.Id;
      dataStore.SaveRootId(rootPathId);
    }
    catch (TaskCanceledException ex)
    {
      logger.LogWarning(ex, ex.Message);
      throw;
    }
```

```
  catch (KeyNotFoundException ex)
  {
    logger.LogWarning("Unable to retrieve data from Graph " +
      "API, it may not exist or there could be a connection " +
      "issue");
    logger.LogWarning(ex, ex.Message);
    throw;
  }
  catch (Exception ex)
  {
    logger.LogWarning("Unable to retrieve root OneDrive
      " + folder");
    logger.LogWarning(ex, ex.Message);
  }
}

return await GetFilesAsync(
  rootPathId, cachedCallback, cancellationToken);
}
```

That completes all the code changes we need to make for the `GraphFileService`. We can start working on the user interface changes. We made a change to the `IGraphFileService` interface to include the `CancellationToken` and a callback, which we will be using in the user interface.

Update Loading Indicators

The service and database layers are now complete, and we can start editing the presentation layer. We want to update the `MyFilesViewModel` to eagerly load the content from the cached data store and render it on the page. Then the application will make the web request to the Microsoft Graph to get the true live data and update the data store.

This means we need to change the current behavior of the loading indicators to handle cached data. If there is cached data, we will not display the loading indicator in the main content area, only that in the status bar. But if there is no cached data for that page, we will render both loading indicators. We will start with the `MyFilesViewModel` and finish with changes in the `MyFilesPage`.

To handle the two different loading indicators, we need to add a new property to the view model to track when we want it to display. Add a new property to the Properties section of your MyFilesViewModel as seen in the code snippet of Listing 18-33.

Listing 18-33. MyFilesViewModel IsMainContentLoading property implementation

```
public bool IsMainContentLoading =>
  IsStatusBarLoading && !FilesAndFolders.Any();
```

The goal of the IsMainContentLoading property is to only render if the status bar loading indicator is visible and there are no files rendered on the page. We can use the FilesAndFolders property to determine what is on the page.

Since the IsMainContentLoading property does not explicitly invoke OnPropertyChanged(), it currently will not tell the user interface that it has changed. We need to update the dependent properties to manually trigger this. You need to add a new line to the setter of FilesAndFolders and IsStatusBarLoading properties to trigger this. See the code snippet in Listing 18-34; the code additions are highlighted in bold.

Listing 18-34. MyFilesViewModel IsMainContentLoading OnPropertyChanged events. Changes are highlighted in bold

```
List<OneDriveItem> filesAndFolders;
public List<OneDriveItem> FilesAndFolders
{
  get => filesAndFolders;
  set
  {
    SetProperty(ref filesAndFolders, value);
    OnPropertyChanged(nameof(CurrentFolderPath));
    OnPropertyChanged(nameof(IsPageEmpty));
    OnPropertyChanged(nameof(IsMainContentLoading));
  }
}

public bool IsMainContentLoading =>
  IsStatusBarLoading && !FilesAndFolders.Any();
```

```
bool isStatusBarLoading;
public bool IsStatusBarLoading
{
  get => isStatusBarLoading;
  set
  {
    SetProperty(ref isStatusBarLoading, value);
    OnPropertyChanged(nameof(IsPageEmpty));
    OnPropertyChanged(nameof(IsMainContentLoading));
  }
}
```

In the `GraphFileService` we changed the method signature to accept a `CancellationToken`, which allows us to cancel the `Task` at any point in time after it has started. This is useful when there is a long-running request and the user does not want to wait. They can click the back button, and it will need to cancel the `Task` and start a new `Task`. The addition of the `CancellationToken` requires some changes into how we process the `LoadDataAsync` method in the `MyFilesViewModel`.

To add `CancellationToken` support, you will need to add instance variables for the `MyFilesViewModel` as the `LoadDataAsync` can be invoked from several code paths. Having the `CancellationToken` as an instance variable allows the method to determine if there is a running task and cancel it as the last one always overrides any existing task. See the updated code for `LoadDataAsync` in Listing 18-35; changes will be highlighted in bold.

Listing 18-35. MyFilesViewModel LoadDataAsync updates to use new API from IGraphFileService and CancellationToken. Changes highlighted in bold

```
CancellationTokenSource cancellationTokenSource;
TaskCompletedSource<bool> currentLoadDataTask;

async Task LoadDataAsync(
  string pathId = null,
  Action presentationCallback = null)
{
  if (cancellationTokenSource != null &&
    !cancellationTokenSource.IsCancellationRequested)
```

```
{
  cancellationTokenSource.Cancel();
  await currentLoadDataTask?.Task;
}

currentLoadDataTask = new TaskCompletionSource<bool>(
  TaskCreationOptions.RunContinuationsAsynchronously);
cancellationTokenSource = new CancellationTokenSource();
var cancellationToken = cancellationTokenSource.Token;

try
{
  IsStatusBarLoading = true;

  IEnumerable<OneDriveData> data;
  Action<IEnumerable<OneDriveItem>, bool> updateFilesCallback =
    (items, isCached) => UpdateFiles(items, null, isCached);

  if (string.IsNullOrEmpty(pathId))
  {
    data = await graphFileService.GetRootFilesAsync(
      updateFilesCallback, cancellationToken);
  }
  else
  {
    data = await graphFileService.GetFiles(
      pathId, updateFilesCallback, cancellationToken);
  }
}
catch (Exception ex)
{
  logger.LogError(ex, ex.Message);
}
finally
{
  cancellationTokenSource = default;
  cancellationToken = default;
```

```
    Forward.NotifyCanExecuteChanged();
    Back.NotifyCanExecuteChanged();

    IsStatusBarLoading = false;

    currentLoadDataTask.SetResult(true);
  }
}
```

Now, we can modify the UpdateFiles method, which has an adjusted method signature to invoke callbacks if the data is cached. This is a method that will be invoked from the MyFilesViewModel and the GraphFileService. The change to this method is relatively small but has impact. You will adjust the method signature and invoke the callback if the data is cached. See the updated code snippet in Listing 18-36 with the changes highlighted in bold.

Listing 18-36. MyFilesViewModel UpdateFiles to invoke callback. Changes highlighted in bold

```
void UpdateFiles(
  IEnumerable<OneDriveItem> files,
  Action presentationCallback,
  bool isCached = false)
{
  if (files == null)
  {
    NoDataMessage = "Unable to retrieve data from API,
      " + "check network connection";
    logger.LogInformation("No data retrieved from API,
      " + "ensure have a stable internet connection");
    return;
  }
  else if (!files.Any())
  {
    NoDataMessage = "No files or folders";
  }

  FilesAndFolders = files.ToList();
```

```
if (isCached)
{
  presentationCallback?.Invoke();
}
}
```

The MyFilesViewModel changes are complete, and now we can update the loading indicator in the MyFilesPage.xaml file. Currently all the indicators are using the property IsStatusBarLoading, and we want to update the not_skia and skia indicator in the main content area to use IsMainContentLoading. Open the MyFilesPage.xaml and find the not_skia:ProgressRing and skia:TextBlock in the Grid.Row="1" section. Update the controls to match the code snippet in Listing 18-37.

Listing 18-37. MyFilesPage.xaml updates – loading indicator for main content area to use IsMainContentLoading. Changes highlighted in bold

```
<not_skia:ProgressRing
  Width="300"
  Height="300"
  IsActive="{Binding IsMainContentLoading}"
  Visibility="{Binding IsMainContentLoading, Converter=
    {StaticResource BoolToVisibilityConverter}}" />

<skia:TextBlock
  Text="Loading . . ."
  FontSize="40"
  Foreground="Black"
  HorizontalAlignment="Center"
  VerticalAlignment="Center"
  Visibility="{Binding IsMainContentLoading, Converter=
    {StaticResource BoolToVisibilityConverter}}" />
```

That completes the updates for the loading indicators for the user interface. You can now launch the application and test it out!

Conclusion

In this chapter we implemented several new concepts to handle offline data access and better page state management. This chapter is really an introduction where we used LiteDB as our local data store to cache data. We then updated the presentation layer to eagerly render any cached data while we wait for the Microsoft Graph to respond with real data.

If you had any trouble following along with the code in this chapter, you can download the completed code from GitHub: `https://github.com/SkyeHoefling/UnoDrive/tree/main/Chapter%2018`.

CHAPTER 19

Complete App

In this chapter we will be finishing the UnoDrive application by using concepts we have already learned in the book. By the end of this chapter, you will have a fully functioning application that you can use as an example for your next project. We will be adding more code to complete the Recent Files and Shared Files pages. This includes complete changes for new APIs that invoke the Microsoft Graph. We will be adding code in ViewModels, the service layer, and the data store.

To implement the changes in the Recent Pages and Shared Pages, we are going to start with the Microsoft Graph integration and work our way into the presentation layer.

Note   Uploading and downloading files are omitted from this book. You can learn more about completing those tasks by looking at the Microsoft Graph documentation: `https://docs.microsoft.com/graph`.

Update the GraphFileService and Data Model

Currently the `IGraphFileService` only supports retrieving the current files at a specified path or root path. This is useful for our `MyFilesPage`, but we are going to be implementing for the methods `GetRecentFilesAsync` and `GetSharedFilesAsync`. The Microsoft Graph implementations will be very similar to the existing implementation with one exception. These pages do not require any navigation like the `MyFilesPage`; they render a flat page of files with no folders.

The new implementations of `GetRecentFilesAsync` and `GetSharedFilesAsync` in the `GraphFileService` will be almost identical to what is currently implemented. The change will be updating the specific API invoked on the Microsoft Graph. The data returned will be in a similar format, which means we can reuse a bunch of code.

© Skye Hoefling 2022
S. Hoefling, *Getting Started with the Uno Platform and WinUI 3*,
https://doi.org/10.1007/978-1-4842-8248-9_19

We can get started by updating the IGraphFileService to support the new APIs needed for RecentFilesPage and SharedFilesPage. Update the IGraphFileService as seen in Listing 19-1.

Listing 19-1. IGraphFileService adds new methods for recent files and shared files. Changes are highlighted in bold

```
public interface IGraphFileService
{
  Task<IEnumerable<OneDriveItem>> GetRootFilesAsync(
    Action<IEnumerable<OneDriveItem>, bool> callback = null,
    CancellationToken cancellationToken = default);

  Task<IEnumerable<OneDriveItem>> GetMyFilesAsync(
    string id,
    Action<IEnumerable<OneDriveItem>, bool> callback = null,
    CancellationToken cancellationToken = default);

  Task<IEnumerable<OneDriveItem>> GetRecentFilesAsync(
    Action<IEnumerable<OneDriveItem>, bool> callback = null,
    CancellationToken cancellationToken = default);

  Task<IEnumerable<OneDriveItem>> GetSharedFilesAsync(
    Action<IEnumerable<OneDriveItem>, bool> callback = null,
    CancellationToken cancellationToken = default);
}
```

Before we can start adding new code in the GraphFileService, we need to add an enum to support the different API code paths. In the UnoDrive.Shared project, under the Models folder, create a new file named GraphRequestType.cs. See the screenshot of the Visual Studio Solution Explorer in Figure 19-1.

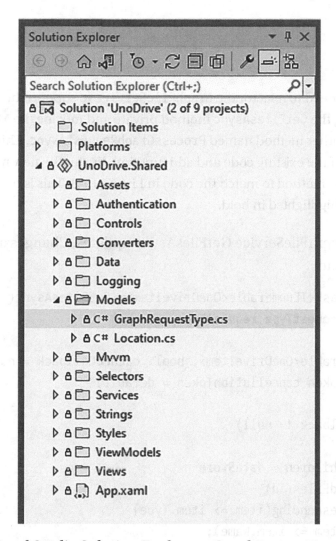

Figure 19-1. *Visual Studio Solution Explorer – GraphRequestType*

Once you have created the new file, create the enum to support MyFiles, Recent, and SharedWithMe. See the full code implementation in Listing 19-2.

Listing 19-2. GraphRequestType enum implementation

```
public enum GraphRequestType
{
  MyFiles,
```

```
  Recent,
  SharedWithMe
}
```

Next, you will need to refactor the GraphFileService to support the new API pattern. We will be making the GetFilesAsync method private and moving the Microsoft Graph invocations to another method named ProcessGraphRequestAsync. This will allow us to leverage most of the existing code and add functionality for the new methods. Update the GetFilesAsync method to match the code in Listing 19-3. This is the entire method with the changes highlighted in bold.

Listing 19-3. GraphFileService GetFilesAsync updates. Changes are highlighted in bold

```
private async Task<IEnumerable<OneDriveItem>> GetFilesAsync(
  Models.GraphRequestType requestType,
  string id,
  Action<IEnumerable<OneDriveItem>, bool> cachedCallback = null,
  CancellationToken cancellationToken = default)
{
  if (cachedCallback != null)
  {
    var cachedChildren = dataStore
      .GetCachedFiles(id)
      .OrderByDescending(item => item.Type)
      .ThenBy(item => item.Name);

    cachedCallback(cachedChildren, true);
  }

  logger.LogInformation(
    $"Network Connectivity: {networkConnectivity.Connectivity}");
  if (networkConnectivity.Connectivity !=
    NetworkConnectivityLevel.InternetAccess)
  {
    return null;
  }
```

504

```
  cancellationToken.ThrowIfCancellationRequested();

#if DEBUG
  await Task.Delay(apiDelayInMilliseconds, cancellationToken)
#endif

  var oneDriveItems = await ProcessGraphRequestAsync(
    requestType,
    id,
    cachedCallback,
    cancellationToken);

  var childrenTable = oneDriveItems
    .Select(driveItem => new OneDriveItem
    {
      Id = driveItem.Id,
      Name = driveItem.Name,
      Path = driveItem.ParentReference.Path,
      PathId = driveItem.ParentReference.Id,
      FileSize = $"{driveItem.Size}",
      Modified = driveItem.LastModifiedDateTime.HasValue ?
        driveItem.LastModifiedDateTime.Value.LocalDateTime :
        DateTime.Now,
      Type = driveItem.Folder != null ?
        OneDriveItemType.Folder :
        OneDriveItemType.File
    })
    .OrderByDescending(item => item.Type)
    .ThenBy(item => item.Name)
    .ToDictionary(item => item.Id);

  cancellationToken.ThrowIfCancellationRequested();

  var children = childrenTable
    .Select(item => item.Value)
    .ToArray();
  if (cachedCallback != null)
```

```
{
  cachedCallback(children, false);
}

dataStore.SaveCachedFiles(children, id);
await StoreThumbnailsAsync(oneDriveItems, childrenTable
  cachedCallback, cancellationToken);
return childrenTable.Select(x => x.Value);
}
```

The notable changes in Listing 19-3 are changing the method signature from
public to private, adding a new parameter GraphRequestType, and then removing the
Microsoft Graph API requests to use the new method ProcessGraphRequestAsync. This
new method uses the GraphRequestType to perform the various Microsoft Graph API
requests and return the DriveItem.

To start implementing the ProcessGraphRequestAsync method, we will need
to define the method signature. Like StoreThumbnailsAsync the method signature
will differ slightly if it is mobile vs. the other platforms. It needs to return UnoDrive.
Models.DriveItem[] if mobile; otherwise, it can use the Microsoft Graph SDK object of
DriveItem[]. See Listing 19-4 for the method signature definition.

Listing 19-4. GraphFileService ProcessGraphRequestAsync method stub

```
#if __ANDROID__ || __IOS__ || __MACOS__
  async Task<UnoDrive.Models.DriveItem[]>
#else
  async Task<DriveItem[]>
#endif
    ProcessGraphRequestAsync(
      UnoDrive.Models.GraphRequestType requestType,
      string id,
      Action<IEnumerable<OneDriveItem>, bool> cachedCallback,
      CancellationToken cancellationToken)
  {
    // TODO - Add implementation
  }
```

The method signature for ProcessGraphRequestAsync is a little odd because of the different return types depending on the platform. Since Uno Platform is using a shared project, this is an easy thing to add, but it can make it a little less readable.

In the implementation of ProcessGraphRequestAsync, it will be using the requestType parameter to determine what Microsoft Graph API to invoke. This method is split into a series of if statements and returns the correct data. See the full implementation in Listing 19-5.

Listing 19-5. GraphFileService ProcessGraphRequestAsync full implementation

```
#if __ANDROID__ || __IOS__ || __MACOS__
  async Task<UnoDrive.Models.DriveItem[]>
#else
  async Task<DriveItem[]>
#endif
    ProcessGraphRequestAsync(
      UnoDrive.Models.GraphRequestType requestType,
      string id,
      Action<IEnumerable<OneDriveItem>, bool> cachedCallback,
      CancellationToken cancellationToken)
  {
#if __ANDROID__ || __IOS__ || __MACOS__
    UnoDrive.Models.DriveItem[] oneDriveItems = null;
#else
    DriveItem[] oneDriveItems = null;
#endif

    if (requestType == Models.GraphRequestType.MyFiles)
    {
      var request = graphClient.Me.Drive
        .Items[id]
        .Children
        .Request()
        .Expand("thumbnails");

#if __ANDROID__ || __IOS__ || __MACOS__
      var response = await request
```

```
          .GetResponseAsync(cancellationToken);
      var data = await response.Content.ReadAsStringAsync();
      var collection = JsonConvert
        .DeserializeObject<UnoDrive.Models.DriveItemCollection>(
          data);
      oneDriveItems = collection.Value;
#else
      oneDriveItems = (await request
        .GetAsync(cancellationToken)).ToArray();
#endif
      return oneDriveItems;
    }
    else if (requestType == Models.GraphRequestType.Recent)
    {
      var request = graphClient.Me.Drive
        .Recent()
        .Request();

#if __ANDROID__ || __IOS__ || __MACOS__
      var response = await request
        .GetResponseAsync(cancellationToken);
      var data = await response.Content.ReadAsStringAsync();
      var collection = JsonConvert
        .DeserializeObject<UnoDrive.Models.DriveItemCollection>(
          data);
      oneDriveItems = collection.Value;
#else
      oneDriveItems = (await request
        .GetAsync(cancellationToken)).ToArray();
#endif
    }
    else if (requestType == Models.GraphRequestType.SharedWithMe)
    {
      var request = graphClient.Me.Drive
        .SharedWithMe()
        .Request();
```

```
#if __ANDROID__ || __IOS__ || __MACOS__
      var response = await request
        .GetResponseAsync(cancellationToken);
      var data = await response.Content.ReadAsStringAsync();
      var collection = JsonConvert
        .DeserializeObject<UnoDrive.Models.DriveItemCollection>(
          data);
      oneDriveItems = collection.Value;
#else
      oneDriveItems = (await request
        .GetAsync(cancellationToken)).ToArray();
#endif
    }

    return oneDriveItems;
  }
```

With the implementation of the Microsoft Graph API invocations complete, we can now implement the new methods we added to the IGraphFileService. Earlier in this chapter in Listing 19-1, we defined the interface that supports the various pages that we want to implement. The implementations of the GetRecentFilesAsync and GetSharedFilesAsync methods invoke the GetFilesAsync method and use the correct GraphRequestType parameter. See implementations for new methods in Listing 19-6.

Listing 19-6. GraphFileService – my files, recent files, and shared files implementations

```
public Task<IEnumerable<OneDriveItem>> GetMyFilesAsync(
  string id,
  Action<IEnumerable<OneDriveItem>, bool> cachedCallback = null,
  CancellationToken cancellationToken = default) =>
    GetFilesAsync(
      GraphRequestType.MyFiles,
      id, cachedCallback, cancellationToken);

public Task<IEnumerable<OneDriveItem>> GetRecentFilesAsync(
  Action<IEnumerable<OneDriveItem>, bool> cachedCallback = null,
  CancellationToken cancellationToken = default) =>
```

```
  GetFilesAsync(
    GraphRequestType.Recent,
    "RECENT-FILES", cachedCallback, cancellationToken);

public Task<IEnumerable<OneDriveItem>> GetSharedFilesAsync(
  Action<IEnumerable<OneDriveItem>, bool> cachedCallback = null,
  CancellationToken cancellationToken = default) =>
    GetFilesAsync(
      GraphRequestType.SharedWithMe,
      "SHARED-FILES", cachedCallback, cancellationToken);
```

That completes our changes to the GraphFileService implementation, and we can start using these changes in our view models.

Note   The GetSharedFilesAsync and GetRecentFilesAsync methods both pass a hard-coded string into the GetFilesAsync method. This string is a unique identifier to store the data in the LiteDB data store so it can be read during offline mode.

Update View Models

The IGraphFileService contract has changed to support MyFilesViewModel, RecentFilesViewModel, and SharedFilesViewModel. In this section we will be updating all the view models to use the correct APIs and get the data we need. These view models all perform similar tasks that we have already implemented, so we can refactor our code to extract an abstract class that is shared among all of them. The RecentFilesViewModel and SharedFilesViewModel do not allow any navigation, and they display a flat list of OneDrive files, whereas the MyFilesViewModel that we already implemented allows for navigation. As we extract out common code, we will need to implement a strategy to handle navigation only in the MyFilesViewModel.

Port Existing Code into BaseFilesViewModel

Most of the structure of the current MyFilesViewModel can be reused in our abstract class. The only parts that will not be included are the direct navigation APIs as the other pages do not support any navigation.

The abstract class will be named BaseFilesViewModel, and it will be inherited in the other view model classes. In the UnoDrive.Shared project under the ViewModels folder, create a new empty class named BaseFilesViewModel. See Figure 19-2 for a screenshot of the Visual Studio Solution Explorer.

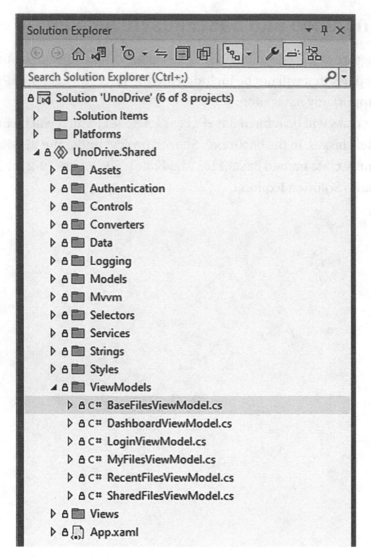

Figure 19-2. *Visual Studio Solution Explorer – BaseFilesViewModel*

We are going to port the existing code from MyFilesViewModel into our abstract class BaseFilesViewModel. This will include

- Dependency Injection properties

- Class properties

- Shared methods

Start by updating the `BaseFilesViewModel` contract to inherit `ObservableObject` and defining it as an abstract class. See Listing 19-7 for the updated class definition.

Listing 19-7. BaseFilesViewModel abstract class definition

```
public abstract class BaseFilesViewModel : ObservableObject
{
  // TODO - add implementation
}
```

> **Note**   Earlier in this book, we learned that `ObservableObject` provides methods to help us notify the user interface of changes to class-level properties. We are going to move this inheritance to the abstract class, which means the children classes will not need to directly inherit `ObservableObject` – they can inherit `BaseFilesViewModel`.

Update the constructor code to inject the Dependency Injection properties. Currently, the properties are stored as private fields in `MyFilesViewModel`. As we port them to the `BaseFilesViewModel,` we will make them `protected` properties. Using the `protected` keyword will allow them to be accessible in the children classes for use. In addition to the Dependency Injection properties, we will need to move the `Location` field and make it `protected` as well. This field is used to store the current location in OneDrive and will be used in all child classes. See constructor code in Listing 19-8.

Listing 19-8. BaseFilesViewModel constructor and Dependency Injection implementation

```
protected Location Location { get; set; } = new Location();
protected IGraphFileService GraphFileService { get; set; }
protected ILogger Logger { get; set; }

public BaseFilesViewModel(
  IGraphFileService graphFileService,
  ILogger<BaseFilesViewModel> logger)
{
```

```
    GraphFileService = graphFileService;
    Logger = logger;
}
```

Next, we will start adding properties from the MyFilesViewModel into our new BaseFilesViewModel class. We will just add the FilesAndFolders in Listing 19-9 because it has some changes to the constructor code. It needs to have a default instantiation. See updated constructor code in Listing 19-9 with changes highlighted in bold.

Listing 19-9. BaseFilesViewModel updated constructor implementation to include FilesAndFolders. Changes highlighted in bold

```
protected Location Location { get; set; } = new Location();
protected IGraphFileService GraphFileService { get; set; }
protected ILogger Logger { get; set; }

public BaseFilesViewModel(
  IGraphFileService graphFileService,
  ILogger<BaseFilesViewModel> logger)
{
  GraphFileService = graphFileService;
  Logger = logger;

  FilesAndFolders = new List<OneDriveItem>();
}

List<OneDriveItem> filesAndFolders;
public List<OneDriveItem> FilesAndFolders
{
  get => filesAndFolders;
  set
  {
    SetProperty(ref filesAndFolders, value);
    OnPropertyChanged(nameof(CurrentFolderPath));
    OnPropertyChanged(nameof(IsPageEmpty));
    OnPropertyChanged(nameof(IsMainContentLoading));
  }
}
```

514

Note   As we move existing code from the `MyFilesViewModel` into the `BaseFilesViewModel`, we still need to access APIs from the `ObservableObject` such as `SetProperty()` and `OnPropertyChanged()`. This is seen in Listings 19-9 and 19-10.

Now we can start porting the remaining properties over from the `MyFilesViewModel` class into our new `BaseFilesViewModel` class. As we copy these properties over, we will be making one change that is different from the original code. We will update the definition of the `CurrentFolderPath` property to include the keyword `virtual`. Using the `virtual` keyword means we can override the behavior in child classes. Not all of our pages will have navigation, and in those pages, we will want a different message to display in the address bar than the path. See the code snippet in Listing 19-10 for all the properties to copy over, and changes will be highlighted in bold.

Listing 19-10. BaseFilesViewModel property implementations

```
public bool IsMainContentLoading =>
  IsStatusBarLoading && !FilesAndFolders.Any();

public bool IsPageEmpty =>
  !IsStatusBarLoading && !FilesAndFolders.Any();

public virtual string CurrentFolderPath =>
  FilesAndFolders.FirstOrDefault()?.Path;

string noDataMessage;
public string NoDataMessage
{
  get => noDataMessage;
  set => SetProperty(ref noDataMessage, value);
}

bool isStatusBarLoading;
public bool IsStatusBarLoading
{
  get => isStatusBarLoading;
  set
```

```
  {
    SetProperty(ref isStatusBarLoading, value);
    OnPropertyChanged(nameof(IsPageEmpty));
    OnPropertyChanged(nameof(IsMainContentLoading));
  }
}
```

Next, we will start working on the various methods that need to be copied over from the `MyFilesViewModel` into the `BaseFilesViewModel`. We will start with the `OnItemClick()` method. The only change to this method is updating the signature to include the virtual keyword. This allows child classes to override the behavior if necessary. See the code snippet in Listing 19-11 for the copied implementation.

Listing 19-11. BaseFilesViewModel OnItemClick method implementation. Changes highlighted in bold

```
public async virtual void OnItemClick(
  object sender, ItemClickEventArgs args)
{
  if (args.ClickedItem is not OneDriveItem oneDriveItem)
    return;

  if (oneDriveItem.Type == OneDriveItemType.Folder)
  {
    try
    {
      Location.Forward = new Location
      {
        Id = oneDriveItem.Id,
        Back = Location
      };
      Location = Location.Forward;

      await LoadDataAsync(oneDriveItem.Id);
    }
    catch (Exception ex)
    {
      Logger.LogError(ex, ex.Message);
```

```
    }
  }
}
```

The next method that we will be porting over from the MyFilesViewModel to the BaseFilesViewModel is the LoadDataAsync() method. This performs the work to retrieve our data and render it onto the page. Since our BaseFilesViewModel now needs to handle various data loading strategies, we need to make some minor updates to it. Instead of invoking the IGraphFileService APIs directly, we will create a special protected abstract method that will invoke the IGraphFileService for us.

Note   An abstract method is a special method defined in an abstract class that defines a contract with any child class that inherits from that abstract class. This means the child classes that inherit from BaseFilesViewModel will need to write their own implementation for our abstract method.

The abstract method will be named GetGraphDataAsync() and will include the necessary properties to retrieve the data. See the abstract method definition in Listing 19-12.

Listing 19-12. BaseFilesViewModel abstract method definition for GetGraphDataAsync()

```
protected abstract Task<IEnumerable<OneDriveItem>>
  GetGraphDataAsync(
    string pathId,
    Action<IEnumerable<OneDriveItem>, bool> callback,
    CancellationToken cancellationToken);
```

Now that the abstract method GetGraphDataAsync() is defined, we can add our implementation for LoadDataAsync(). We do not need to worry about the implementation for the abstract method GetGraphDataAsync() since that will be handled in any child class implementation. We can assume it will take the parameters and return a value. See the LoadDataAsync() updated implementation in Listing 19-13, and the changes will be highlighted in bold.

517

Listing 19-13. BaseFilesViewModel LoadDataAsync method implementation.
Changes highlighted in bold

```
CancellationTokenSource cancellationTokenSource;
CancellationToken cancellationToken;
TaskCompletionSource<bool> currentLoadDataTask;
protected virtual async Task LoadDataAsync(
  string pathId = null,
  Action presentationCallback = null)
{
  if (cancellationTokenSource != null &&
    !cancellationTokenSource.IsCancellationRequested)
  {
    cancellationTokenSource.Cancel();
    await currentLoadDataTask.Task;
  }

  currentLoadDataTask = new TaskCompletionSource<bool>(
    TaskCreationOptions.RunContinuationsAsynchronously);
  cancellationTokenSource = new CancellationTokenSource();
  cancellationToken = cancellationTokenSource.Token;

  try
  {
    IsStatusBarLoading = true;

    IEnumerable<OneDriveItem> data;
    Action<IEnumerable<OneDriveItem>, bool> updateFilesCallback =
      (items, isCached) => UpdateFiles(items, null, isCached);

    if (string.IsNullOrEmpty(pathId))
    {
      data = await GraphFileService.GetRootFilesAsync(
        updateFilesCallback, cancellationToken);
    }
    else
    {
      data = await GetGraphDataAsync(
```

```
    pathId, updateFilesCallback, cancellationToken);
  }

  UpdateFiles(data, presentationCallback);
  }
catch (Exception ex)
{
  Logger.LogError(ex, ex.Message);
}
finally
{
  cancellationTokenSource = default;
  cancellationToken = default;

  IsStatusBarLoading = false;

  currentLoadDataTask.SetResult(true);
  }
}
```

The final method we need to port over from MyFilesViewModel to the BaseFilesViewModel is the UpdateFiles() method, which is a helper method used in the LoadDataAsync() method. See the implementation in Listing 19-14.

Listing 19-14. BaseFilesViewModel UpdateFiles method implementation

```
protected void UpdateFiles(
  IEnumerable<OneDriveItem> files,
  Action presentationCallback,
  bool isCached = false)
{
  if (files == null)
  {
    NoDataMessage = "Unable to retrieve data from API, " +
    "check network connection";
    Logger.LogInformation("No data retrieved from API, " +
    "ensure you have a stable internet connection";
  }
```

```
else if (!files.Any())
{
  NoDataMessage = "No files or folders";
}

FilesAndFolders = files.ToList();

if (isCached)
{
  presentationCallback?.Invoke();
}
}
```

The abstract class BaseFilesViewModel is now implemented, and we will start adding implementations to the view models: MyFilesViewModel, RecentFilesViewModel, and SharedFilesViewModel.

Update MyFilesViewModel

The original implementation has been ported over to BaseFilesViewModel, and the MyFilesViewModel will shrink in size as most of the code is no longer needed. In this section we are going to start from the beginning and reimplement it. You can start by deleting the entire contents of MyFilesViewModel.

The first thing we need to do is add our class definition, which will now inherit from BaseFilesViewModel instead of ObservableObject. See Listing 19-15 for the MyFilesViewModel class definition.

Listing 19-15. MyFilesViewModel class definition

```
public class MyFilesViewModel : BaseFilesViewModel, IInitialize
{
  // TODO - add implementation
}
```

Just like the original implementation, we will need to inject the properties into the constructor that we want to resolve and use. The major difference is they are not stored in this class but as properties in the parent class BaseFilesViewModel. As you implement the constructor, you will need to invoke the base constructor and pass the parameters along. See the constructor code snippet in Listing 19-16.

Listing 19-16. MyFilesViewModel constructor injection implementation

```
public MyFilesViewModel(
  IGraphFileService graphFileService,
  ILogger<MyFilesViewModel> logger)
  : base(graphFileService, logger)
{
}
```

The MyFilesViewModel performs basic navigation forward and back, and that is not included in the parent class BaseFilesViewModel. Next, we will add our IRelayCommand properties and method implementations. See Listing 19-17 for navigation implementation.

Listing 19-17. MyFilesViewModel navigation IRelayCommand and method implementations

```
public MyFilesViewModel(
  IGraphFileService graphFileService,
  ILogger<MyFilesViewModel> logger)
  : base(graphFileService, logger)
{
  Forward = new AsyncRelayCommand(OnForwardAsync,
    () => location.CanMoveForward);
  Back = new AsyncRelayCommand(OnBackAsync,
    () => location.CanMoveBack);
}

public IRelayCommand Forward { get; }
public IRelayCommand Back { get; }

Task OnForwardAsync()
{
  var forwardId = Location.Forward.Id;
  Location = Location.Forward;
  return LoadDataAsync(forwardId);
}
```

```
Task OnBackAsync()
{
  var backId = Location.Back.Id;
  Location = Location.Back;
  return LoadDataAsync(backId);
}
```

When we implemented the BaseFilesViewModel, we defined the abstract method GetGraphDataAsync(), which we need to implement. This method will invoke the correct API on the IGraphFileService to retrieve the files for our page. See Listing 19-18 for the abstract method implementation.

Listing 19-18. MyFilesViewModel GetGraphDataAsync method implementation

```
protected override Task<IEnumerable<OneDriveItem>>
  GetGraphDataAsync(
    string pathId,
    Action<IEnumerable<OneDriveItem>, bool> callback,
    CancellationToken cancellationToken) =>
      GraphFileService.GetMyFilesAsync(
        pathId, callback, cancellationToken);
```

The method OnItemClick() uses x:Bind from the page, and it needs to have a reference here in the child class to be properly invoked from the XAML.

Note   We need to override the OnItemClick() method on Uno Platform targets. The code generation will fail to read the method in the parent classes.

To resolve this, we will create an override of the method OnItemClick from the parent class BaseFilesViewModel and just invoke the parent implementation. See the override implementation in Listing 19-19.

Listing 19-19. MyFilesViewModel OnItemClick method override implementation

```
public override void OnItemClick(
  object sender, ItemClickEventArgs args) =>
    base.OnItemClick(sender, args);
```

MyFilesViewModel is the only ViewModel that allows for navigation through the structure of OneDrive. We still have the IRelayCommand for both forward and back, and they are in this class. After the LoadDataAsync base implementation completes, we will need to use the NotifyCanExecuteChanged() method to check if any navigation action can occur. See the code snippet for method override in Listing 19-20.

Listing 19-20. MyFilesViewModel LoadDataAsync override for NotifyCanExecuteChanged

```
protected override async Task LoadDataAsync(
  string pathId = null,
  Action presentationCallback = null)
{
  await base.LoadDataAsync(pathId, presentationCallback);
  Forward.NotifyCanExecuteChanged();
  Back.NotifyCanExecuteChanged();
}
```

In the original MyFilesViewModel implementation, the class implemented IInitialize, and that code does not change at all. We already included the interface in the class definition. You can see this in Listing 19-15. Now, add the IInitialize implementation and invoke the LoadDataAsync() method. See Listing 19-21 for the InitializeAsync() method implementation.

Listing 19-21. MyFilesViewModel IInitialize interface implementation

```
public Task InitializeAsync() =>
  LoadDataAsync();
```

That completes our updates to the MyFilesViewModel. There is no need to change anything in the user interface.

Implement RecentFilesViewModel

The RecentFilesViewModel is a new implementation in this chapter and will be almost identical to the SharedFilesViewModel. This page does not allow any navigation and just displays a list of files that the user recently viewed.

To implement the RecentFilesViewModel, you will need to complete the following tasks:

- Define the constructor and inject properties.
- Override CurrentFolderPath to display the message "Recent Files."
- Override GetGraphDataAsync() to invoke the correct API.
- Override the OnItemClick() method to invoke the base method.
- Implement IInitialize.

See complete RecentFilesViewModel code in Listing 19-22.

Listing 19-22. RecentFilesViewModel complete implementation

```
public class RecentFilesViewModel :
  BaseFilesViewModel, IInitialize
{
  public RecentFilesViewModel(
    IGraphFileService graphFileService,
    ILogger<RecentFilesViewModel> logger)
    : base(graphFileService, logger)
  {
  }

  public override string CurrentFolderPath => "Recent Files";

  protected override Task<IEnumerable<OneDriveItem>>
    GetGraphDataAsync(
      string pathId,
      Action<IEnumerable<OneDriveItem>, bool> callback,
      CancellationToken cancellationToken) =>
        GraphFileService.GetRecentFilesAsync(
          callback, cancellationToken);
```

```
public override void OnItemClick(
  object sender, ItemClickEventArgs args) =>
    base.OnItemClick(sender, args);

public Task InitializeAsync() =>
  LoadDataAsync("RECENT");
}
```

Implement SharedFilesViewModel

The SharedFilesViewModel is a new implementation in this chapter and will be almost identical to the RecentFilesViewModel. This page does not allow any navigation and just displays a list of files shared to the user.

To implement the SharedFilesViewModel, you will need to complete the following tasks:

- Define the constructor and inject properties.

- Override CurrentFolderPath to display the message "Shared Files."

- Override GetGraphDataAsync() to invoke the correct API.

- Override the OnItemClick() method to invoke the base method.

- Implement IInitialize.

See complete SharedFilesViewModel code in Listing 19-23.

Listing 19-23. SharedFilesViewModel complete implementation

```
public class SharedFilesViewModel :
  BaseFilesViewModel, IInitialize
{
  public SharedFilesViewModel(
    IGraphFileService graphFileService,
    ILogger<SharedFilesViewModel> logger)
    : base(graphFileService, logger)
  {
  }

  public override string CurrentFolderPath => "Shared Files";
```

525

```
protected override Task<IEnumerable<OneDriveItem>>
  GetGraphDataAsync(
    string pathId,
    Action<IEnumerable<OneDriveItem>, bool> callback,
    CancellationToken cancellationToken) =>
      GraphFileService.GetSharedFilesAsync(
        callback, cancellationToken);

public override void OnItemClick(
  object sender, ItemClickEventArgs args) =>
    base.OnItemClick(sender, args);

public Task InitializeAsync() =>
  LoadDataAsync("SHARED-WITH-ME");
}
```

Update the User Interface

The service layer changes and view model changes are complete, and we can start working on the user interface changes. The `MyFilesPage.xaml` and `MyFilesPage.xaml.cs` implementations are valid and do not need any changing. We only updated the `MyFilesViewModel` code to work with our new abstract class.

We do need to implement both `RecentFilesPage` and `SharedFilesPage,` which are going to be carbon copies of `MyFilesPage` for both the XAML and the code behind.

Both the `RecentFilesPage` and `SharedFilesPage` code behinds have the constructor defined. We will need to add the following to each code behind:

- `ViewModel` reference for `x:Bind` usages

- `OnNavigatedTo` override to invoke the `IInitialize` interface

See the code implementation for `RecentFilesPage` in Listing 19-24 and `SharedFilesPage` in Listing 19-25.

Listing 19-24. RecentFilesPage.xaml.cs code behind complete implementation

```
public sealed partial class RecentFilesPage : Page
{
  public RecentFilesPage()
  {
    this.InitializeComponent();
  }

  public RecentFilesViewModel ViewModel =>
    (RecentFilesViewModel)DataContext;

  protected override async void OnNavigatedTo(
    NavigationEventArgs e)
  {
    base.OnNavigatedTo(e);

    if (ViewModel is IInitialize initializeViewModel)
      await initializeViewModel.InitializeAsync();
  }
}
```

Listing 19-25. SharedFilesPage.xaml.cs code behind complete implementation

```
public sealed partial class SharedFilesPage : Page
{
  public SharedFilesPage()
  {
    this.InitializeComponent();
  }

  public SharedFilesViewModel ViewModel =>
    (SharedFilesViewModel)DataContext;

  protected override async void OnNavigatedTo(
    NavigationEventArgs e)
  {
    base.OnNavigatedTo(e);
```

```
    if (ViewModel is IInitialize initializeViewModel)
      await initializeViewModel.InitializeAsync();
  }
}
```

The implementations of both RecentFilesPage.xaml and SharedFilesPage.xaml are identical to MyFilesPage.xaml with the one change that the x:Class definition at the top must reference the correct class. For the remainder of this section, the code snippets will apply to both RecentFilesPage.xaml and SharedFilesPage.xaml.

To start our implementation of the RecentFilesPage.xaml and SharedFilesPage.xaml, you will need to update the xmlns section. See Listing 19-26 for RecentFilesPage.xaml and SharedFilesPage.xaml xmlns definitions.

Listing 19-26. RecentFilesPage.xaml and SharedFilesPage.xaml xmlns definitions code snippet

```
xmlns:mvvm="using:UnoDrive.Mvvm"
mvvm:ViewModelLocator.AutoWireViewModel="True"
xmlns:not_skia="http://schemas.microsoft.com/winfx/2006/xaml/presentation"
xmlns:skia="http://uno.ui/skia"
mc:Ignorable="d skia"
```

Next, we can add the entire XAML needed to define the page. This can be copied from the MyFilesPage.xaml as it is the same XAML. See code in Listing 19-27.

Listing 19-27. RecentFilesPage.xaml and SharedFilesPage.xaml complete XAML

```
<Grid x:Name="rootGrid">
  <Grid.RowDefinitions>
    <RowDefinition Height="Auto" />
    <RowDefinition Height="*" />
  </Grid.RowDefinitions>

  <Grid Grid.Row="0" Margin="0, 0, 0, 20">
    <Grid.ColumnDefinitions>
      <ColumnDefinition />
    </Grid.ColumnDefinitions>

    <TextBox
```

```
        Grid.Column="0"
        Margin="10, 0, 0, 0"
        Padding="10, 6, 36, 5"
        IsReadOnly="True"
        IsFocusEngaged="False"
        IsEnabled="False"
        Foreground="Black"
        Background="#F2F2F2"
        Text="{Binding CurrentFolderPath}" />

    <not_skia:ProgressRing
        Grid.Column="0"
        Style="{StaticResource AddressBarProgressRing}"
        HorizontalAlignment="Right"
        Margin="0, 0, 10, 0"
        IsActive="{Binding IsStatusBarLoading}"
        Visibility="{Binding IsStatusBarLoading,
          Converter={StaticResource BoolToVisibilityConverter}}" />

    <skia:TextBlock
        Grid.Column="0"
        Text="Loading . . ."
        FontSize="12"
        Margin="0, 0, 10, 0"
        Foreground="Black"
        HorizontalAlignment="Right"
        VerticalAlignment="Center"
        Visibility="{Binding IsStatusBarLoading,
          Converter={StaticResource BoolToVisibilityConverter}}" />
</Grid>

<ScrollViewer Grid.Row="1">
  <StackPanel>
    <GridView
      ItemsSource="{Binding FilesAndFolders}"
      ItemClick="{x:Bind ViewModel.OnItemClick}"
      Visibility="{Binding IsPageEmpty, Converter=
```

```
          {StaticResource BoolNegationToVisibilityConverter}}"
        ScrollViewer.VerticalScrollMode="Enabled"
        ScrollViewer.VerticalScrollBarVisibility="Visible"
        ScrollViewer.HorizontalScrollMode="Disabled" />

      <TextBlock
        Text="No data found"
        Visibility="{Binding IsPageEmpty, Converter=
          {StaticResource BoolToVisibilityConverter}}" />

      <not_skia:ProgressRing
        Width="300"
        Height="300"
        IsActive="{Binding IsMainContentLoading}"
        Visibility="{Binding IsMainContentLoading, Converter=
          {StaticResource BoolToVisibilityConverter}}" />

      <skia:TextBlock
        Text="Loading . . ."
        FontSize="40"
        Foreground="Black"
        HorizontalAlignment="Center"
        VerticalAlignment="Center"
        Visibility="{Binding IsMainContentLoading, Converter=
          {StaticResource BoolToVisibilityConverter}}" />

    </StackPanel>
  </ScrollViewer>
</Grid>
```

That completes our changes for the RecentFilesPage and SharedFilesPage. You can now launch the application and navigate to those pages, and it will render your recent files or shared files in a flat list. If you navigate to the original MyFilesPage, it will still work just as it has always done.

Conclusion

That completes all the final changes to our application. In this chapter we applied concepts we learned throughout this book to finish our implementation, which gives us a working OneDrive clone application built using Uno Platform targeting Windows, WASM, WPF, GTK (Linux), iOS, Android, and macOS!

If you had trouble following along with any of the code in this chapter, you can view the chapter 19 code available on GitHub: `https://github.com/SkyeHoefling/UnoDrive/tree/main/Chapter%2019`.

Index

A

Accessor, 199

Access techniques
    application implementation, 453
    caching strategies, 455, 456
    modern applications, 453
    order of operations, 454
    presentation code, 454
    stable connection, 454
    user interface, 455

Access token, 259–261, 285, 288, 292, 296,
    304, 308, 321, 337, 347, 348, 404

AcquireInteractiveTokenAsync, 285, 286,
    288, 292, 304

AcquireSilentTokenAsync, 291–295, 300

AcquireTokenAsync, 286, 292, 308

AcquireTokenInteractive, 288

AddAuthentication, 280, 281

AddConsole(), 226, 231

AddDebug(), 226, 231

Address bar, 378–385, 388, 389, 391, 450,
    451, 515

AddressBarProgressRing, 383

AfterAccessNotification, 464–466

Android, 2, 6, 136–138
    application, 28, 71, 72
    custom fonts, 176–178
    Device Manager, 27
    ecosystem, 25
    emulator, 26, 27
    folder, 24
    images, 432

logging, 232–237
    Microsoft Graph, 397
    page header, 152–155, 165
    pre-processor directives, 104
    project, 25
    test authentication, 317, 318
    user interface, 416

AndroidAsset, 176

Android-specific configurations, 25

AppKit, 34

Application
    object, 213
    code flow, 304–312
    flow, 269, 304
    scope, 82, 84, 287
    styles, 77–95, 172, 332, 333
    window, 230, 240

App.xaml, 18, 36, 80, 85–87, 89, 90, 95, 216

App.xaml.cs, 22, 29, 32, 56, 216, 220, 252,
    281, 298, 305, 361, 460

App.xaml.cs ConfigureServices method,
    220, 281, 298, 361, 460

App.xaml styles
    benefits, 85
    disadvantages, 86
    XAML code, 85

Architecture, 4–5, 7, 191, 195, 205–207,
    218, 239, 243

Assets, 18, 21, 25, 38, 165, 168–170, 175,
    176, 179, 180, 190, 291, 419–422,
    426, 440, 457

Asset scaling table, 420

G

J, K

L

X, Y, Z

Printed in the United States
by Baker & Taylor Publisher Services